Basic Spanish Grammar

Fifth Edition

Basic Spanish Grammar

Ana C. Jarvis
Chandler-Gilbert Community College

Raquel Lebredo
California Baptist College

Francisco Mena-Ayllón
University of Redlands

D. C. Heath and Company
Lexington, Massachusetts   Toronto

Address editorial correspondence to:

D. C. Heath and Company
125 Spring Street
Lexington, MA 02173

Acquisitions Editor: Denise St. Jean
Developmental Editor: Sheila McIntosh
Production Editor: Julie Lane
Designer: Alwyn R. Velásquez
Photo Researcher: Kathleen Carcia
Production Coordinator: Richard Tonachel

Cover photo: *Presencias* by Wilfredo Chiesa.

Photo Credits: p. 1, Peter Menzel Photography; p. 13, Ulrike
Welsch; p. 21, Robert Frerck/Tony Stone Images; p. 35, Robert
Fried/D. Donne Bryant Stock Photo; p. 45, Cameramann
International, Ltd.; p. 57, Beryl Goldberg; p. 69, Peter Menzel;
p. 89, José Luis Dorado/Godo Foto; p. 101, Peter Menzel;
p. 113, Beryl Goldberg; p. 127, Robert Fried/D. Donne Bryant
Stock Photo; p. 141, Beryl Goldberg; p. 159, D. Donne Bryant
Stock Photo; p. 171, Chip and Rosa Maria de la Cueva Peterson;
p. 181, Beryl Goldberg; p. 191, Peter Menzel; p. 201, Doug
Bryant; p. 223, Peter Menzel; p. 233, Cameramann
International, Ltd.; p. 243, Chip and Rosa Maria de la Cueva
Peterson; p. 251, Robert Frerck/Woodfin Camp & Associates;
p. 259, Beryl Goldberg

International Standard Book Number: 0–669–35451–1

Library of Congress Catalog Number: 95–79602

10 9 8 7 6 5

Preface

Basic Spanish Grammar, Fifth Edition, presents the essential points of Spanish grammar to students or professionals seeking a working knowledge of Spanish. Grammatical structures and high-frequency vocabulary that are indispensable for communication are presented clearly and concisely and reinforced through a variety of practice exercises.

The Student's Edition

The organization of this central component of the *Basic Spanish Grammar* program reflects its emphasis on the acquisition of Spanish fundamentals for practical use. The Student's Edition consists of two preliminary lessons, twenty regular lessons, and four self-tests, organized as follows:

◆ The preliminary lessons enable students to communicate in Spanish using basic, high-frequency language from the outset of the course.

◆ The twenty regular lessons contain the features listed below.

A core vocabulary list of essential words and expressions, organized by parts of speech. Since this vocabulary is used in the lesson's grammar explanations and activities, students should familiarize themselves with these terms before proceeding.

Three to six grammar structures per lesson, explained clearly and concisely in English so that the explanations may be used independently as an out-of-class reference. All explanations are followed by numerous examples of their practical use in natural Spanish. After each explanation, the *Práctica* offers immediate reinforcement of new concepts through a variety of structured and open-ended activities.

En el laboratorio exercises to be completed in conjunction with the Cassette Program. Signalled by a cassette icon, the laboratory exercises include *Vocabulario* and *Práctica* (grammar) sections, as well as a *Para escuchar y entender* (listening comprehension) section.

◆ *¿Cuánto sabe usted ahora?* self-tests after Lessons 5, 10, 15, and 20 allow students to review the structures and vocabulary of the five preceding lessons. Organized by lesson and by grammar structure, the self-tests enable students to determine quickly what material they have mastered and which concepts to target for further review. An answer key is provided in Appendix D for immediate verification.

◆ Reference Materials: The following sections provide students with useful reference tools throughout the course:

Maps: Up-to-date maps of the Spanish-speaking world appear at the front of the textbook for quick reference.

Appendixes: Appendix A summarizes the sounds and key pronunciation features of the Spanish language, with abundant examples. Conjugations of high-frequency regular, stem-changing, and irregular Spanish verbs constitute Appendix B. Appendix C provides a list of the Spanish names of more than 100 professions and occupations to facilitate personalized classroom discussion. Appendix D is the answer key to the *¿Cuánto sabe usted ahora?* self-tests.

Vocabularies: Spanish-English and English-Spanish glossaries list all active vocabulary introduced in the *Vocabulario* lists and in the grammar explanations. Each word or expression is followed by the number of the lesson in which it becomes active.

Cassette Program

The complete Cassette Program to accompany *Basic Spanish Grammar,* Fifth Edition, is available for student purchase. Recorded by native speakers, the seven 60-minute audiocassettes contain the vocabulary lists and laboratory activities from *Basic Spanish Grammar.* Vocabulary and grammar exercises, plus two or three listening comprehension passages, accompany each student text lesson.

Other Components of the Basic Spanish Grammar Program

The *Basic Spanish Grammar* program features a full range of components designed to meet the needs of students who wish to learn Spanish for specific purposes. To maximize students' exposure to natural spoken Spanish, each of the seven companion manuals is accompanied by its own cassette program.

Companion Manuals

Students studying Spanish for professional reasons have specific needs and limited study time. In response to these issues, all components of the *Basic Spanish Grammar* program have been designed to facilitate individualized instruction and independent study. Seven manuals develop practical communication skills for both general and professional use. All may be used in conjunction with the core text in introductory Spanish classes or as stand-alone texts in a one-semester course for students who have had at least one year of Spanish. In each lesson, realistic dialogues and activities present and reinforce vocabulary specific to particular situations or professions and provide practical applications of the grammatical structures introduced in the corresponding lesson of *Basic Spanish Grammar*, Fifth Edition.

Getting Along in Spanish, Fourth Edition

This communication manual develops practical vocabulary for everyday situations by emphasizing common themes such as travel, eating in a restaurant, shopping, running errands, and going to the doctor. Realistic dialogues, personalized questions, situational role-plays, and realia-based activities prepare students to carry out normal daily interactions in Spanish.

Spanish for Communication, Fourth Edition

Spanish for Communication covers the same themes as *Getting Along in Spanish*, but at a more advanced level.

Spanish for Business and Finance, Fifth Edition

Spanish for Business and Finance presents and practices business and finance vocabulary in realistic contexts. Tax preparation, banking operations, real estate, and insurance are among the topics addressed, along with the essentials of business travel such as renting a car, staying in a hotel, and ordering meals. *Suplemento* sections after every few lessons introduce the basics of commercial correspondence and provide both models and practice activities.

Spanish for Law Enforcement, Fifth Edition

Designed specifically for law enforcement personnel, *Spanish for Law Enforcement* introduces and reinforces vocabulary and communicative functions essential to police officers, firefighters, court clerks, and other professionals who interact with the Spanish-speaking community.

Spanish for Medical Personnel, Fifth Edition
Spanish for Medical Personnel presents situations and vocabulary that medical personnel encounter in the course of their daily work. New *Notas culturales* highlight Hispanic customs and traditions relevant to health care, as well as information on medical conditions and concerns affecting Hispanics in the United States. Supplementary readings on illnesses such as diabetes, cancer, heart disease, and AIDS reflect some of the most urgent concerns of the medical community.

Spanish for Social Services, Fifth Edition
Extensive in its coverage of vocabulary and themes requisite to social services professionals or those who are planning a career in the field, *Spanish for Social Services* develops and reinforces communication skills within a context of cultural sensitivity, preparing students for such tasks as explaining available services and eligibility requirements, conducting home visits, and taking family histories.

Spanish for Teachers, Fourth Edition
Spanish for Teachers prepares current and prospective elementary and secondary school teachers, including ESL teachers, to communicate effectively with Spanish-speaking students and their parents. Key vocabulary related to a full range of subject areas and administrative duties is presented.

Cassette Programs

Each companion manual of the *Basic Spanish Grammar* program has its own Cassette Program, available for student purchase. The cassette programs include an introduction to Spanish sounds followed by the dialogues (paused and unpaused versions) and vocabulary lists for each lesson, and the *Práctica oral* questions from the four *Repaso* sections.

Supplementary Materials for the Instructor

Instructor's Edition
The Introduction to the Instructor's Edition provides a detailed description of the entire *Basic Spanish Grammar* program, suggestions for its implementation in the classroom, and a complete answer key to textbook exercises with discrete answers.

Testing Program/Transparency Masters

Completely revised, this supplement includes twenty quizzes (one for each regular lesson), two in-class midterms, two take-home midterms, and two final exams for *Basic Spanish Grammar*. It also contains a sample vocabulary quiz and comprehensive final exams for *Getting Along in Spanish*, the career manuals, and *Spanish for Communication*. Suggestions for grading and scheduling quizzes and tests complete the program. For vocabulary review, a set of twenty transparency masters containing art from *Getting Along in Spanish* and five transparency masters with diagrams of the human body from *Spanish for Medical Personnel* are bound with the *Testing Program*.

Tapescripts

Complete transcripts for the cassette programs to accompany *Basic Spanish Grammar*, *Getting Along in Spanish*, the career manuals, and *Spanish for Communication* are bound together in one volume.

We would like to hear your comments on and reactions to the *Basic Spanish Grammar*, Fifth Edition, program. Reports on your experiences using this program would be of great interest and value to us. Please write us in care of D. C. Heath and Company, College Division, 125 Spring Street, Lexington, MA 02173.

Acknowledgments

We wish to thank our colleagues who have used previous editions of *Basic Spanish Grammar* for their many constructive comments and recommendations. We especially appreciate the valuable suggestions of the following reviewers of *Basic Spanish Grammar*, Fourth Edition:

Dan Adams, Snow College
Peter R. Alfieri, Salve Regina University
Richard Appelbaum, Broward Community College
Gertrudis D. Caminero, Bethune Cookman College
Irene Corso, Stanford University
Guadalupe C. Gómez, University of Texas at El Paso
Donald B. Gibbs, Creighton University
Monica D. Lavosky, State University of New York College
    at New Paltz
Oswaldo A. López, Miami-Dade Community College
Hugo Muñoz-Ballesteros, Tarleton State University
John D. Nesbitt, Eastern Wyoming College
Maria Rugeles-Smith, Rider University

We also extend our sincere appreciation to the Modern Languages Staff of D. C. Heath and Company, College Division: Denise St. Jean, Senior Acquisitions Editor; Sheila McIntosh, Developmental Editor; Julie Lane, Production Editor; Michael O'Dea, Production Manager; Richard Tonachel, Production Supervisor; and Alwyn Velásquez, Senior Designer.

Ana C. Jarvis
Raquel Lebredo
Francisco Mena-Ayllón

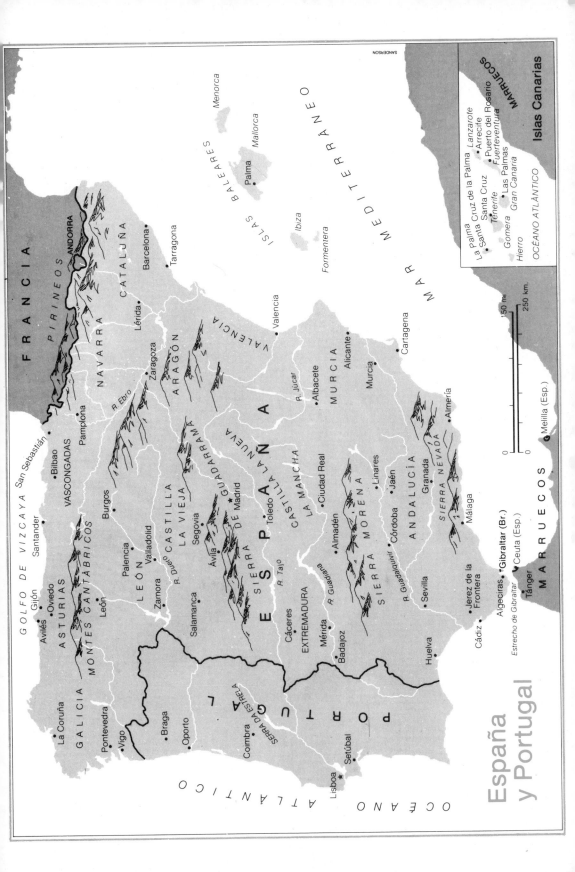

España y Portugal

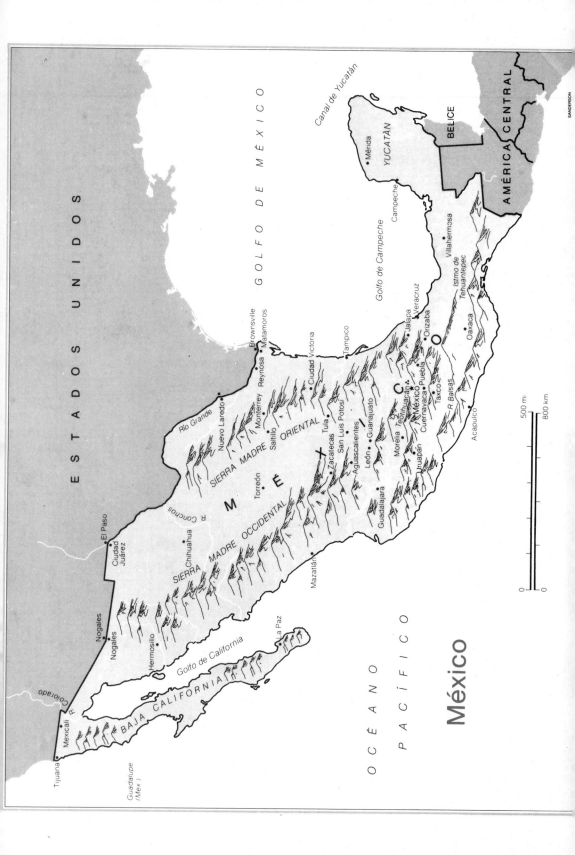

México

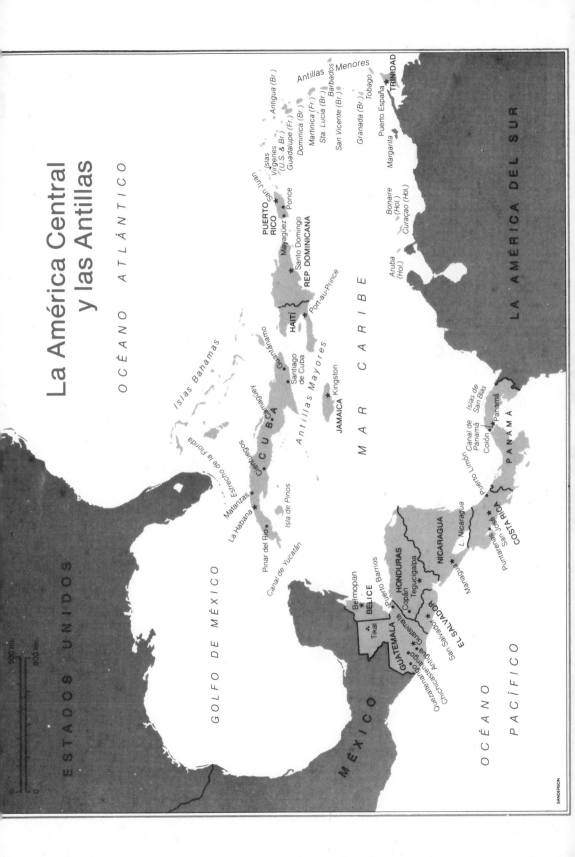

La América Central y las Antillas

OCÉANO ATLÁNTICO

ESTADOS UNIDOS

GOLFO DE MÉXICO

Islas Bahamas

Estrecho de la Florida

Pinar del Río
Isla de Pinos
La Habana
Matanzas
Cienfuegos
C U B A
Camagüey
Santiago de Cuba
Guantánamo

Canal de Yucatán

MÉXICO

Tikal
Belmopan
BELICE
Puerto Barrios
Copán
HONDURAS
Tegucigalpa
Quezaltenango
Chichicastenango
Antigua
Guatemala
GUATEMALA
San Salvador
EL SALVADOR
Managua
NICARAGUA
L. Nicaragua
San José
Puntarenas
COSTA RICA
Puerto Limón

OCÉANO PACÍFICO

Canal de Panamá
Islas de San Blas
Colón
Panamá
PANAMÁ

MAR CARIBE

Antillas Mayores
JAMAICA
Kingston

HAITÍ
Port-au-Prince
Santo Domingo
REP. DOMINICANA

PUERTO RICO
San Juan
Mayagüez • Ponce

Antillas Menores
Islas Vírgenes (U.S. & Br.)
Guadalupe (Fr.)
Antigua (Br.)
Dominica (Br.)
Martinica (Fr.)
Sta. Lucía (Br.)
Barbados (Br.)
San Vicente (Br.)
Granada (Br.)
Tobago
TRINIDAD
Puerto España
Margarita

Aruba (Hol.)
Bonaire (Hol.)
Curaçao (Hol.)

LA AMÉRICA DEL SUR

500 mil.
800 km.

SANDERSON

MAR CARIBE

OCÉANO ATLÁNTICO

Barranquilla
Cartagena
Maracaibo
Caracas
TRINIDAD
Puerto España
VENEZUELA
GUAYANA
Georgetown
SURINAM
Paramaribo
GUAYANA FRAN.
Cayenne
Medellín
R. Orinoco
Bogotá
COLOMBIA
Cali
Quito
Ecuador
ECUADOR
Guayaquil
Iquitos
Manaus
R. Amazonas
Belem
CORDILLERA DE LOS ANDES
R. Madeira
B R A S I L
Recife
PERÚ
Machu Picchu
Lima
Cuzco
BOLIVIA
Salvador
Arequipa
L. Titicaca
La Paz
Brasília
Arica
Sucre
Belo Horizonte
Iquique
PARAGUAY
Rio de Janeiro
Antofagasta
Asunción
São Paulo
Santos
Trópico de Capricornio
Tucumán
CHILE
CORDILLERA DE LOS ANDES
Córdoba
Pôrto Alegre
OCÉANO PACÍFICO
Rosario
R. Paraná
URUGUAY
Valparaíso
Mendoza
Buenos Aires
Montevideo
Santiago
A R G E N T I N A
La Plata
Río de la Plata
Concepción
Bahía Blanca
Puerto Montt
0   1000 mi.
0   1600 km.
Islas Malvinas
Punta Arenas
Estrecho de Magallanes
La América del Sur
Tierra del Fuego
Cabo de Hornos

SANDERSON

Contents

Lección 2

Lección 3

Lección 4

Lección 5

Lección 6

Lección 7

Lección 8

Lección 9

Lección 10

Lección 11

Lección 12

Lección 13

1. The preterit of stem-changing verbs (**e:i** and **o:u**) 182
2. The expression **acabar de** 184
3. Special construction with **gustar, doler,** and **hacer falta** 185
4. **¿Qué?** and **¿cuál?** used with **ser** 187
   En el laboratorio 188

Lección 14

1. **Hace** meaning *ago* 192
2. The past participle 193
3. The present perfect tense 195
4. The past perfect (pluperfect) tense 196
   En el laboratorio 198

Lección 15

1. The future tense 202
2. The conditional tense 205
3. Some uses of the prepositions **a, de,** and **en** 208
   En el laboratorio 211
   ¿Cuánto sabe usted ahora?
   Lecciones 11–15 214

Lección 16

1. The present subjunctive 224
2. The subjunctive with verbs of volition 228
3. The absolute superlative 230
   En el laboratorio 231

Lección 17

Lección 18

Lección 19

Lección 20

Appendixes/Vocabularies

Lección preliminar

I

1. Greetings and farewells

Saludos y despedidas

—Buenos días, doctor Rivas. ¿Cómo está usted?	*"Good morning, Doctor Rivas. How are you?"*
—Muy bien, gracias. ¿Y usted?	*"Very well, thank you. And you?"*
—Bien, gracias. Hasta luego.	*"Fine, thank you. See you later."*
—Adiós.	*"Good-bye."*
—Buenas tardes, señora.	*"Good afternoon, madam."*
—Buenas tardes, señor.	*"Good afternoon, sir."*
—Pase y tome asiento, por favor.	*"Come in and sit down, please."*
—Gracias.	*"Thank you."*
—Buenas noches, señorita. ¿Cómo está usted?	*"Good evening, miss. How are you?"*
—No muy bien.	*"Not very well."*
—Lo siento. Hasta mañana.	*"I'm sorry. I'll see you tomorrow."*
—Muchas gracias, señor.	*"Thank you very much, sir."*
—De nada, señora. Adiós.	*"You're very welcome, madam. Good-bye."*
—Mucho gusto, profesor Vera.	*"Pleased to meet you, Professor Vera."*
—El gusto es mío, señorita Reyes.	*"The pleasure is mine, Miss Reyes."*

Vocabulario: Saludos y despedidas

SALUDOS Y DESPEDIDAS

Buenos días.	*Good morning. (Good day.)*
Buenas tardes.	*Good afternoon.*
Buenas noches.	*Good evening. (Good night.)*
Hasta luego.	*I'll see you later. (lit., until later)*
Hasta mañana.	*I'll see you tomorrow.*
Adiós.	*Good-bye.*

TÍTULOS

doctor (Dr.)[1]	*doctor* (masc.)
doctora (Dra.)	*doctor* (fem.)

---

[1] Notice that in Spanish, titles are not capitalized except when they are abbreviated.

profesor	*professor, teacher* (masc.)
profesora	*professor, teacher* (fem.)
señor (Sr.)	*Mr., sir, gentleman*
señora (Sra.)	*Mrs., madam, lady*
señorita (Srta.)	*Miss, young lady*

EXPRESIONES ÚTILES

¿Cómo está usted?	*How are you?*
Bien.	*Well. (Fine.)*
Muy bien, ¿y usted?	*Very well, and you?*
No muy bien.	*Not very well.*
Lo siento.	*I'm sorry.*
Mucho gusto.	*It's a pleasure to meet you.*
El gusto es mío.	*The pleasure is mine.*
Pase.	*Come in.*
Por favor.	*Please.*
Tome asiento.	*Sit down. (Take a seat.)*

Práctica

A. Familiarize yourself with each of the dialogues on page 2, and then act them out with another student.

B. What would you say in the following situations?
1. You meet Mr. García in the morning and ask him how he is.
2. You thank Miss Vera for a favor and tell her you will see her tomorrow.
3. You greet Mrs. Nieto in the afternoon and ask her to come in and sit down.
4. A young woman is introduced to you.
5. Someone thanks you for a favor.
6. Someone asks you how you are and you are not feeling well.

2. Cardinal numbers 0–39
Los números cardinales 0–39

0	cero	5	cinco
1	uno[1]	6	seis
2	dos	7	siete
3	tres	8	ocho
4	cuatro	9	nueve

[1] **Uno** changes to **un** before a masculine singular noun: *un* **libro** (*one book.*). **Uno** changes to **una** before a femine singular noun: *una* **silla** (*one chair*). All other numbers ending in **-uno** or **-una** follow the same pattern: *veintiún* **libros** (*twenty-one books*), *veintiuna* **sillas** (*twenty-one chairs*).

10 diez	25 veinticinco
11 once	26 veintiséis
12 doce	27 veintisiete
13 trece	28 veintiocho
14 catorce	29 veintinueve
15 quince	30 treinta
16 dieciséis	31 treinta y uno
17 diecisiete	32 treinta y dos
18 dieciocho	33 treinta y tres
19 diecinueve	34 treinta y cuatro
20 veinte	35 treinta y cinco
21 veintiuno[1]	36 treinta y seis
22 veintidós	37 treinta y siete
23 veintitrés	38 treinta y ocho
24 veinticuatro	39 treinta y nueve

Práctica

A. Read the following numbers aloud in Spanish.

0	10	9	31	25	19	7	33
15	37	16	11	21	20	29	17
28	14	13	8	4	12	30	22

B. Read the following telephone numbers in Spanish. Say each number one by one.

383–5079	254–2675	792–5136	689–0275
985–0746	765–1032	985–7340	872–0695

C. Find out the phone number of three classmates. Ask: **¿Cuál es tu número de teléfono?** (*What is your phone number?*).

3. Personal information
Información personal

—**¿Nombre y apellido?**	*"Name and surname?"*
—**María Valdés.**	*"Maria Valdes."*
—**¿Estado civil?**	*"Marital status?"*
—**Casada.**	*"Married."*

[1] The numbers 16 to 29 may also be written as separate words: **diez y seis, veinte y uno,** and so on. The most common spelling, however, is the single word form used in this text.

—¿Apellido de soltera?[1]   *"Maiden name?"*
—Rivas.   *"Rivas."*

—¿Nacionalidad?   *"Nationality (citizenship)?"*
—Norteamericana.[2]   *"North American (U.S.)."*

—¿Lugar de nacimiento?   *"Place of birth?"*
—La Habana, Cuba.   *"Havana, Cuba."*

—¿Edad?   *"Age?"*
—Veintinueve años.   *"Twenty-nine years (old)."*

—¿Ocupación?[3]   *"Occupation?"*
—Enfermera.   *"Nurse."*

—¿Dirección?   *"Address?"*
—Calle Magnolia,[4]   *"Number twenty-three*
    número veintitrés.   *Magnolia Street."*

—¿Ciudad?   *"City?"*
—Riverside.   *"Riverside."*

—¿Número de teléfono?   *"Phone number?"*
—682–7530.   *"682–7530."*

—¿Número de seguro   *"Social Security number?"*
    social?
—566–14–9023.   *"566–14–9023."*

Vocabulario: Información personal

el nombre   *name*
el apellido   *surname*
el apellido de soltera   *maiden name*
el estado civil   *marital status*
   soltero(a)   *single*
   casado(a)   *married*
   separado(a)   *separated*
   divorciado(a)   *divorced*
   viudo(a)   *widowed*
la nacionalidad   *nationality*

---

[1] The preposition **de** + *noun* in Spanish is the equivalent of two nouns used together in English. Notice that the first noun functions as an adjective in English.
[2] Native Spanish speakers use **norteamericano(a)** or **americano(a)** to refer to people from the United States.
[3] See Appendix C for a list of occupations.
[4] In Spanish, the name of the street is placed before the number.

norteamericano(a)　*North American (from the U.S.)*
el lugar de nacimiento　*place of birth*
la edad　*age*
el año, los años　*year(s)*
la ocupación　*occupation*
el (la) enfermero(a)　*nurse*
el lugar donde trabaja　*place of work*
la dirección, el domicilio　*address*
la calle　*street*
la ciudad　*city*
el número　*number*
el número de teléfono　*phone number*
el número de seguro social　*Social Security number*
el número de la licencia　*driver's license number*
para conducir (manejar)
el sexo　*sex*
　femenino　*feminine*
　masculino　*masculine*

Práctica

Interview a classmate, using the following questions. When you have finished, switch roles.

1. ¿Nombre y apellido?
2. ¿Estado civil?
3. ¿Apellido de soltera? *(If you are talking to a married woman.)*
4. ¿Nacionalidad?
5. ¿Lugar de nacimiento?
6. ¿Ocupación?
7. ¿Lugar donde trabaja?
8. ¿Dirección? (¿Domicilio?)
9. ¿Ciudad?
10. ¿Número de teléfono?
11. ¿Número de seguro social?
12. ¿Número de la licencia para conducir?

4. Days of the week
Los días de la semana

—¿Qué día es hoy?　　*"What day is it today?"*
—Hoy es lunes.　　*"Today is Monday."*

—Hoy es martes, ¿no?	*"Today is Tuesday, isn't it?"*
—No, hoy es miércoles.	*"No, today is Wednesday."*

—¿Qué día es hoy?	*"What day is it today?*
¿Jueves?	*Thursday?"*
—No, hoy es viernes.	*"No, today is Friday."*

—Hoy es... sábado...	*"Today is . . . Saturday*
¡no! domingo...	*. . . no! Sunday . . ."*
—Sí, hoy es domingo.	*"Yes, today is Sunday."*

Los días de la semana

lunes	*Monday*	**viernes**	*Friday*
martes	*Tuesday*	**sábado**	*Saturday*
miércoles	*Wednesday*	**domingo**	*Sunday*
jueves	*Thursday*		

ATENCIÓN: The days of the week are not capitalized in Spanish, and in Spanish-speaking countries, the week begins on Monday. **El** and **los** are frequently used with the days of the week to express *on*: **el lunes** *(on Monday)*, **los martes** *(on Tuesdays)*, etc.

Práctica

The people asking the following questions are always a day ahead. Tell them the correct day.

Modelo: —Hoy es lunes, ¿no?
         —**No, hoy es domingo.**

1. Hoy es miércoles, ¿no?	4. Hoy es martes, ¿no?
2. Hoy es domingo, ¿no?	5. Hoy es sábado, ¿no?
3. Hoy es viernes, ¿no?	6. Hoy es jueves, ¿no?

5. Months and seasons of the year
Los meses y las estaciones del año

Los meses del año

enero	*January*	**abril**	*April*
febrero	*February*	**mayo**	*May*
marzo	*March*	**junio**	*June*

julio	*July*	octubre	*October*
agosto	*August*	**noviembre**	*November*
septiembre	*September*	**diciembre**	*December*

ATENCIÓN: The names of the months are not capitalized in Spanish.

◆ To talk about the date, use the following expressions.

—**¿Qué fecha es hoy?**	*"What's the date today?"*
—**Hoy es el quince de enero.**	*"Today is January fifteenth."*
—**¿Hoy es el primero de mayo?**	*"Is today May first?"*
—**No, hoy es el dos de mayo.**	*"No, today is May second."*

ATENCIÓN: Spanish uses cardinal numbers to refer to dates. The only exception is **primero** (*first*).

◆ When telling the date, always begin with the expression **Hoy es el...**

Hoy es el veinte de mayo.   *Today is May twentieth.*

◆ Complete the expression by saying the number followed by the preposition **de** (*of*), and then the month.

el **quince de mayo**   *May 15th*
el **diez de septiembre**   *September 10th*
el **doce de octubre**   *October 12th*

ATENCIÓN: Notice that the day precedes the month. Thus, 3–6–96 means June 3rd, 1996. In Spanish, the article (**el**) is usually included when giving the date orally, although it is sometimes omitted in writing.

Las estaciones del año

la primavera	*spring*	**el verano**	*summer*
el otoño	*fall*	**el invierno**	*winter*

Práctica

A. The following are important dates to remember. Say them in Spanish.

1. the 4th of July
2. the 31st of October
3. March 21st
4. April 1st
5. the first of January
6. February 14th
7. December 25th
8. May 5th
9. your birthday
10. today's date

B. In which season does each of these months fall?

1. febrero
2. agosto
3. mayo
4. enero
5. octubre
6. julio
7. abril
8. noviembre

6. Colors
Los colores

amarillo *yellow*
anaranjado *orange*
azul *blue*
blanco *white*
gris *gray*
marrón (café) *brown*
morado *purple*
negro *black*
rojo *red*
rosado *pink*
verde *green*

Práctica

To ask a classmate whether he or she likes something, you say: **¿Te gusta...?**[1] To say that you like something, say: **Me gusta...** Conduct a survey of your classmates to find out which color is the most popular in class, following the model.

Modelo: —¿Qué color te gusta?
　　　　　—**Me gusta el color rojo.**

---

[1] When addressing someone as **usted**, use, **¿Le gusta...?**

Información personal

Provide the information requested.

Apellido y nombres

_____

Dirección

_____

Ciudad

_____

Teléfono

_____

Estado civil	Sexo	Edad
1. _____ soltero(a)	Masculino _____	_____
2. _____ casado(a)	Femenino _____	
3. _____ separado(a)		
4. _____ divorciado(a)		
5. _____ viudo(a)		

Nacionalidad _____

Ocupación[1] _____

Lugar donde trabaja _____

Número de seguro social _____

Número de la licencia para conducir _____

[1] See Appendix C for a list of occupations.

📼 *En el laboratorio*

The following material is to be used with the tape in the language laboratory.

I. *Vocabulario*

Repeat each word or phrase after the speaker.

SALUDOS Y DESPEDIDAS:	Buenos días. Buenas tardes. Buenas noches. Hasta luego. Hasta mañana. Adiós.
TÍTULOS:	doctor profesor señor señora señorita
EXPRESIONES ÚTILES:	¿Cómo está usted? Bien. Muy bien, ¿y usted? No muy bien. Lo siento. Mucho gusto. El gusto es mío. Pase. Por favor. Tome asiento.
INFORMACIÓN PERSONAL:	nombre apellido apellido de soltera estado civil soltero casado separado divorciado viudo nacionalidad norteamericano lugar de nacimiento edad año fecha de nacimiento ocupación enfermero lugar donde trabaja dirección domicilio calle ciudad número número de teléfono número de seguro social número de la licencia para conducir sexo femenino masculino
LOS DÍAS DE LA SEMANA:	lunes martes miércoles jueves viernes sábado domingo
LOS MESES:	enero febrero marzo abril mayo junio julio agosto septiembre octubre noviembre diciembre
LAS ESTACIONES:	primavera verano otoño invierno

II. Práctica

A. You find yourself in the following situations. What would you say? Repeat the correct answer after the speaker's confirmation. Listen to the model.

Modelo: You meet Mr. Vega in the morning.
Buenos días, señor Vega.

B. Answer each of the addition problems you hear in Spanish. Repeat the correct answer after the speaker's confirmation. Listen to the model.

Modelo: tres y dos
cinco

C. The speaker will tell you what day today is. Respond by saying what day tomorrow is. Repeat the correct answer after the speaker's confirmation. Listen to the model.

Modelo: Hoy es lunes
Mañana es martes.

D. The speaker will name several holidays. Name the date on which each holiday falls. Repeat the correct answer after the speaker's confirmation. Listen to the model.

Modelo: Flag Day
el catorce de junio

E. The speaker will name several familiar objects. State the colors of each object in Spanish. Repeat the correct answer after the speaker's confirmation. Listen to the model.

Modelo: a violet
morado

Lección preliminar

II

1. **The alphabet**
2. **Gender and number**
3. **The definite article**
4. **The indefinite article**
5. **Uses of** hay
6. **Cardinal numbers 40–299**

Vocabulario

COGNADOS[1]

la **conversación** conversation
la **decisión** decision
la **idea** idea
la **lección** lesson
la **libertad** liberty
el **problema** problem
el **programa** program
el **progreso** progress

el (la) **secretario(a)**
  secretary
el **sistema** system
el **teléfono** telephone
el **telegrama** telegram
la **televisión** television
la **universidad** university

NOMBRES

la **amistad** friendship
la **casa** house
el **clima** climate
el **día** day
el **dinero** money
el **español** Spanish (*language*)
el **hombre** man
el **idioma**, la **lengua**
  language
la **lámpara** lamp
el **lápiz** pencil

el **libro** book
la **luz** light
la **mano** hand
el (la) **médico(a)**, **doctor(a)**
  M.D., doctor
la **mesa** table
la **mujer** woman
la **pluma** pen
la **puerta** door
la **silla** chair

1. The alphabet
El alfabeto

Letter	Name	Letter	Name	Letter	Name	Letter	Name
a	a	h	hache	ñ	eñe	u	u
b	be	i	i	o	o	v	ve
c	ce	j	jota	p	pe	w	doble ve
ch	che	k	ka	q	cu	x	equis
d	de	l	ele	r	ere	y	y griega
e	e	ll	elle	rr	erre	z	zeta
f	efe	m	eme	s	ese		
g	ge	n	ene	t	te		

[1] Cognates are words that resemble one another and have similar meanings in Spanish and English. Note that English cognates often have different spellings and always have different pronunciations than their Spanish counterparts.

Práctica

A Spanish-speaking person may not know how to spell your name. He or she might ask: ¿**Cómo se escribe?** *(How do you spell it?).* Learn how to spell your name in Spanish and ask other members of the class how to spell theirs.

2. Gender and number
Género y número

Género

> **Gender**   the classification of nouns, pronouns, and adjectives as masculine or feminine.

In Spanish, all nouns, including abstract nouns and those denoting nonliving things, are either masculine or feminine.

masculine	*feminine*
año	puerta
señor	señora
teléfono	lámpara
progreso	idea

Here are some practical rules to use to determine the gender of Spanish nouns.

◆ Nouns denoting females and most nouns ending in **-a** are feminine. Nouns referring to males and most nouns ending in **-o** are masculine.

masculine	*feminine*
hombre	mujer
teléfon**o**	sill**a**
diner**o**	cas**a**
libr**o**	mes**a**

ATENCIÓN: Two important exceptions to this rule are **día** *(day)*, which is masculine, and **mano** *(hand)*, which is feminine.

◆ Some nouns that end in **-a** are masculine. These nouns are of Greek origin and have kept the gender they had in that language.

problem**a**	sistem**a**
progr**a**ma	telegram**a**
ʾidiom**a**	clim**a**

◆ Nouns ending in **-sión, -ción, -tad,** and **-dad** are feminine.

televi**sión**	lec**ción**
deci**sión**	conversa**ción**
liber**tad**	universi**dad**
amis**tad**	ciu**dad**

◆ The gender of some nouns must be learned.

masculine	*feminine*
español	calle

◆ Many masculine nouns ending in **-o** have a corresponding feminine form ending in **-a.**

masculine	*feminine*
enfermer**o**	enfermer**a**
secretari**o**	secretari**a**

◆ Certain masculine nouns ending in a consonant add **-a** to form the corresponding feminine noun.

masculine	*feminine*
profesor	profesor**a**
doctor	doctor**a**

◆ Colors, numbers, and days of the week are masculine.

Práctica

Are the following nouns feminine or masculine?

1. teléfono
2. día
3. televisión
4. enfermera
5. problema
6. calle
7. mesa
8. universidad
9. dinero
10. idioma
11. silla
12. amistad
13. mano
14. ciudad
15. lección
16. progreso
17. señor
18. profesora
19. programa
20. clima

Número

Number   a term that identifies words as singular or plural: chair, chairs

Nouns are made plural in Spanish by adding **-s** to those ending in a vowel and **-es** to those ending in a consonant. Nouns ending in **-z** are made plural by changing the **z** to **c** and adding **-es**.

teléfon**o**	teléfono**s**	lápi**z**	lápi**ces**
mesa	mesa**s**	lu**z**	lu**ces**
profeso**r**	profesor**es**	lección	leccio**nes**

ATENCIÓN: Accent marks that fall on the last syllable of singular words are omitted in the plural form: **lección, lecciones.**

Práctica

What are the plural forms of the following nouns?

1. silla
2. libro
3. lápiz
4. universidad
5. telegrama
6. ciudad
7. lección
8. señor
9. clima
10. conversación
11. profesor
12. luz
13. decisión
14. doctor
15. amistad
16. lámpara

3. The definite article
El artículo definido

> **Definite article**   a word used before a noun to indicate a definite person or thing: **the** woman, **the** money

Spanish has four forms that are equivalent to the English definite article *the*.

	Masculine	*Feminine*
Singular	el	la
Plural	los	las

el profesor	**la** profesora
los profesores	**las** profesoras
el lápiz	**la** lámpara
los lápices	**las** lámparas

ATENCIÓN: Learning each noun's definite article will help you to remember the noun's gender.

Práctica

What are the definite articles for the following nouns?

1. universidades
2. problema
3. profesor
4. doctor
5. señora
6. señores
7. día
8. televisión
9. silla
10. mujeres
11. dinero
12. profesores
13. idea
14. telegrama
15. libertad

4. The indefinite article
El artículo indefinido

Indefinite article   a word used before a noun to indicate an indefinite person or object: **a** child, **an** apple, **some** students

The indefinite article in Spanish has four forms; they are equivalent to *a*, *an*, and *some*.

	Masculine	*Feminine*
Singular	un	una
Plural	unos	unas

un profesor
unos profesores
un lápiz
unos lápices

una profesora
unas profesoras
una pluma
unas plumas

Práctica

How would you name the following items in Spanish?

1. a pen
2. a man
3. some days
4. some chairs
5. a problem
6. a house
7. a light
8. a program
9. some pencils
10. a lesson
11. a friendship
12. a decision

5. Uses of hay
Usos de hay

The form **hay** means *there is* or *there are*. It has no subject and must not be confused with **es** (*it is*) and **son** (*they are*).

Hay un lápiz en la mesa.	*There is a pencil on the table.*
Hay diez libros en la mesa.	*There are ten books on the table.*

Práctica

Say how many of the following items there are in the classroom, using **hay.**

1. profesor(a)
2. hombres
3. mujeres
4. sillas
5. mesas
6. puertas

6. Cardinal numbers 40–299
Números cardinales 40–299

40	cuarenta	90	noventa	
41	cuarenta y uno...	100	cien (ciento)	
50	cincuenta	101	ciento uno... [1]	
60	sesenta	150	ciento cincuenta	
70	setenta	200	doscientos	
80	ochenta	250	doscientos cincuenta...	

ATENCIÓN: **Ciento** becomes **cien** before a noun.

cien telegramas
cien casas

Remember that **uno** becomes **un** before a masculine noun and **una** before a feminine noun, even in compound numbers.

ciento **un** telegramas
ciento **una** sillas

Práctica

Read the following numbers aloud in Spanish.

86	48	57	123	42	69	74	214
80	91	100	65	111	234	200	261
197	136	115	175	169	185	101	299

[1] Notice that the word **y** (*and*) is not used after hundreds: **ciento uno, ciento dos, doscientos veinte,** and so on.

En el laboratorio

The following material is to be used with the tape in the language laboratory.

I. Vocabulario

Repeat each word after the speaker. When repeating words that are cognates, notice the difference in pronunciation between English and Spanish.

COGNADOS: la conversación   la decisión   la idea
la lección   la libertad   el problema
el programa   el progreso   el secretario
el sistema   el teléfono   el telegrama
la televisión   la universidad

NOMBRES: la amistad   la casa   el clima   el día
el dinero   el español   el hombre   el idioma
la lengua   la lámpara   el lápiz   el libro
la luz   la mano   el médico   la mesa
la mujer   la pluma   la puerta   la silla

II. Práctica

A. Say each of the acronyms you hear in Spanish. Repeat the correct answer after the speaker's confirmation. Listen to the model.

Modelo: USA
u-ese-a

B. You will hear some nouns. Repeat each noun, adding the appropriate singular or plural definite article. Repeat the correct answer after the speaker's confirmation. Listen to the model.

Modelo: silla
la silla

C. You will hear several singular nouns, each preceded by an indefinite article. Make the nouns and the articles plural. Repeat the correct answer after the speaker's confirmation. Listen to the model.

Modelo: un alumno
unos alumnos

D. Say the numbers you hear in Spanish. Repeat the correct answer after the speaker's confirmation. Listen to the model.

Modelo: 157
ciento cincuenta y siete

Lección

1

1. **Subject pronouns**
2. **The present indicative of regular -ar verbs**
3. **Interrogative and negative sentences**
4. **Cardinal numbers 300–1,000**
5. **Telling time**

Vocabulario

COGNADOS

la cafetería cafeteria	**el restaurante** restaurant
el italiano Italian *(language)*	

NOMBRES
la cerveza beer
la cuchara spoon
la cuenta bill, check
el francés French
  (language)
el inglés English
  (language)
el mantel tablecloth
la mañana morning
la noche evening
el refresco soft drink, soda
la servilleta napkin
la tarde afternoon
el tenedor fork
el vino wine

VERBOS
  desear to want, to wish
  estudiar to study

hablar to speak, to talk
necesitar to need
pagar to pay (for)
tomar to drink
trabajar to work

**OTRAS PALABRAS Y
EXPRESIONES**
  ¿a qué hora...? at
  what time?
  en in, at
  pero but
  ¿Qué hora es? What
  time is it?
  sí yes

1. Subject pronouns
Pronombres usados como sujetos

Subject   person or thing about which something is said in a sentence or phrase: **Mary** works. **The car** is new.
Pronoun   a word that replaces a noun: **she, them, us, it**
Subject pronoun   a personal pronoun that is used as a subject: **They** work. **It** is small.

Singular		*Plural*[1]	
yo	I	{ **nosotros** we (*masculine*) { **nosotras** we (*feminine*)	
tú	you (*familiar*)	**ustedes**[3] you	
usted[2]	you (*formal*)		
él	he	**ellos**	they (*masculine*)
ella	she	**ellas**	they (*feminine*)

◆ The masculine plural pronoun may refer to the masculine gender alone or to both genders together.

Juan y Roberto: **ellos**   *Juan and Roberto:* **they**
Juan y María: **ellos**   *Juan and María:* **they**

◆ Use the **tú** form as the equivalent of *you* when addressing a close friend, a relative, or a child. Use the **usted** form in all other instances. Notice that **ustedes** is used for both familiar and polite plural.

Práctica

Complete the following sentences with the appropriate subject pronoun.

Modelo: You refer to *Mr. Gómez* as . . . **él.**

1. You point to yourself and say . . .
2. You refer to Mrs. Gómez as . . .
3. You are talking to a little boy and you call him . . .
4. You are talking to a woman you've just met and you call her . . .
5. Your mother refers to herself and her sister as . . .
6. Your father refers to himself and his sister as . . .
7. You are talking to a few people and you call them . . .
8. You refer to Mr. Gómez and his daughter as . . .
9. You refer to Mrs. Gómez and her daughter as . . .
10. You refer to Mr. and Mrs. Gómez as . . .
11. You are talking with one of your professors and you call him . . .
12. You are talking with one of your friends and you call her . . .

[1] The second-person plural subject pronoun **vosotros,** used only in Spain, is not taught in this text. In all other Spanish-speaking countries, **ustedes** is used for both the familiar and the formal plural form of *you.*
[2] Abbreviated **Ud.**
[3] Abbreviated **Uds.**

2. The present indicative of regular -ar verbs

El presente de indicativo de los verbos regulares terminados en -ar

> **Verb**   a word that expresses an action or a state: We **sleep.** The baby **is** sick.
> **Infinitive**   the form of a verb showing no subject or number, preceded in English by the word *to*: **to do, to bring**

The infinitive of all Spanish verbs consists of a stem (such as habl-) and an ending (such as **-ar**). When looking up a verb in the dictionary, you will always find it listed under the infinitive (*e.g.,* **hablar:** *to speak*). Spanish verbs are classified according to their endings. There are three conjugations: **-ar, -er,** and **-ir.** The stem of regular verbs does not change; the endings change to agree with the subjects. Regular verbs ending in **-ar** are conjugated like **hablar.**

hablar *(to speak)*		
Singular		
Stem	*Ending*	
yo	habl-**o**	Yo **hablo** español.[1]
tú	habl-**as**	Tú **hablas** español.
Ud.	habl-**a**	Ud. **habla** español.
él	habl-**a**	Juan **habla** español. Él **habla** español.
ella	habl-**a**	Ana **habla** español. Ella **habla** español.
Plural		
nosotros	habl-**amos**	Nosotros **hablamos** español.
Uds.	habl-**an**	Uds. **hablan** español.
ellos	habl-**an**	Ellos **hablan** español.
ellas	habl-**an**	Ellas **hablan** español.

◆   The present tense in Spanish is equivalent to three forms in English.

Yo **hablo** *italiano.*
$\begin{cases} \textit{I speak Italian.} \\ \textit{I do speak Italian.} \\ \textit{I am speaking Italian.} \end{cases}$

[1] Names of languages and nationalities are not capitalized in Spanish.

◆ Since the verb endings indicate who the speaker is, the subject pronouns are frequently omitted.

—**Hablas** inglés, ¿no?   *"You (familiar) speak English, don't you?"*

—Sí, **hablo** inglés.   *"Yes, I speak English."*

However, subject pronouns may be used for emphasis or clarification:

—**Ellos hablan** inglés, ¿no?   *"They speak English, don't they?"*
—**Ella habla** inglés.   *"She speaks English."*
—**Él habla** español.   *"He speaks Spanish."*

◆ Some common verbs that follow the regular **-ar** pattern are:

desear	to want, to wish	**pagar**	to pay
estudiar	to study	**tomar**	to drink
necesitar	to need	**trabajar**	to work

—El Sr. Paz **trabaja** en una cafetería, ¿no?   *"Mr. Paz works at a cafeteria, doesn't he?"*
—No, él **trabaja** en un restaurante.   *"No, he works at a restaurant."*

—Ud. **desea** una cerveza, ¿no?   *"You want a beer, don't you?"*
—Sí, y ella **desea** tomar[1] un refresco. Yo pago la cuenta.   *"Yes, and she wants to drink a soda. I'm paying the bill."*

—Ud. **necesita** el mantel, ¿no?   *"You need the tablecloth, don't you?"*
—Sí, **necesito** el mantel y las servilletas.   *"Yes, I need the tablecloth and the napkins."*

—Uds. **estudian** francés en la universidad, ¿no?   *"You study French at the university, don't you?"*
—No, pero **estudiamos** inglés.   *"No, but we study English."*

ATENCIÓN: When speaking about a third person (indirect address) and using a title with the last name, the definite article is placed before the title (*El Sr. Paz habla español.*) It is not used when speaking directly to someone (**Buenos días, *Sr.* Paz.**).

---

[1] When two verbs are used together, the second verb is in the infinitive.

Práctica

A. Form sentences that tell where these people work, what they study, what they need, and what they want.

1. **trabajar:**   yo / un restaurante *yo trabajo un restaurante.*
   Anita / la cafetería *Anita trabajo la cafetería*
   tú / Los Ángeles *Tu trabajen Los Ángeles*
   nosotros / la universidad *Nosotros trabajes la universidad*

2. **estudiar:**   Uds. / francés *Uds estudian frances.*
   Carlos / italiano *Carlos estudia italiano*
   Ud. / la lección dos *Ud estudian la lección dos*
   él y yo / español *El y yo estudio español.*

3. **necesitar:**   Ana y Rosa / dinero *Ana y Rosa necesitas dinero*
   nosotras / una mesa *Nosotras necesitas una mesa*
   yo / pagar la cuenta *yo necesito pagar la cuenta.*
   tú / una servilleta *tú necesitas un servilleta*

4. **desear:**   ellos / cerveza *ellos desean cerveza*
   nosotros / un refresco *nosotros deseos un refresco.*
   yo / tomar Coca-Cola *yo deseo tomar Coca-Cola*
   Elsa / estudiar inglés

B. Provide the missing information about yourself and other people.

1. Ella trabaja en Los Ángeles y yo... *Yo trabajen los Angeles*
2. Tú y yo trabajamos en la cafetería y ellos... *trabajan en la cafetería*
3. Carlos estudia italiano y nosotros... *nos estudiamos italiano*
4. Yo deseo estudiar francés y ellos... *desean estudiar frances*
5. Nosotros hablamos inglés y el profesor... *el profesor hablaingles*
6. Ellos hablan francés y yo... *hablo frances*
7. Yo necesito una pluma y tú... *tú necesita una pluma*
8. María necesita sillas y nosotros... *nosotros necesitamos sillas*
9. Tú tomas refrescos y yo... *yo tomo refrescos*
10. Ella toma cerveza y Uds... *uds toman cerveza*

3. Interrogative and negative sentences

Oraciones interrogativas y negativas

Interrogative sentences

There are three ways of asking a question in Spanish to elicit a yes / no answer. These three questions ask for the same information and have the same meaning.

1. ¿**Uds.** necesitan el mantel? ⎫
2. ¿Necesitan **Uds.** el mantel? ⎬ Sí, nosotros necesita-
3. ¿Necesitan el mantel **Uds.**? ⎭ mos el mantel.

◆ Example 1 is a declarative sentence that is made interrogative by a change in intonation.

Uds. necesitan el mantel.   ¿Uds. necesitan el mantel?

◆ Example 2 is an interrogative sentence formed by placing the subject (**Uds.**) after the verb.

◆ Example 3, another interrogative sentence, is formed by placing the subject (**Uds.**) at the end of the sentence.

ATENCIÓN: An auxiliary verb such as *do* or *does* is not used in Spanish to form an interrogative sentence.

　　　　¿Uds.　toman　vino?
　(Do)　you　drink　wine?

Notice that in Spanish interrogative sentences have a question mark at the end and an inverted question mark at the beginning.

Práctica

Ask the following questions in two other ways, using the model as an example.

Modelo: ¿**Elena** trabaja en Buenos Aires?
　　　　¿Trabaja **Elena** en Buenos Aires?
　　　　¿Trabaja en Buenos Aires **Elena**?

1. ¿Tú tomas vino?　　　　4. ¿Pedro necesita el mantel?
2. ¿Ella estudia inglés?　　5. ¿Tú pagas la cuenta?
3. ¿Uds. hablan español?　6. ¿Ud. desea tomar un refresco?

Negative sentences

To make a sentence negative, simply place the word **no** in front of the verb.

Ella　　habla inglés.　　　*She　　　speaks English.*
Ella **no** habla inglés.　*She **doesn't** speak English.*

ATENCIÓN: Spanish does not use an auxiliary verb such as the English *do* or *does* in a negative sentence.

◆ If the answer to a question is negative, the word **no** appears twice: at the beginning of the sentence, as in English, and also in front of the verb.

—¿Necesitas las cucharas?	*"Do you need the spoons?"*
—**No,** (yo) **no** necesito las cucharas, pero necesito los tenedores.	*"No, I don't need the spoons, but I need the forks."*

ATENCIÓN: The subject pronoun need not appear in the answer because the verb ending identifies the speaker.

Práctica

Answer the following questions in the negative, using the information provided in parentheses. Then create two original questions to ask a classmate.

Modelo: —¿Ud. trabaja en un restaurante? (cafetería)
     —**No, (yo) no trabajo en un restaurante; trabajo en una cafetería.**

1. ¿Uds. necesitan los tenedores? (cucharas)
2. ¿Ellos necesitan el mantel? (servilletas)
3. ¿Tú deseas tomar cerveza? (un refresco)
4. ¿Uds. toman Pepsi? (Sprite)
5. ¿Tú pagas la cerveza? (vino)

4. Cardinal numbers 300–1,000
Números cardinales 300–1.000

300 trescientos	700 setecientos
400 cuatrocientos	800 ochocientos
500 quinientos	900 novecientos
600 seiscientos	1.000 mil[1]

In Spanish, one does not count in hundreds beyond 1,000; thus, 1,100 is expressed as **mil cien**. Note that a period is used instead of a comma to indicate thousands.

1.996	**mil novecientos noventa y seis**
32.418	**treinta y dos mil cuatrocientos dieciocho**

---

[1] Notice that the indefinite article is not used before the word **mil**.

Práctica

Read the following numbers aloud in Spanish.

896	380	519	937	722
1.305	451	978	643	504
1.000	15.893	11.906	27.567	565.736

5. Telling time
La hora

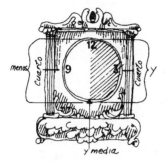

◆ Here are some important points to remember when telling time in Spanish.

1. **Es** is used with **una** and **son** is used with all the other hours.

Es la **una** y cuarto.	*It is a quarter after one.*
Son las **cinco** y diez.	*It is ten after five.*

2. The feminine definite article is always used before the hour, since it refers to **la hora.**

Es **la** una y veinte.	*It is twenty after one.*
Son **las** cuatro y media.	*It is four-thirty.*

3. The hour is given first, then the minutes.

Son las **cuatro** y **diez.**	*It is ten after four* (literally: *four and ten*).

4. The equivalent of *past* or *after* is **y.**

Son las doce **y** cinco.	*It's five after twelve.*

5. The equivalent of *to* or *till* is **menos.**

Son las ocho **menos** veinte.	*It's twenty to eight.*

6. When telling time, follow this order.

    a. **Es** or **Son**
    b. **la** or **las**
    c. the hour
    d. **y** or **menos**
    e. the minutes

Es
la
una
y
veinte.

Son
las
cinco
menos
diez.

♦ The equivalent of *at + time* is **a** + **las** + *time*.

A la una.   *At one o'clock.*
A las tres y media.   *At three-thirty.*

♦ While both **por la** and **de la** mean *in the* when used with time, they are used differently and are not interchangeable. When a specific time is mentioned, **de la (mañana, tarde, noche)** should be used.

Yo estudio a las dos   *I study at two in the afternoon.*
  de la tarde.

When a specific time is *not* mentioned, **por la (mañana, tarde, noche)** should be used.

Yo estudio **por la** mañana.   *I study in the morning.*

—¿A qué hora estudias tú?   *"At what time do you study?"*
—Yo estudio a las dos   *"I study at two in the after-*
  de la tarde.   *noon."*

—¿Trabajas **por la** noche?   *"Do you work in the evening?"*
—No, yo trabajo **por la**   *"No, I work in the morning."*
  mañana.

Práctica

A. ¿Qué hora es?   (*What time is it?*)   Say the time given on the following clocks, and then write the times in Spanish.

B. With a partner, act out the following dialogues in Spanish.

1. "What time is it?"

   "It's a quarter to six."

2. "At what time does he work?"

   "He works at two-thirty in the afternoon."

3. "Do you study in the morning or in the afternoon?"

   "We study in the evening."

4. "Is it one-thirty?"

   "No, it's twenty-five to two."

C. Interview a classmate to find out the time of day at which he or she does the following things. When you have finished, switch roles.

1. studies
2. works
3. speaks Spanish

🔲 *En el laboratorio*

The following material is to be used with the tape in the language laboratory.

I. Vocabulario

Repeat each word after the speaker. When repeating words that are cognates, notice the difference in pronunciation between English and Spanish.

COGNADOS:	la cafetería　el italiano　el restaurante
NOMBRES:	la cerveza　la cuchara　la cuenta el francés　el inglés　el mantel la mañana　la noche　el refresco la servilleta　la tarde　el tenedor el vino
VERBOS:	desear　estudiar　hablar　necesitar pagar　tomar　trabajar
OTRAS PALABRAS Y EXPRESIONES:	¿a qué hora...?　en　pero ¿Qué hora es?　sí

II. Práctica

A. Repeat each sentence, then substitute the new subject given by the speaker. Be sure the verb agrees with the new subject. Repeat the correct answer after the speaker's confirmation. Listen to the model.

Modelo: Yo estudio español. (nosotros)
　　　　Nosotros estudiamos español.

1. Yo estudio español. (nosotros / Ud. / ellos)
2. Ella trabaja en la cafetería. (Yo / Uds. / tú.)
3. Tú necesitas dinero. (Él / nosotros / ellas)
4. Nosotros tomamos refrescos. (Tú / Elsa / yo)
5. Él paga la cuenta. (nosotros / tú / Uds.)

B. Change each sentence to the interrogative form by placing the subject at the end of the sentence. Repeat the correct answer after the speaker's confirmation. Listen to the model.

Modelo: Teresa necesita dinero.
　　　　¿Necesita dinero Teresa?

1. La Sra. López estudia inglés.
2. El Sr. Vega habla francés.

3. La Srta. Díaz necesita los tenedores.
4. Uds. trabajan en el restaurante.
5. Tú deseas estudiar francés.

C. Change each of the following sentences to the negative. Repeat the correct answer after the speaker's confirmation. Listen to the model.

Modelo: Yo hablo inglés.
     Yo no hablo inglés.

1. Eva y Luis hablan español.
2. Nosotros estudiamos en la universidad.
3. Ella trabaja en un restaurante.
4. Yo necesito una cuchara.
5. Tú tomas cerveza.
6. Uds. desean trabajar en un restaurante.

D. Read the following numbers in Spanish. Repeat the correct answer after the speaker's confirmation. Listen to the model.

Modelo: 1.581
     Mil quinientos ochenta y uno.

1. 322	6. 878	11. 5.873
2. 430	7. 985	12. 9.108
3. 547	8. 1.000	13. 12.920
4. 659	9. 543	14. 15.008
5. 761	10. 2.715	15. 23.192

III. Para escuchar y entender

1. Listen carefully to the dialogue. It will be read twice.

(*Diálogo 1*)

Now the speaker will make statements about the dialogue you just heard. Tell whether each statement is true (**verdadero**) or false (**falso**). The speaker will confirm the correct answer.

2. Listen carefully to the dialogue. It will be read twice.

(*Diálogo 2*)

Now the speaker will ask some questions about the dialogue you just heard. Answer each question, omitting the subject. The speaker will confirm the correct answer. Repeat the correct answer.

Lección

2

1. **Position of adjectives**
2. **Forms of adjectives**
3. **Agreement of articles, nouns, and adjectives**
4. **The present indicative of regular -er and -ir verbs**
5. **The present indicative of** ser

Vocabulario

COGNADOS

el **champán** champagne
el **cheque** check
el **chocolate** chocolate
 inteligente intelligent

el **menú** menu
mexicano(a) Mexican
el **té** tea

NOMBRES
el **café** coffee
la **comida** meal, food
el **huevo** egg
la **leche** milk
el **mozo**, el **(la)**
 camarero(a), el **(la)**
 mesero(a) (*Méx.*) waiter,
 waitress
la **muchacha**, la **chica** girl,
 young woman
el **muchacho**, el **chico** boy,
 young man
la **papa**, la **patata** (*Esp.*)
 potato
el **pastel**[1] pie
el **pescado** fish
el **pollo** chicken

VERBOS
 abrir to open
 aprender to learn
 beber to drink
 comer to eat
 decidir to decide
 escribir to write
 leer to read
 recibir to receive
 ser to be
 vivir to live

ADJETIVOS
 alemán (alemana)
 German
 alto(a) tall
 asado(a) roasted, baked
 bueno(a) good

caliente hot
español(a) Spanish
feliz happy
francés (francesa)
 French
frito(a) fried
grande big, large
guapo(a) handsome,
 attractive
inglés (inglesa) English
malo(a) bad

**OTRAS PALABRAS Y
EXPRESIONES**
 ¿cuántos(as)? how many?
 ¿de dónde es...? where
 is . . . from?
 ¿dónde? where?
 me gusta I like
 mucho a lot, very much
 o or
 ¿qué? what?
 solamente, sólo only
 tarde late
 ¿te gusta? do you like?
 temprano early
 el **vino tinto** red wine

---

[1] In Mexico, **pastel** is more commonly used for *cake* rather than *pie*.

1. Position of adjectives
Posición de los adjetivos

> **Adjective**   a word that modifies a noun or a pronoun: **tall**
> girl, **difficult** lesson

◆ Descriptive adjectives (such as adjectives of color, size, etc.)
generally follow the noun in Spanish.

el mantel **rojo**	*the red tablecloth*
la casa **grande**	*the big house*
el muchacho **guapo**	*the handsome young man*
el hombre **alto**	*the tall man*

◆ Adjectives denoting nationality always follow the noun.

el mozo **español**	*the Spanish waiter*

◆ Other kinds of adjectives (possessive, demonstrative, numerical,
etc.) precede the noun, as in English.

tres pasteles   *three pies*   **mi** cheque   *my check*

—¿Cuántos menús necesitas?	*"How many menus do you need?"*
—Necesito solamente **un** menú.	*"I need only one menu."*
—¿Uds. toman vino **tinto**?	*"Do you drink red wine?"*
—No, tomamos vino **blanco**.	*"No, we drink white wine."*

Práctica

How would you say the following in Spanish?

1. three waiters
2. a handsome man
3. a big restaurant
4. a tall girl
5. my pie
6. twenty-five checks
7. five menus

2. Forms of adjectives
Formas del adjetivo

Adjectives whose masculine singular form ends in **-o** have four
forms, ending in **-o, -a, -os, -as.** Most other adjectives have only

two forms, a singular and a plural. Like nouns, adjectives are made plural by adding **-s, -es,** or by changing **z** to **c** and adding **-es.**

Singular		Plural	
Masculine	**Feminine**	**Masculine**	**Feminine**
negro	negra	negros	negras
inteligente	inteligente	inteligentes	inteligentes
feliz	feliz	felices	felices
azul	azul	azules	azules

♦   Adjectives of nationality that end in a consonant are made feminine by adding **-a** to the masculine singular form.

español   española
alemán   alemana
inglés   inglesa
francés   francesa

—¿Dónde trabaja Elsa?   *"Where does Elsa work?*
—Trabaja en un   *"She works at a*
  restaurante **alemán**.   *German restaurant."*

—¿Uds. comen comida   *"Do you eat Mexican food?"*
  mexicana?
—No, comemos comida   *"No, we eat Italian or French*
  italiana o **francesa**.   *food."*

—¿Te gusta el champán   *"Do you like French*
  francés?   *champagne?"*
—Sí, me gusta mucho.   *"Yes, I like it a lot."*

Práctica

A. Supply the three missing forms of the following adjectives.

1. blanco   _____   _____   _____

2. _____   _____   amarillos   _____

3. _____   guapa   _____   _____

4. _____   _____   _____   alemanas

5. feliz   _____   _____   _____

B. Match the nouns in column A with the adjectives in column B.

A	B
1. señor _____	a. rojo
2. mesa _____	b. inteligentes
3. señoritas _____	c. feliz
4. libros _____	d. tinto
5. muchachos _____	e. mexicana
6. lápiz _____	f. verdes
7. vino _____	g. negra
8. comida _____	h. guapos

3. Agreement of articles, nouns, and adjectives

Concordancia de artículos, nombres y adjetivos

> **Agreement**   the correspondence in number and gender between an article, a noun, and the adjective that modifies the noun

In Spanish, the article, the noun, and the adjective agree in number and gender.

la pap**a** asad**a**	*the baked potato*
el poll**o** asad**o**	*the roasted chicken*
las pap**as** asad**as**	*the baked potatoes*
los poll**os** asad**os**	*the roasted chickens*
—¿Deseas huev**os** frit**os** o pesca**do** frit**o**?	*"Do you want fried eggs or fried fish?"*
—Huev**os** frit**os**. No me gusta el pescado.	*"Fried eggs. I don't like fish."*

Práctica

Make the adjectives agree with the nouns in the list and add the corresponding definite article.

1. _____ pollo frito
   _____ papas _____
2. _____ servilletas blancas
   _____ vino _____
3. _____ muchacho alemán
   _____ mujeres _____
4. _____ champán francés
   _____ vinos _____

5. _____ mozos mexicanos
   _____ comida _____
6. _____ restaurante italiano
   _____ muchachas _____
7. _____ hombre feliz
   _____ camareras _____
8. _____ manteles azules
   _____ servilleta _____

4. The present indicative of regular -er and -ir verbs

El presente de indicativo de los verbos regulares terminados en -er e -ir

Regular verbs ending in **-er** are conjugated like **comer.** Regular verbs ending in **-ir** are conjugated like **vivir.**

comer *(to eat)*		vivir *(to live)*	
yo	com- **o**	yo	viv- **o**
tú	com- **es**	tú	viv- **es**
Ud.		Ud.	
él }	com- **e**	él }	viv- **e**
ella		ella	
nosotros	com- **emos**	nosotros	viv- **imos**
Uds.		Uds.	
ellos }	com- **en**	ellos }	viv- **en**
ellas		ellas	

◆ Some other common verbs that follow the same **-er** and **-ir** patterns are:

aprender	to learn	**decidir**	to decide
beber	to drink	**escribir**	to write
leer	to read	**recibir**	to receive
abrir	to open		

—¿Qué **bebes** tú: leche, café o té?
"*What do you drink: milk, coffee or tea?*"

—**Bebo** café o chocolate caliente.
"*I drink coffee or hot chocolate.*"

—¿**Comen** Uds. temprano?
"*Do you eat early?*"

—No, **comemos** tarde.
"*No, we eat late.*"

—¿Dónde **vive** Ud.?
"*Where do you live?*"

—**Vivo** en la calle Unión.
"*I live on Union Street.*"

—¿**Escriben** Uds. en español?
"*Do you write in Spanish?*"

—Sí, **escribimos** en español.
"*Yes, we write in Spanish.*"

Práctica

A. Conjugate the verbs in the following sentences, using the subjects provided.

1. Yo abro la puerta. (nosotros, Uds., Ana, tú, Ud.) *abri, abrimos, uds, ud*
2. Eva decide leer. (Ud., ellos, yo, nosotras, tú)

B. Interview a classmate, using the following questions. When you have finished, switch roles.

1. ¿Qué bebes por la mañana: leche, café o chocolate caliente? *bebo un vaso de leche por la mañana*
2. ¿Qué comes por la noche: pollo asado, pescado o huevos? *Como soup de pollo por la noche*
3. ¿Uds. comen temprano o tarde? *Como Como temprano*
4. ¿En qué calle vives? *Yo vivo en Hawii*
5. ¿Cuánto dinero recibes? *recibo ciautro mil.*
6. ¿Lees muchos libros? *Yo leo libros muchos*
7. ¿Aprendemos mucho en la clase (*class*)? *yo aprendo mucho en la clase*
8. ¿Escribes en español o solamente en inglés? *yo siempre escribir en español*

5. The present indicative of ser
El presente de indicativo del verbo ser

The verb **ser** (*to be*) is an irregular verb. Its forms are not like the forms of regular **-er** verbs.

The Verb SER (*to be*)		
yo	**soy**	I am
tú	**eres**	you are (*familiar*)
Ud.		you are (*formal*)
él	**es**	he is
ella		she is
nosotros	**somos**	we are
Uds.		you are
ellos	**son**	they are (*masculine*)
ellas		they are (*feminine*)

—¿De dónde **son** Uds.?   *"Where are you from?"*
—Yo **soy** de México y   *"I'm from Mexico and Graciela*
　Graciela **es** de Cuba.   *is from Cuba."*

—¿De dónde **eres** tú?   *"Where are you from?"*
—Yo **soy** de Buenos Aires.   *"I'm from Buenos Aires."*

—¿**Son** Uds.   *"Are you North American?"*
   norteamericanos?
—Sí, **somos**   *"Yes, we are North American."*
   norteamericanos.

—¿La comida **es** buena aquí?   *"Is the food good here?"*
—No, **es** mala.   *"No, it is bad."*

Práctica

A. Use the verb **ser** to complete the following conversations. Then act them out with a partner.

1. —¿De dónde _____ tú, Anita?
   —_____ de Buenos Aires. ¿De dónde _____ Ud., señora?
   —Yo _____ de Montevideo.
2. —¿Uds. _____ norteamericanos?
   —Sí, _____ de California.
3. —¿Te gusta el restaurante Azteca?
   —Sí, me gusta mucho. _____ muy bueno.
4. —¿Qué día _____ hoy?
   —Hoy _____ miércoles.

B. Answer the following questions using complete sentences.

1. ¿Qué fecha es hoy?
2. ¿Qué día es hoy?
3. ¿Uds. son norteamericanos?
4. ¿De dónde es Ud.?
5. ¿De dónde es el profesor (la profesora) de español?
6. ¿La comida de la cafetería es buena o mala?

En el laboratorio

The following material is to be used with the tape in the language laboratory.

I. Vocabulario

Repeat each word after the speaker. When repeating words that are cognates, notice the difference in pronunciation between English and Spanish.

COGNADOS: el champán   el cheque   el chocolate
                   inteligente   el menú   mexicano   el té

NOMBRES:	el café la comida el huevo la leche el mozo el camarero el mesero la muchacha la chica el muchacho el chico la papa la patata el pastel el pescado el pollo
VERBOS:	abrir aprender beber comer decidir escribir leer recibir ser vivir
ADJETIVOS:	alemán alto asado bueno caliente español feliz francés frito grande guapo inglés malo
OTRAS PALABRAS Y EXPRESIONES:	¿cuántos? ¿de dónde? ¿dónde? me gusta mucho o ¿qué? solamente sólo tarde te gusta temprano vino tinto

II. Práctica

A. Change each phrase you hear according to the new cue. Repeat the correct answer after the speaker's confirmation. Listen to the model.

Modelo: un señor español (señorita)
   una señorita española

1. (manteles)
2. (servilletas)
3. (señora)
4. (menú)
5. (pollos)
6. (mozos)
7. (profesora)
8. (chocolate)
9. (muchacho)
10. (hombres)

B. Answer the questions, always using the second choice. Omit the subject. Repeat the correct answer after the speaker's confirmation. Listen to the model.

Modelo: —¿Ana vive en la calle Cinco o en la calle Siete?
   —Vive en la calle Siete.

C. Answer the questions, always using the second choice. Omit the subject. Repeat the correct answer after the speaker's confirmation. Listen to the model.

Modelo: —¿Tú eres de Argentina o de los Estados Unidos?
   —Soy de los Estados Unidos.

III. Para escuchar y entender

1. Listen carefully to the dialogue. It will be read twice.

   (*Diálogo 1*)

   Now the speaker will make statements about the dialogue you just heard. Tell whether each statement is true (**verdadero**) or false (**falso**). The speaker will confirm the correct answer.

2. Listen carefully to the dialogue. It will be read twice.

   (*Diálogo 2*)

   Now the speaker will make statements about the dialogue you just heard. Tell whether each statement is true (**verdadero**) or false (**falso**). The speaker will confirm the correct answer.

3. Listen carefully to the dialogue. It will be read twice.

   (*Diálogo 3*)

   Now the speaker will make statements about the dialogue you just heard. Answer each question, omitting the subject. The speaker will confirm the correct answer. Repeat the correct answer.

Lección

3

Vocabulario

COGNADOS

argentino(a) Argentinian
el dólar dollar
el hospital hospital
el metal metal

el museo museum
la profesión profession
el taxi taxi

NOMBRES
el (la) abuelo(a) grandfather, grandmother
el (la) amigo(a) friend
la bebida drink
**el coche, el carro, el
automóvil, el auto**
car, automobile
los Estados Unidos
United States
la fiesta party
el (la) hermano(a)
brother, sister
el (la) hijo(a) son,
daughter
la madera wood
la mamá, la madre mom,
mother
el (la) novio(a) boyfriend,
girlfriend
el ómnibus, el autobús
bus
los padres parents
el papá, el padre dad,
father
el (la) primo(a) cousin

VERBOS
dar to give
deber (+ *inf.*) must, to
have to, should
estar to be
ir to go
llamar to call
llevar to take (*something
or someone to someplace*)

tomar to take (*i.e.,
the bus*)
visitar to visit

ADJETIVOS
bonito(a) pretty
cansado(a) tired
enfermo(a) sick

**OTRAS PALABRAS Y
EXPRESIONES**
a to
a menudo often
¿adónde? where (to)?
¿a quién? to whom?
ahora now
aquí here
¿cómo? how?
¿cómo es? what is he
(she, it) like?
con with
¿con quién? with
whom?
¿cuál? what,? which
one?
de of, from
¿de quién? whose?
muy very
¿por qué? why?
porque because
¿quién(es)? who?,
whom?
siempre always

1. Possession with de
El caso posesivo

De + *noun* is used to express possession or relationship. Unlike English, Spanish does not use the apostrophe.

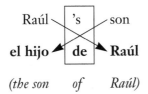

Raúl 's son

el hijo de Raúl

(the son   of   Raúl)

—¿De quién es el libro?   *"To whom does the book belong?"*
—Es **el** libro **de** Julio.   *"It is Julio's book."*

—¿Quién es Julio?   *"Who is Julio?"*
—Es **el** primo **de** Ana.   *"He is Ana's cousin."*

Práctica

With a partner, act out the following dialogues in Spanish.

1. "Who is she?"
   "She is Robert's cousin."
2. "I need Mrs. Prado's address."
   "It's 125 Magnolia Street."
3. "Teresa's last name is Vega?"
   "No, it's not Vega, it's Vera."
4. "Where does María's son live?"
   "He lives at Mrs. Nieto's house."

2. Possessive adjectives
Los adjetivos posesivos

Possessive   a word that denotes ownership or possession: **our** house, **their** mother

Forms of the Possessive Adjectives

Singular	Plural	
mi	mis	my
tu	tus	your (*familiar*)
su	sus	his her its your (*formal*) their
nuestro(a)	nuestros(as)	our

Possessive adjectives agree in number with the nouns they modify.

—¿Ud. necesita hablar
  con **mi** abuelo?
"*Do you need to speak with
  my grandfather?*"

—No, no necesito hablar
  con **su** abuelo. Necesito
  hablar con **sus** padres.
"*No, I don't need to speak with
  your grandfather. I need to
  speak with your parents.*"

—**Mis** padres no viven aquí.
"*My parents don't live here.*"

ATENCIÓN: These forms of the possessive adjectives always precede
the nouns they introduce and are never stressed.

◆ Since both **su** and **sus** may have different meanings, the form **de
él (de ella, de ellos, de ellas, de Ud., de Uds.)** may be substi-
tuted to avoid confusion.

su abuelo ——— el abuelo **de Ud. (de Uds.)**
el abuelo **de él (de ellos)**
el abuelo **de ella (de ellas)**

—¿Ellas son **sus** hijas,
  señora?
"*Are they your daughters,
  madam?*"

—No, no son **mis** hijas;
  son las hijas **de él.**
"*No, they are not my daughters;
  they are his daughters.*"

◆ **Nuestro** is the only possessive adjective that has the feminine
endings **-a, -as.** The others use the same endings for both the
masculine and feminine genders.

—¿Con quién debemos
  hablar?
"*With whom should we speak?*"

—Deben hablar con
  nuestras amigas.
"*You should speak with our
  friends.*"

Práctica

A. Fill in the blanks with the appropriate form of the possessive adjective in Spanish. Whenever **su (sus)** is required, give the alternate form with **de**.

> *Modelo:* (*his*) _____ silla
> **su** silla/**la** silla **de él**

1. (*my*) _____ amiga
2. (*his*) _____ abuela / _____ abuela _____ _____
3. (*our*) _____ casa
4. (*her*) _____ idioma / _____ idioma _____ _____
5. (*your*—**Ud.**) _____ dinero /
   _____ dinero _____ _____
6. (*my*) _____ padres
7. (*our*) _____ mantel
8. (*your*—**tú**) _____ ocupación
9. (*your*—**Uds.**) _____ primos _____
   primos _____ _____
10. (*their*—*fem.*) _____ lecciones /
    _____ lecciones _____ _____

B. Ask a classmate the following questions. When you have finished, switch roles.

1. ¿Dónde viven tus padres?
2. ¿Cuál es el número de teléfono de tus padres?
3. ¿Quién es nuestro profesor (nuestra profesora)?
4. ¿A qué hora es nuestra clase (*class*) de español?
5. ¿Tú necesitas mi libro?

3. The personal a
La a personal

In Spanish, as in English, a verb has a subject and may have one or more objects. The function of the object is to complete the idea expressed by the verb.

In English, the direct object cannot be separated from the verb by a preposition: *She killed **the burglar**. He sees **the nurse**.* In the preceding sentences, *the burglar* and *the nurse* are direct objects.

In Spanish, the preposition **a** is used before a direct object that refers to a specific person. This preposition is called "the personal **a**" and has no equivalent in English.

Yo visito **a** Carmen.
　I visit　Carmen.

◆　The personal **a** is not used when the direct object is not a person.

—¿**A** quién llevas a la
　fiesta?
—Llevo **a** mi hermana.
—¿Ella lleva las bebidas?
—No, lleva los pasteles.

*"Whom are you taking to the
　party?"*
"I'm taking my sister."
"Is she taking the drinks?"
"No, she is taking the pies."

—¿Tú visitas **a** tus abuelos
　a menudo?
—Sí, yo visito **a** mis
　abuelos los domingos.

*"Do you visit your grandparents
　often?"*
*"Yes I visit my grandparents on
　Sundays."*

—¿Qué visitan los chicos
　hoy?
—Visitan el museo.

*"What are the boys visiting
　today?"*
*"They are visiting the
　museum."*

—¿**A** quién llama Ud.?
—Llamo **a** la profesora.

"Whom are you calling?"
"I'm calling the professor."

—¿Desea llamar un taxi?
—No, siempre tomo el
　ómnibus.

"Do you want to call a taxi?"
"No, I always take the bus."

Práctica

With a partner, act out the following dialogues in Spanish.

1. "Do you want to take the bus, Mrs. Peña?"
　"No, I want to call a taxi."
2. "Paco, are you taking your cousin Teresa to María's party?"
　"No, I'm taking my friends."
3. "Whom are you calling, Anita?"
　"I'm calling my sister."
　"Do you visit your sister often?"
　"No, but I always call my sister on Saturdays."

4. The irregular verbs ir, dar, and estar

Los verbos irregulares ir, dar y estar

	ir *(to go)*	dar *(to give)*	estar *(to be)*
yo	**voy**	**doy**	**estoy**
tú	**vas**	**das**	**estás**
Ud. él ella	**va**	**da**	**está**
nosotros	**vamos**	**damos**	**estamos**
Uds. ellos ellas	**van**	**dan**	**están**

—¿**Vas** a la fiesta que **dan**
  Rosa y David?
—No, no **voy** porque
  estoy muy cansada.
  ¿Con quién **van** Uds.?
—**Vamos** con Raúl. Él
  está en mi casa ahora.
—¿Tú **das** dinero para
  la fiesta?
—No, yo no **doy** dinero,
  pero Raúl **da** diez
  dólares.

"Are you going to the party that
Rosa and David are giving?"
"No, I'm not going because I'm
very tired. With whom are
you going?"
"We are going with Raúl. He's
at my house now."
"Are you giving money for the
party?"
"No, I'm not giving money, but
Raúl is giving ten dollars."

Práctica

A. Complete the following dialogues with the present indicative of
ir, dar, and **estar**. Then act them out with a partner.

1. —Buenos días, ¿cómo _____ Ud., señora?
  —_____ muy bien, gracias.
  —¿Adónde _____ Ud.?
  —_____ a la fiesta que _____ la Dra. Sánchez.
2. —¿Cuánto dinero _____ Uds. para la fiesta?
  —Nosotros _____ diez dólares. ¿Cuánto _____ tú?
  —Yo _____ solamente cinco dólares.
3. —¿No _____ Uds. a la fiesta?
  —No, no _____ porque _____ muy cansados.
4. —¿Los chicos _____ aquí?
  —No, _____ en el museo.

B. Interview a classmate, using the following questions. When you have finished, switch roles.

1. ¿Dónde estás ahora?
2. ¿Dónde están tus amigos?
3. ¿Dónde está tu familia?
4. ¿Adónde vas los viernes?
5. ¿Con quién vas?
6. ¿Vas a la biblioteca (*library*) los sábados?
7. ¿Van Uds. (tú y tus amigos) a la universidad los domingos?
8. ¿Das tu número de teléfono?

5. Uses of the verbs ser and estar
Usos de los verbos ser y estar

Although both **ser** and **estar** are equivalent to the English verb *to be*, they are not interchangeable. They are used to indicate the following.

ser	estar
1. Possession or relationship	1. Current condition (usually the product of a change)
2. Profession	2. Location
3. Nationality	
4. Origin	
5. Basic characteristics (color, shape, size, etc.)	
6. Marital status	
7. Expressions of time and dates	
8. Material (metal, wood, glass, etc.)	
9. Events taking place	

—El coche **es** de Pedro, ¿no?   "*The car is Pedro's, isn't it?*"

—No, **es** de Juan.   "*No, it's Juan's.*"

—¿Cuál **es** la profesión de tu madre?   "*What is your mother's profession?*"

—**Es** profesora.   "*She is a professor.*"

—Elena **es** muy inteligente.	*"Elena is very intelligent."*
—Ella **es** de Argentina, ¿no?	*"She's from Argentina, isn't she?"*
—Sí, **es** argentina, pero ahora **está** en los Estados Unidos.	*"Yes, she's an Argentinian, but now she's in the United States."*
—¿Cómo **es** tu papá?	*"What is your Dad like?"*
—**Es** muy guapo.	*"He's very handsome."*
—¿**Es** Ud. casada?	*"Are you married?"*
—No, **soy** soltera.	*"No, I am single."*
—¿Qué día **es** hoy?	*"What day is today?"*
—Hoy **es** martes.	*"Today is Tuesday."*
—¿**Es** de madera la mesa?	*"Is the table made of wood?"*
—No, **es** de metal.	*"No, it is made of metal."*
—¿Dónde **es** la fiesta?	*"Where's the party?"*
—**Es** en el hotel Azteca.	*"It's at the Azteca hotel."*
—¿Cómo **está** Ud.?	*"How are you?"*
—**Estoy** bien, gracias.	*"I am fine, thanks."*
—¿Dónde **está** tu novio?	*"Where is your boyfriend?"*
—**Está** en el hospital. **Está** enfermo.	*"He is in the hospital. He is sick."*

Práctica

A. Complete the following dialogues with **ser** or **estar**, as appropriate. Then act them out with a partner.

1. —¿Cómo _____ Amelia?
   —_____ muy inteligente y muy bonita.
   —¿De dónde _____ ella?
   —_____ argentina, pero ahora _____ en los Estados Unidos.
   —¿_____ soltera?
   —No, _____ casada.
   —¿Hoy no trabaja?
   —No... , _____ enferma. _____ en el hospital.
2. —¿Las sillas _____ de metal?
   —No, _____ de madera.
   —¿_____ de tu novia?
   —No, _____ de Raquel.

3. —¿Cuál _____ su profesión, Sr. Paz?
—_____ profesor.
4. —¿Cómo _____ sus hijos?
—_____ altos y guapos.
5. —¿Qué fecha _____ hoy?
—Hoy _____ el veinte de mayo.
—¿_____ lunes?
—No, hoy _____ martes.
6. —¿Dónde _____ las bebidas?
—_____ en el auto de Jorge.
7. —¿La fiesta _____ en el hotel México?
—No, _____ en el hotel Hilton.

B. How would you describe Alberto in Spanish?

Alberto is a very handsome young man. He's not an American; he's from Buenos Aires, but now he's in California. His father is a professor and his mother is a doctor. He's single. Alberto studies at the University of California. Today he's at home (*en casa*); he is very sick.

C. Use **ser** or **estar** to tell a classmate the following information about yourself.

1. nationality and origin
2. profession (student)
3. marital status
4. basic characteristics (i.e., appearance, qualities)
5. state of health
6. location

D. Go to the map of South America on page xiv and say what the capital of each Spanish-speaking country is.

Modelo: **Buenos Aires es la capital de Argentina.**

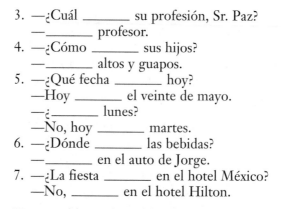 # En el laboratorio

The following material is to be used with the tape in the language laboratory.

I. Vocabulario

Repeat each word after the speaker. When repeating words that are cognates, notice the difference in pronunciation between English and Spanish.

Cognados: argentino   el dólar   el hospital
el metal   el museo   la profesión   el taxi

NOMBRES:	el abuelo el amigo la bebida
	el coche el carro el automóvil
	el auto los Estados Unidos la fiesta
	el hermano el hijo la madera
	la mamá la madre el novio
	el ómnibus el autobús los padres
	el papá el padre el primo

VERBOS	dar deber estar ir llamar llevar
	tomar visitar

ADJETIVOS:	bonito cansado enfermo

OTRAS PALABRAS Y EXPRESIONES:	a a menudo ¿a quién? ¿adónde?
	ahora aquí ¿cómo? ¿cómo es?
	con ¿con quién? ¿cuál? de
	¿de quién? muy ¿por qué? porque
	¿quién? siempre

II. Práctica

A. Using the cues provided, say to whom the following items belong. Repeat the correct answer after the speaker's confirmation. Listen to the model.

Modelo: el libro (Susana)
      Es el libro de Susana.

1. (Antonio)
2. (mi primo)
3. (Juan)
4. (la profesora)
5. (Estela)

B. Answer the questions, using the cues provided. Remember to use the personal **a** when needed. Repeat the correct answer after the speaker's confirmation. Listen to the model.

Modelo: —¿A quién visitas? (Rosa)
      —**Visito a Rosa.**

1. (el museo)
2. (la Sra. Vega)
3. (el ómnibus)
4. (dinero)
5. (la profesora)

C. Answer the questions, always using the second choice. Omit the subject. Repeat the correct answer after the speaker's confirmation. Listen to the model.

Modelo: —¿Tú eres de Argentina o de los Estados Unidos?
—**Soy de los Estados Unidos.**

III. Para escuchar y entender

1. Listen carefully to the narration. It will be read twice.

(*Narración 1*)

Now the speaker will make statements about the narration you just heard. Tell whether each statement is true (**verdadero**) or false (**falso**). The speaker will confirm the correct answer.

2. Listen carefully to the narration. It will be read twice.

(*Narración 2*)

Now the speaker will make statements about the narration you just heard. Tell whether each statement is true (**verdadero**) or false (**falso**). The speaker will confirm the correct answer.

3. Listen carefully to the dialogue. It will be read twice.

(*Diálogo*)

Now the speaker will ask you some questions about the dialogue you just heard. Answer each question, omitting the subject. The speaker will confirm the correct answer. Repeat the correct answer.

Lección

4

Vocabulario

COGNADOS

la clase class	**el (la) supervisor(a)**
el (la) estudiante student	supervisor
el hotel hotel	

NOMBRES
la biblioteca library
la esposa wife
el esposo husband
el (la) gerente manager
el gimnasio gym
la habitación, el cuarto
  room
los hijos children [son(s)
  and daughter(s)]
la llave key
la maleta suitcase
el mercado market
la pensión boarding
  house
la piscina, la alberca
  (*Méx.*) swimming pool
la tienda store

VERBOS
creer to think, to
  believe
esperar to wait (for)
llegar to arrive

tener to have
venir to come

ADJETIVOS
barato(a) inexpensive
caro(a) expensive
mayor older, bigger
mejor better
menor younger, smaller
peor worse
pequeño(a) small, little
  (*size*)
poco(a) little (*quantity*)
solo(a) alone

**OTRAS PALABRAS Y
EXPRESIONES**
mal badly
más more
menos less, fewer
que than, that
también also, too
tener éxito to be
  successful

1. The irregular verbs tener and venir

venir

Los verbos irregulares tener y venir

tener *(to have)*		venir *(to come)*	
yo	**tengo**	yo	**vengo**
tú	**tienes**	tú	**vienes**
Ud.		Ud.	
él }	**tiene**	él }	**viene**
ella		ella	
nosotros	**tenemos**	nosotros	**venimos**
Uds.		Uds.	
ellos }	**tienen**	ellos }	**vienen**
ellas		ellas	

—¿El hotel **tiene** piscina?   *"Does the hotel have a pool?"*
—Sí, y también **tiene**   *"Yes, and it also has a gym."*
   gimnasio.

—¿Con quién **viene** Ud.?   *"With whom are you coming?*
   ¿Con su hijo?   *With your son?"*
—No, **vengo** sola.   *"No, I'm coming alone."*

—¿Cuántos hijos **tiene** Ud.?   *"How many children do you*
                                have?"
—**Tengo** tres hijos y   *"I have three sons and one*
   una hija.   *daughter."*

ATENCIÓN: The personal **a** is not used with the verb **tener**.

—Ana, ¿**tienes** novio?   *"Ana, do you have a boyfriend?"*
—No, no **tengo** novio.   *"No, I don't have a boyfriend."*

ATENCIÓN: **Un** and **una** are not used with the verb **tener** when the
numerical concept is not emphasized.

No **tengo** novio.   *I don't have a boyfriend.*

Práctica

A. Complete the dialogues with the present indicative of **tener** and
venir, as appropriate. Then act them out with a partner.

   1. —Teresa, ¿tu hermano _____ a la universidad con su
      novia?
      —Él no _____ novia.

2. —¿A qué hora _____ Uds. mañana?
   —_____ a las cinco de la tarde. ¿A qué hora _____
     Ud.?
   —Yo _____ a las cinco también.
3. —¿Cuántos hijos _____ Uds.?
   —_____ dos hijos. ¿Cuántos hijos _____ tú?
   —Yo _____ un hijo.

B. Interview a classmate, using the following questions. When you have finished, switch roles.

1. ¿A qué hora vienes a la universidad?
2. ¿Vienes solo(a)?
3. ¿Cuántas clases tienes?
4. ¿Tienes clases los sábados?
5. ¿Qué días tenemos clase de español?
6. ¿Vienes a la universidad los domingos?
7. ¿La universidad tiene piscina? (¿gimnasio?)
8. ¿Tú y tus amigos vienen a la universidad los sábados?

2. **Uses of** tener que **and** hay que
Usos de tener que **y** hay que

◆ The Spanish equivalent of *to have to* (*do something*) is **tener que.**

Yo **tengo que** trabajar.
I   have   to work.

—¿Uds. **tienen que ir** a   *"Do you have to go to the library*
   la biblioteca hoy?   *today?"*
—Sí, porque **tenemos**   *"Yes, because we have to study.*
   que estudiar. ¿Tú   *Do you have to work?"*
   tienes que trabajar?
—Sí, **tengo que trabajar**   *"Yes, I have to work in the*
   por la mañana.   *morning."*

◆ The Spanish equivalent of *one must* is **hay que.**

Hay que estudiar mucho.
One must study   a lot.

—¿Qué **hay que** hacer   *"What must one do to succeed?"*
   para tener éxito?
—**Hay que** trabajar.   *"One must work."*

ATENCIÓN: Note that **tener que** and **hay que** are followed by the infinitive. Note also that no subject is used with **hay que;** it is an invariable expression.

Práctica

A. Complete the following sentences with **hay que** or the correct form of **tener que,** as appropriate.

1. _____ estudiar mucho en la universidad.
2. Nosotros _____ ir a la biblioteca mañana.
3. Mi hermano _____ llamar a las diez de la noche.
4. Uds. no _____ venir hoy.
5. Para tomar el ómnibus, _____ pagar un dólar.

B. Use your imagination to explain what these people have to do.

Modelo: José / en la biblioteca / mañana.
José **tiene que trabajar** en la biblioteca mañana.

1. yo / por la noche
2. mi papá / el sábado
3. nosotros / el domingo
4. Uds. / el lunes
5. tú / mañana por la tarde
6. mis padres / hoy

3. Contractions
Contracciones

> **Contraction**   the combination of two or more words into one, with certain sounds or letters missing: **isn't, don't, can't, I'm**

In Spanish there are only two contractions: **al** and **del.**

◆ The preposition **de** (*of, from*) plus the article **el** is contracted to form **del.**

Leen los libros **de + el** profesor.   Leen los libros **del** profesor.

◆ The preposition **a** (*to, toward*) or the personal **a** plus the article **el** is contracted to form **al.**

Esperamos **a + el** profesor.   Esperamos **al** profesor.

ATENCIÓN: None of the other combinations of prepositions and definite articles (**de la, de los, de las, a la, a los, a las**) is contracted.

—¿Llaman Uds. **al**   *"Are you calling the hotel*
   gerente **del** hotel?   *manager?"*
—No, llamamos **a la**   *"No, we're calling the*
   supervisora.   *supervisor."*

—¿Vas **a la** tienda?   *"Are you going to the store?"*
—No, voy **al** mercado.   *"No, I'm going to the market."*

—Las maletas son **del**   *"The suitcases are the teacher's,*
   profesor, ¿no?   *aren't they?"*
—No, son **de los**   *"No, they are the students'."*
   estudiantes.

—¿Necesitan ellos la   *"Do they need the key to the*
   llave **del** cuarto?   *room?"*
—Sí.   *"Yes."*

Práctica

Complete the following dialogues, using one of the following: **de la, de las, del, de los, a la, a las, al,** or **a los.** Then act them out with a partner.

1. —¿Por qué llamas _____ gerente?
   —Porque necesito la llave _____ cuarto _____
   Sra. Reyes.
2. —¿Uds. van _____ mercado o _____ tienda?
   —Vamos _____ restaurante _____ hotel.
3. —¿Dónde están las maletas _____ estudiantes?
   —Están en el cuarto _____ profesor.
4. —¿A quiénes llevas a la fiesta? ¿_____ muchachos?
   —No, _____ muchachas.
5. —¿A quién esperan Uds.?
   —_____ supervisor.

4. Comparative forms
Las formas comparativas

Comparisons of inequality

◆ In Spanish, the comparative of most adjectives, adverbs, and nouns is formed by placing **más** (*more*) or **menos** (*less*) before the adjective, adverb, or noun and **que** after.

Ella es **más bonita que** Rosa.
She is   prettier than   Rosa.

		adjective		
más		or		
	+	*adverb*	+	**que**
menos		or		
		noun		

In the construction shown in the chart, **que** is equivalent to *than*.

—El hotel Azteca es **barato**.	*"The Azteca hotel is inexpensive."*
—Sí, pero creo que es **más caro que** el hotel Torres.	*"Yes, but I think it is more expensive than the Torres hotel."*
—Yo tengo muy **poco** dinero.	*"I have very little money."*
—¡Yo tengo **menos dinero que** tú!	*"I have less money than you!"*
—¿Quién llega **más tarde?** ¿Tú o ella?	*"Who arrives later? You or she?"*
—Ella llega **más tarde que** yo.	*"She arrives later than I."*

Comparisons of equality

◆ To form comparisons of equality with adjectives, adverbs, and nouns, use the adverb **tan** or the adjective **tanto, -a, -os, -as** and **como**.

When comparing adjectives or adverbs:	When comparing nouns:
tan (*as*) < **bonita** / **tarde** + **como**	**tanto** (*as much*) dinero ⎤ **tanta** plata (*money*) **tantos** (*as many*) libros ⎬ + **como** **tantas** plumas ⎦

—¿Te gusta el hotel California?   *"Do you like the California hotel?"*

—Sí, pero no es **tan bonito como** el hotel Victoria.   *"Yes, but it's not as pretty as the Victoria hotel."*

—Tu casa es muy grande.   *"Your house is very big."*

—Sí, pero no tiene **tantas habitaciones como** la casa de tus padres.   *"Yes, but it doesn't have as many rooms as your parents' house."*

The Superlative

◆ The superlative construction is similar to the comparative. It is formed by placing the definite article before the person or thing being compared.

definite article	+	*noun*	+	**más** or **menos**	+ *adjective* + **de**

—¿Cuál es **la habitación más grande de** la pensión?   *"Which is the biggest room in the boarding house?"*

—La habitación número 5.   *"Room number 5."*

ATENCIÓN: After a superlative construction, *in* is expressed by **de** in Spanish. In many instances, the noun may not be expressed in a superlative.

La habitación número 5 es **la más grande.**   *Room number 5 is the biggest (one).*

Práctica

A. With a partner, act out the following dialogues in Spanish.
    1. "Are you taller than your sister, Anita?"
       "No, she is as tall as I."

2. "Is the Azteca hotel very large?"
   "Yes, it's the largest in the city."
3. "I have to work."
   "Why?"
   "Because I don't have as much money as you."
4. "How many suitcases do you need, Miss Peña?"
   "One or two . . . I don't need as many as you, Paco."
5. "I think that the Mexico hotel is very inexpensive."
   "Yes, but it's more expensive than the boarding house."

B. Compare these people, places, or things to each other.

   Modelo: Vermont / California (pequeño)
                Vermont **es más pequeño que** California.
   1. Texas / Rhode Island (grande)
   2. tú / tu amigo (alto)
   3. Tom Cruise (Meg Ryan) / tú (guapo/bonita)
   4. Chile / Brasil (pequeño)
   5. un Rolls Royce / un Ford (caro)

5. Irregular comparative forms
Las formas comparativas irregulares

Adjectives	Adverbs	Comparative	Superlative
bueno	bien	mejor	el (la) mejor
malo	mal	peor	el (la) peor
grande		mayor	el (la) mayor
pequeño		menor	el (la) menor

◆ When the adjectives **grande** and **pequeño(a)** refer to size, their regular forms are generally used.

   Tu clase es **más grande**   *Your class is bigger than*
     que la de Antonio.   *Antonio's.*

◆ When these adjectives refer to age, the irregular forms are used.

   —¿Felipe es **mayor** que tú?   *"Is Felipe older than you?"*
   —No, es **menor** que yo.   *"No, he is younger than I (am)."*

   —¿Quién es **mayor**? ¿Ud.   *"Who is older? You or Elsa?"*
     o Elsa?
   —Elsa. Ella es **la mayor**   *"Elsa. She is the oldest in the*
     de la clase.   *class."*

—¿Su esposo habla
   español tan **bien**
   como Ud.?

"_Does your husband speak Spanish
as well as you do?_"

—No, él habla español
   mucho **mejor** que yo.

"_No, he speaks Spanish much
better than I._"

—La casa de Ana es **más**
   grande que la casa
   de Eva, ¿no?

"_Ana's house is bigger than Eva's
house, isn't it?_"

—No, la casa de Ana es
   más pequeña que la
   casa de Eva.

"_No, Ana's house is smaller than
Eva's house._"

Práctica

A. Answer the following questions.

1. ¿Es Ud. menor o mayor que su mejor amigo o amiga?
2. ¿Tiene Ud. un hermano mayor (un hermano menor)?
3. ¿Cuál es la mejor universidad de los Estados Unidos?
4. ¿Quién habla mejor el español: Ud. o el profesor (la profesora)?
5. ¿Cuál cree Ud. que es el peor restaurante de la ciudad donde Ud. vive?

B. With a partner, act out the following dialogues in Spanish.

1. "Is your wife older or younger than you, Mr. Vega?"
   "She's younger than I."
2. "The Azteca hotel is very good."
   "Yes, it's the best in the city."
3. "My Spanish is very bad."
   "My Spanish is worse!"

En el laboratorio

The following material is to be used with the tape in the language laboratory.

I. Vocabulario

Repeat each word after the speaker. When repeating words that are cognates, notice the difference in pronunciation between English and Spanish.

Cognados: la clase   el estudiante   el hotel
                   el supervisor

NOMBRES:	la biblioteca la esposa el esposo el gerente el gimnasio la habitación el cuarto los hijos la llave la maleta el mercado la pensión la piscina la alberca la tienda
VERBOS:	creer esperar llegar tener venir
ADJECTIVES:	barato caro mayor mejor menor peor pequeño poco solo
OTRAS PALABRAS Y EXPRESIONES:	mal más menos que también tener éxito

II. Práctica

A. Answer the questions, using the cues provided. Omit the subject. Repeat the correct answer after the speaker's confirmation. Listen to the model.

Modelo: —¿Cuántos hijos tienes? (tres)
      —**Tengo tres hijos.**

1. (cuatro)
2. (no)
3. (los martes y los jueves)
4. (no)
5. (sí)
6. (cinco)
7. (los domingos)

B. Answer the questions, always using the first choice. Omit the subject. Repeat the correct answer after the speaker's confirmation. Listen to the model.

Modelo: —¿Alberto tiene que trabajar o tiene que estudiar?
      —**Tiene que trabajar.**

C. Answer the questions, always using the second choice. Omit the subject. Repeat the correct answer after the speaker's confirmation. Listen to the model.

Modelo: —¿Quién es más bonita, Rosa o Ana?
      —**Ana es más bonita que Rosa.**

III. Para escuchar y entender

1. Listen carefully to the dialogue. It will be read twice.

   (*Diálogo 1*)

   Now the speaker will make statements about the dialogue you just heard. Tell whether each statement is true (**verdadero**) or false (**falso**). The speaker will confirm the correct answer.

2. Listen carefully to the dialogue. It will be read twice.

   (*Diálogo 2*)

   Now the speaker will make statements about the dialogue you just heard. Tell whether each statement is true (**verdadero**) or false (**falso**). The speaker will confirm the correct answer.

3. Listen carefully to the dialogue. It will be read twice.

   (*Diálogo 3*)

   Now the speaker will make statements about the dialogue you just heard. Tell whether each statement is true (**verdadero**) or false (**falso**). The speaker will confirm the correct answer.

Lección

5

1. **Expressions with** tener
2. **Stem-changing verbs** (e:ie)
3. Ir a + **infinitive**
4. **Some uses of the definite article**
5. **Ordinal numbers**

Vocabulario

COGNADOS

el concierto concert	**la oficina** office
la educación education	**las vacaciones**[1] vacation
importante important	

NOMBRES
el almuerzo lunch
la cárcel jail
la cena dinner
el cine movie theater, movies
el desayuno breakfast
el (la) dueño(a) owner
la escuela school
la iglesia church
el jabón soap
el mes month
el piso floor, story
la revista magazine
la semana week
la toalla towel

VERBOS
cerrar (e:ie) to close
comenzar (e:ie) to begin, to start

comprar to buy
desayunar to have breakfast
empezar (e:ie) to begin, to start
entender (e:ie) to understand
perder (e:ie) to lose
preferir (e:ie) to prefer
querer (e:ie) to want
viajar to travel

ADJETIVO
próximo(a) next

OTRAS PALABRAS Y EXPRESIONES
esta noche tonight
para to, in order to
primero first
ya lo creo I'll say

Resumen de palabras interrogativas

¿a quién? to whom?	¿A quién llamas?	
¿adónde? where to?	¿Adónde vas?	
¿cuál(es)? which?	¿Cuál prefieres?	
¿cuándo? when?	¿Cuándo vienen ellos?	
¿cuánto(a)? how much?	¿Cuánto dinero necesitas?	
¿cuántos(as)? how many?	¿Cuántas toallas quieres?	
¿de dónde? from where?	¿De dónde es Ud.?	
¿de quién(es)? whose?	¿De quién es la revista?	
¿dónde? where?	¿Dónde está el cine Rex?	
¿por qué? why?	¿Por qué no van al concierto?	
¿qué? what?	¿Qué desea comprar, señora?	
¿quién(es)? who?	¿Quiénes van a venir a la fiesta?	

---

[1] **Vacaciones** is always used in the plural.

1. Expressions with tener
Las expresiones con tener

In Spanish, many useful idiomatic expressions are formed with the verb **tener** and a noun, while English uses *to be* and an adjective.

tener calor *to be hot*	**tener hambre** *to be hungry*
tener frío *to be cold*	**tener sed** *to be thirsty*
tener cuidado *to be careful*	**tener prisa** *to be in a hurry*
tener sueño *to be sleepy*	**tener razón** *to be right*
tener miedo *to be afraid*	
tener... años (de edad) *to be . . . years old*	

◆ The equivalent of *I am very hungry*, for example, is **Tengo mucha hambre.**

—¿**Tienes hambre,** María?　　*"Are you hungry, María?"*
—No, pero **tengo** mucha　　　*"No, but I am very thirsty."*
　sed.

—¿**Tienes calor,** Carlos?　　*"Are you hot, Carlos?"*
—Sí, **tengo** mucho **calor.**　　*"Yes, I'm very hot."*

—¿Cuántos **años tiene**　　　*"How old is your daughter?"*
　su hija?
—Mi hija **tiene** seis **años.**　　*"My daughter is six years old."*

—Deseo hablar con el　　　　*"I wish to speak with the*
　dueño, por favor.　　　　　　*owner, please."*
—Ahora no, lo siento. Él　　　*"Not now, I'm sorry. He's in*
　tiene mucha **prisa.**　　　　　*a big hurry."*
—**Tiene razón.** Es tarde.　　　*"You're right. It's late."*

Práctica

A. Tell what is happening in each of the pictures. Follow the model.

Modelo:

Ella...
Ella tiene hambre.

1. Carlos...

2. Él...

5. ¿Ud... ?

3. Yo...

6. Tú...

4. Ellas...

7. Nélida...

B. With a partner act out the following dialogues in Spanish.

1. "I'm hungry and I'm also very thirsty."
   "Me too."
2. "Aren't you cold, Paquito?"
   "No, I'm hot."

3. "How old are you, Anita?"
   "I'm six years old."
4. "Are you in a hurry, Miss Vega?"
   "Yes, it's very late."
5. "You must be careful, Mrs. Lopez."
   "You are right."

C. Interview a classmate, using the following questions. When you have finished, switch roles.

1. ¿Qué bebes cuando tienes sed? ¿Y cuando tienes frío?
2. ¿Qué comes cuando tienes hambre?
3. ¿Cuántos años tienes?
4. ¿Cuántos años tiene tu madre? ¿Y tu padre?
5. En tu familia, ¿quién tiene razón siempre? ¿Y en la clase?
6. ¿Tienes miedo a veces *(sometimes)*?

2. Stem-changing verbs (e:ie)
Verbos que cambian en la raíz (e:ie)

In Spanish, some verbs undergo a stem change in the present indicative. For these verbs, when **e** is the last stem vowel and it is stressed, it changes to **ie** as follows.

preferir *(to prefer)*	
prefiero	preferimos
prefieres	
prefiere	prefieren

◆ Notice that the stem vowel is not stressed in the verb form corresponding to **nosotros,** and therefore the **e** does not change to **ie: nosotros preferimos.**

◆ Stem-changing verbs have regular endings like other -ar, -er, and -ir verbs.

◆ Some other verbs that undergo the same change are:

cerrar	to close	**entender**	to understand
comenzar[1]	to start, to begin	**perder**	to lose
empezar[1]	to start, to begin	**querer**	to want

—¿**Quieres** ir al cine esta noche?

"Do you want to go to the movies tonight?"

—No, **prefiero** ir al concierto.

"No, I prefer to go to the concert."

—¿A qué hora **empieza**?

"At what time does it begin?"

—**Comienza** a las nueve.

"It starts at nine."

—Pedro **entiende** el francés y el alemán, ¿no?

"Pedro understands French and German, doesn't he?"

—**Entiende** el francés, pero no **entiende** el alemán.

"He understands French, but he doesn't understand German."

Práctica

A. Finish the following sentences in your own words, matching the verbs to the new subjects:

1. Luis comienza a trabajar a las siete y nosotros...
2. Tú prefieres ir al cine y yo...
3. Nosotros cerramos a las nueve y ellos...
4. Yo empiezo a trabajar el lunes y Uds...
5. Rafael quiere aprender francés y nosotros...
6. Yo no entiendo inglés y Uds...

B. Interview a classmate, using the following questions and two of your own. When you have finished, switch roles.

1. ¿Cuándo comienzan las clases en la universidad?
2. ¿A qué hora empieza la clase de español?
3. Cuando el profesor (la profesora) habla español, ¿tú entiendes?
4. ¿A qué hora cierran la biblioteca?
5. ¿Prefieres ir al cine o a un concierto?
6. ¿Quieres ir al cine el sábado?
7. ¿Quieres ir a un restaurante italiano o prefieres comer comida mexicana?
8. ¿Tú pierdes las llaves a menudo?

---

[1] When **comenzar** and **empezar** are followed by an infinitive, the preposition **a** is used: **Yo comienzo (empiezo) a trabajar a las seis.** Notice that these two verbs are synonymous.

3. Ir a + infinitive
Ir a + infinitivo

The construction **ir a** + *infinitive* is used to express future time. It is equivalent to the English expression *to be going to*. The formula is:

ir	+ a + *infinitive*		
Yo voy	a	**viajar**	**a Chile.**
I'm going		*to travel*	*to Chile.*

—¿Qué **vas a comprar?**   *"What are you going to buy?"*
—**Voy a comprar** jabón   *"I'm going to buy soap and a*
  y una toalla.   *towel."*
—Nosotros **vamos a**   *"We are going to buy a magazine."*
  comprar una revista.

—¿Van Uds. ahora?   *"Are you going now?"*
—No, primero **vamos a**   *"No, first we are going to have*
  desayunar.   *breakfast."*

Práctica

A. Make new sentences using the subjects provided.

   1. Tú vas a desayunar. (Nosotros, Mi amigo, Yo, Ud., Ellos)
   2. El dueño va a hablar con ella. (Yo, Uds., Nosotros, Tú)

B. Use your imagination to describe what these people are going to do.

   Modelo: yo / mañana
        Yo **voy a estudiar** mañana.

   1. mi hermano / por la noche
   2. nosotras / el lunes
   3. tú / mañana por la tarde
   4. los muchachos / el sábado
   5. Ud. / el viernes

C. Interview a classmate, using the following questions and two of your own. When you have finished, switch roles.

   1. ¿Qué vas a hacer esta noche?
   2. ¿A qué hora vas a desayunar mañana?
   3. ¿Qué van a comprar mañana?
   4. ¿Qué van a hacer tú y tus amigos el sábado?
   5. ¿Tus padres van a ir también?
   6. ¿Adónde vas a viajar este verano?

4. Some uses of the definite article
Algunos usos del artículo definido

The definite article is used in the following instances in Spanish.

◆ with expressions of time, the seasons, and the days of the week

—¿Cuándo es su clase de español? — *"When is your Spanish class?"*

—Tengo clase de español **los**[1] lunes, miércoles y viernes, a **las** nueve. — *"I have a Spanish class on Mondays, Wednesdays, and Fridays at nine."*

ATENCIÓN: The definite article is omitted with the seasons and days of the week when used after the verb **ser:**

—¿Es primavera ahora en Argentina? — *"Is it spring in Argentina now?"*

—Sí es primavera. — *"Yes, it is spring."*

—¿Qué día es hoy? — *"What day is today?"*

—Hoy es domingo. — *"Today is Sunday."*

◆ before nouns used in a general sense

—¿Te gusta **el café?** — *"Do you like coffee?"*

—Sí, pero prefiero **el té.** — *"Yes, but I prefer tea."*

◆ with abstract nouns

—**La educación** es muy importante. — *"Education is very important."*

—Ya lo creo. — *"I'll say."*

◆ before próximo(a) (next) with expressions of time

—¿Tus vacaciones comienzan **la** semana **próxima?** — *"Does your vacation start next week?"*

—Sí, comienzan el lunes. — *"Yes, it starts on Monday."*

◆ with the nouns **iglesia, escuela,** and **cárcel** when they are preceded by a preposition

—¿Vas a **la iglesia** los viernes? — *"Do you go to church on Fridays?"*

—No, los viernes voy a **la escuela.** — *"No, I go to school on Fridays."*

---

[1] Notice that the definite article is used here as the equivalent of *on.*

◆ before the words **desayuno, almuerzo,** and **cena**

—¿**El desayuno** es a las ocho?   *"Is breakfast at eight?"*

—Sí, y **el almuerzo** es a las doce.   *"Yes, and lunch is at twelve."*

Práctica

A. Is the definite article needed or not? Complete the following dialogues, then act them out with a partner.

1. —¿Tú vas a _____ iglesia hoy?
—No, hoy es _____ sábado, y yo voy a _____ iglesia _____ domingos.
—¿Vas a _____ escuela _____ lunes?
—No, _____ lunes no tengo clases.

2. —¿Uds. van a viajar a Argentina en julio?
—No, porque cuando en los Estados Unidos es _____ verano, en Argentina es _____ invierno y nosotros preferimos _____ verano.

3. —_____ hombres son más inteligentes que _____ mujeres.
—¡No! _____ mujeres somos tan inteligentes como _____ hombres.

4. —¿Adónde vas a ir _____ domingo próximo?
—Voy a ir a visitar a Julio, que está en _____ cárcel.

5. —¿Qué es muy importante para ti?
—_____ educación.

B. Interview a classmate, using the following questions. When you have finished, switch roles.

1. ¿Qué días tienes clases de español?
2. ¿A qué hora es la clase en la universidad?
3. ¿A qué hora es la cena en tu casa? (¿y el desayuno? ¿ y el almuerzo?)
4. ¿Van a ir Uds. de vacaciones la semana próxima?
5. ¿Vas a la iglesia los domingos?
6. ¿Qué crees que es más importante, el amor **(love)** o el dinero?
7. ¿Quiénes crees tú que son más inteligentes, los hombres o las mujeres?
8. Cuando en los Estados Unidos es primavera, ¿qué estación es en Argentina?

5. Ordinal numbers

Los números ordinales

primero(a)	*first*	**sexto(a)**	*sixth*
segundo(a)	*second*	**séptimo(a)**	*seventh*
tercero(a)	*third*	**octavo(a)**	*eighth*
cuarto(a)	*fourth*	**noveno(a)**	*ninth*
quinto(a)	*fifth*	**décimo(a)**	*tenth*

Ordinal numbers agree in gender and number with the nouns they modify.

—¿Qué oficina prefiere?   *"Which office do you prefer?"*
—Prefiero **la** quint**a** oficina.   *"I prefer the fifth (one)."*

◆ The ordinal numbers **primero** and **tercero** drop the final **-o** before masculine singular nouns.

—¿Qué día llegan Uds.?   *"What day are you arriving?"*
—Llegamos el **primer** día   *"We are arriving the first day*
   del mes.   *of the month."*

◆ Ordinal numbers are seldom used after *the tenth*.

—¿En qué piso viven Uds.?   *"On which floor do you live?"*
—Vivimos en el piso **doce.**   *"We live on the twelfth floor."*

◆ Remember that cardinal numbers are used in Spanish for dates except for *the first*.

—¿Qué día es hoy?   *"What day is it today?"*
—Hoy es el **treinta** de abril.   *"Today is April 30th.*
   Mañana es **el primero**   *Tomorrow is the first (day)*
   de mayo.   *of May."*

Práctica

Complete the following dialogues with the correct ordinal numbers. Then act them out with a partner.

1. —¿La oficina de Alberto está en el _____ piso? *(third)*
   —No, está en el _____ piso. *(second)*
   —Yo quiero una en el _____ piso. *(fifth)*
2. —¿Uds. viajan la _____ semana? *(fourth)*
   —Sí, pero no viajamos el _____ día. *(first)*
3. —¿Septiembre es el _____ mes del año? *(tenth)*
   —No, es el _____. *(ninth)*

En el laboratorio

The following material is to be used with the tape in the language laboratory.

I. Vocabulario

Repeat each word after the speaker. When repeating words that are cognates, notice the difference in pronunciation between English and Spanish.

COGNADOS:	el concierto la educación importante la oficina las vacaciones
NOMBRES:	el almuerzo la cárcel la cena el cine el desayuno el dueño la escuela la iglesia el jabón el mes el piso la revista la semana la toalla
VERBOS:	cerrar comenzar comprar desayunar empezar entender perder preferir querer viajar
ADJETIVO:	próximo
OTRAS PALABRAS Y EXPRESIONES:	esta noche para primero ya lo creo

II. Práctica

A. Answer the questions in the affirmative, always using **mucho** or **mucha** as appropriate. Repeat the correct answer after the speaker's confirmation. Listen to the model.

Modelo: —¿Tienes hambre?
  —**Sí tengo mucha hambre.**

B. Change the verb in each sentence according to the new subject. Repeat the correct answer after the speaker's confirmation. Listen to the model.

Modelo: Nosotros comenzamos temprano. (yo)
  Yo comienzo temprano.

1. (Uds.)
2. (tú)
3. (ella)
4. (ellos)
5. (Ud.)
6. (él)

C. Answer the questions, using the cue provided. Repeat the correct answer after the speaker's confirmation. Listen to the model.

Modelo: —¿Cuándo vas a venir tú? (el viernes)
　　　　 —**Voy a venir el viernes.**

1. (al cine)　　　　4. (el quinto)　　　7. (con mi padre)
2. (jabón)　　　　 5. (con mi primo)　8. (a la cárcel)
3. (a las nueve)　　6. (al dueño)

D. Say the ordinal number that corresponds to each cardinal number. Repeat the correct number after the speaker's confirmation. Listen to the model.

Modelo: cuatro **cuarto**

III. Para escuchar y entender

1. Listen carefully to the dialogue. It will be read twice.

   (Diálogo 1)

   Now the speaker will make statements about the dialogue you just heard. Tell whether each statement is true **(verdadero)** or false **(falso)**. The speaker will confirm the correct answer.

2. Listen carefully to the narration. It will be read twice.

   (Narración)

   Now the speaker will make statements about the narration you just heard. Tell whether each statement is true **(verdadero)** or false **(falso)**. The speaker will confirm the correct answer.

3. Listen carefully to the dialogue. It will be read twice.

   (Diálogo 2)

   Now the speaker will ask you some questions about the dialogue you just heard. Answer each question, omitting the subject. The speaker will confirm the correct answer. Repeat the correct answer.

¿Cuánto sabe usted ahora?

LECCIONES 1–5

A. Subject pronouns

Lección 1

Replace the subjects below with the appropriate subject pronouns.

1. tú y yo
2. los estudiantes
3. Ana y Rosa
4. Ud., Ud., Ud. y Ud.
5. Teresa y Roberto
6. la profesora y yo

B. The present indicative of regular **-ar** verbs

Complete the sentences below with the Spanish equivalent of the verbs provided.

1. Ellos _____ una cerveza. (*want*)
2. Nosotros _____ el mantel y las servilletas. (*need*)
3. ¿Tú _____ francés? (*study*)
4. Yo _____ un refresco (*drink*)
5. Carlos _____ en un restaurante. (*works*)

C. Interrogative and negative sentences

How would you say the following in Spanish?

1. "Does she need the spoons?"
   "No, she doesn't need the spoons; she needs the forks."
2. "Do you (*pl.*) speak Italian?"
   "No, we don't speak Italian; we speak Spanish."
3. "Does Mr. Vega work in Lima?"
   "No, he doesn't work in Lima; he works in Santiago."

D. Cardinal numbers (300–1,000)

Write the following numbers in Spanish.

1. 341   4. 575
2. 783   5. 467
3. 1,000   6. 896

E. Telling time

Give the Spanish equivalent of the words in parentheses.

1. Estudiamos _____. (*at seven-thirty in the morning*)
2. Nosotros trabajamos _____. (*in the afternoon*)
3. Elsa estudia _____. (*at one o'clock*)
4. La clase (*class*) es _____. (*at a quarter after seven in the evening*)
5. Son _____. (*twenty-five to nine*)

F. Vocabulary

Complete the following sentences, using words learned in **Lección 1.**

1. Necesito las servilletas y el _____.
2. En California hablan _____, en Roma hablan _____ y en París hablan _____.
3. Necesito una cuchara y un _____.
4. ¿Trabaja en una cafetería o en un _____?
5. Yo _____ un refresco y Jorge _____ tomar cerveza.
6. Ellos _____ la cuenta.

Lección 2   **A.** Position and forms of adjectives; agreement of articles, adjectives and nouns

How would you say the following in Spanish?

1. We need the white chairs and the black table.
2. I need two red pencils.
3. I study with two very intelligent girls.
4. Do you need to talk with the German girl, sir?

B. The present indicative of regular **-er** and **-ir** verbs

Complete the following sentences using the present indicative of the verbs provided

beber   vivir   recibir   comer   leer   escribir

1. Yo _____ Coca-Cola y ellos _____ Pepsi.
2. Nosotros _____ y _____ en español.
3. ¿Tú _____ en la cafetería?
4. Ellos _____ veinte pesos.
5. Yo _____ en la calle Magnolia y Ana _____ en la calle Universidad.

C. The present indicative of the verb **ser**

Use the present indicative of the verb **ser** to complete the following sentences.

1. ¿Qué día _____ hoy?
2. ¿Tú _____ de California?
3. Nosotros _____ estudiantes y ella _____ profesora.
4. Ellos _____ de Cuba.
5. Yo _____ de Venezuela. ¿De dónde _____ Ud.?

D. Vocabulary

Complete the sentences, using words learned in **Lección 2**.

1. ¿Tú _____ café o té?
2. Nosotros _____ en la cafetería.
3. Yo _____ en la calle Magnolia.
4. Ella _____ con una pluma negra.
5. No es tarde; es _____.
6. Tomamos café con _____.
7. ¿_____ estudiantes hay? ¿Veinte?
8. ¿De _____ es Ana? ¿De Paraguay?
9. Nosotros _____ la puerta.
10. No es malo. Es _____.

Lección 3

A. Possession with **de**

How would you say the following in Spanish?

1. Carlos is María Iriarte's son.
2. Ana's cousin is from Colombia.
3. The girl's last name is Torres.
4. She needs Mrs. Madera's phone number.
5. David's house is green.

B. Possessive adjectives

How would you say the following in Spanish?

1. Do you need his address or her address?
2. Miss Vega is our friend.
3. I need my car.
4. Do you need to speak with your sons, Mr. Varela?
5. Do you call your parents, Paquito?

C. The personal **a**

How would you say the following in Spanish?

1. I wish to visit Miss Arévalo.
2. Do you call Mary?
3. The students visit the museum.

D. The irregular verbs **ir, dar,** and **estar**

Use the present indicative of **ir, dar,** or **estar** to complete the following sentences.

1. Ella no _____ su número de teléfono y nosotros no _____ nuestra dirección.
2. ¿Adónde _____ tú los sábados? ¿Adónde _____ ellos?
3. Yo _____ en el hotel Acapulco. ¿En qué hotel _____ Uds.?
4. Nosotros _____ a la universidad los martes y jueves.
5. ¿Dónde _____ tú?

E. Uses of the verb **ser** and **estar**

Use the present indicative of **ser** or **estar** to complete the following sentences.

1. Ella _____ de Buenos Aires, pero ahora _____ en California.
2. Nosotros _____ norteamericanos.
3. Ella _____ alta y _____ muy bonita.
4. Hoy _____ jueves.
5. Yo _____ muy bien, gracias.
6. ¿Las sillas _____ de madera o de metal?
7. Teresa _____ profesora.
8. ¿Tú _____ enfermo, Luis?
9. Alicia _____ la hermana de Rosa.
10. Elba no va a la fiesta porque _____ muy cansada.

F. Vocabulary

Complete the following sentences, using words learned in **Lección 3.**

1. Es de Buenos Aires; es _____.
2. Es el papá de mi mamá; es mi _____.
3. David es de los _____ Unidos.
4. ¿Su _____? Él es ingeniero.
5. No voy en mi coche. Voy a _____ un taxi.
6. Voy a _____ a mi novia a la fiesta.
7. ¿_____ es él? ¿Tu novio?
8. ¿De _____ es el libro? ¿De Teresa?
9. ¿_____ es él? ¿Es guapo?
10. Ellos _____ veinte dólares para la fiesta.

A. The irregular verbs **tener** and **venir**

Use the present indicative of **tener** or **venir** to complete the following sentences.

1. Aníbal no _____ novia. ¿Tú _____ novia, Ariel?
2. Yo _____ a la fiesta con mi esposa y con mis hijos.
3. Mi prima y yo _____ doscientos pesos.
4. ¿Uds. _____ la dirección de Ana? Nosotros _____ a California el sábado.
5. ¿Tú _____ a la piscina mañana?
6. Ellos no _____ tu llave.

B. Contractions

How would you say the following in Spanish?

1. I need Mr. Soto's phone number.
2. She goes to the university on Fridays.
3. I call the manager on Tuesdays.
4. She is Mr. Miranda's daughter.
5. We go to the gym on Saturdays.

C. Comparative Forms

How would you say the following in Spanish?

1. She is as tall as my son.
2. The Azteca Hotel is the most expensive in the city. It's the best.
3. Is she younger or older than David?
4. Colombia is smaller than the United States.
5. I have little money, but he has less money than I.
6. We are as tired as you (*are*), Anita.
7. I don't have as many books as you (*do*), Ana.
8. My wife needs as many suitcases as I (*need*).

D. Vocabulary

Complete the following sentences, using words learned in **Lección 4.**

1. El hotel Regina, ¿es caro o es _____?
2. ¿Es un hotel o una _____?
3. ¿Es grande o _____?
4. Alicia es mayor que yo. Yo soy _____ que ella.
5. Yo no hablo muy bien el inglés. Ella habla inglés muy bien. Ella habla inglés _____ que yo.
6. El hotel tiene _____ y gimnasio.
7. Ellos no tienen la _____ de mi habitación.
8. Tu coche es malo, pero mi coche es _____.
9. No tenemos mucho dinero. Tenemos muy _____.
10. En la _____ hay muchos libros.

Lección 5   **A.** Expressions with **tener**

How would you say the following in Spanish?

1. I'm not hungry, but I'm very thirsty.
2. Darío is nineteen years old. How old are you, Paco?
3. Are you in a hurry, Miss Perales?
4. Are you cold, Dad? I'm hot!
5. We are very sleepy.
6. You're right, Mrs. Vega! Paquito is very scared.

B. Stem-changing verbs (**e:ie**)

Complete the following sentences using the present indicative of the verbs provided.

1. —¿Tú _____ ir hoy? (querer)
   —No, _____ ir mañana. (preferir)
2. —¿A qué hora _____ ellos la cafetería? (cerrar)
   —A las nueve. ¿A qué hora _____ el concierto? (empezar)
   —A las diez y media.
3. —¿Uds. _____? (entender)
   —No, no _____ mucho... (entender)

C. Ir a + infinitive

Use the subjects and the cues provided to describe what everyone is going to do.

1. tú / el libro
2. nosotros / los sándwiches
3. ellos / la lección dos
4. yo / café
5. ella / francés

D. Uses of the definite article

How would you say the following in Spanish?

1. Today is Wednesday.
2. I don't like tea.
3. Education is important.
4. We're going to school next week.
5. I don't have classes on Fridays.

E. Ordinal numbers

Complete the following sentences using the ordinal number that corresponds to the number in parentheses.

1. Ella vive en el _____ piso. (3)
2. Llegan el _____ de mayo. (1)

3. ¿Tú quieres la _____ o la _____ mesa? (5 / 6)
4. Ellos viven en el _____ piso. (8)
5. No tenemos clases la _____ semana. (7)

F. Vocabulary

Complete the following sentences using words learned in
Lección 5.

1. Nosotros _____ a las siete de la mañana. La cena es a
   las ocho de la noche.
2. Ella lee la _____ *Time.*
3. El concierto _____ a las nueve de la noche.
4. Necesito _____ y jabón.
5. ¿Quieres ir al cine o _____ ir al concierto?
6. ¿Tú _____ una conversación en francés?
7. En junio no tenemos clases. Tenemos _____.
8. La oficina está en el tercer _____.
9. Ellos _____ mucho dinero en Las Vegas.
10. Enero es el primer _____ del año.

Lección

6

1. **Stem-changing verbs** (o:ue)
2. **Affirmative and negative expressions**
3. **Pronouns as object of a preposition**
4. **Uses of** *se*
5. **The present progressive**

Vocabulario

COGNADOS

alcohólico(a) alcoholic	**la excursión** excursion, tour
el banco bank	**la farmacia** pharmacy

NOMBRES
la cama bed
el colchón mattress
la estampilla, el sello, el timbre (*Méx.*) stamp
la frazada, la manta, la cobija blanket
el guía guide
la librería book store
los lugares de interés places of interest
el mar ocean
la oficina de correos post office
el periódico, el diario newspaper
la playa beach
el pueblo town
el regalo present, gift
el teatro theater

VERBOS
almorzar (o:ue) to have lunch
costar (o:ue) to cost
decir (e:i) to say, to tell
dormir (o:ue) to sleep

pedir (e:i) to request, to ask for, to order
poder (o:ue) to be able
recordar (o:ue) to remember
servir (e:i) to serve
traer to bring
volar (o:ue) to fly
volver (o:ue) to return, to come (go) back

ADJETIVO
este(a) this

OTRAS PALABRAS Y EXPRESIONES
allí there
cerca de near to
¿cómo se dice... ? how do you say . . . ?
con vista al mar with an ocean view
mañana tomorrow
por noche per night
que viene next
se dice one says

1. Stem-changing verbs (o:ue)
Verbos que cambian en la raíz (o:ue)

As you learned in **Lección 5,** certain verbs undergo a change in the stem in the present indicative. When the last stem vowel is a stressed **o,** it changes to **ue.**

volver *(to return)*	
vuelvo	volvemos
vuelves	
vuelve	vuelven

◆ Notice that the stem vowel is not stressed in the verb form corresponding to **nosotros**; therefore, the **o** does not change to **ue**.

—¿Cuándo **vuelven** Uds. de la excursión?	*"When are you coming back from the excursion?"*
—**Volvemos** a las siete.	*"We are coming back at seven."*
—¿A qué hora **vuelves** tú?	*"What time are you coming back?"*
—**Vuelvo** a las nueve.	*"I'm coming back at nine."*

Some other common verbs that undergo the same change in the stem are:

almorzar	to have lunch	**poder**	to be able
costar	to cost	**recordar**	to remember
dormir	to sleep	**volar**	to fly

—¿Cuánto **cuesta** una habitación con vista al mar?	*"How much does a room with an ocean view cost?"*
—Cien dólares por noche.	*"One hundred dollars per night."*
—**¿Puede** Ud. comprar el colchón mañana?	*"Can you buy the mattress tomorrow?"*
—Sí. ¡Ah!, no, ahora **recuerdo** que no tengo dinero.	*"Yes. Oh!, no, now I remember that I have no money."*
—¿Cuándo **vuela** Ud.?	*"When are you flying?"*
—**Vuelo** la semana que viene.	*"I'm flying next week."*
—¿Cuándo **pueden** ir Uds. a la farmacia?	*"When can you go to the pharmacy?"*
—**Podemos** ir esta noche.	*"We can go tonight."*
—No **duermo** bien.	*"I don't sleep very well."*
—¿Cuántas horas **duermes**?	*"How many hours do you sleep?"*
—**Duermo** solamente tres o cuatro horas.	*"I sleep only three or four hours."*

Práctica

A. Complete the following dialogues with the correct verb forms. Then act them out with a partner.

1. *almorzar*   —¿Dónde _____ Uds.?
                —Nosotros _____ en la cafetería y mis hijos _____ en la escuela.

2. *volver*   —¿Cuándo _____ tú de la excursión?
                —Yo _____ a las ocho. ¿Y Uds.?
                —Nosotros _____ mañana a las diez.

3. *costar*   —¿Cuánto _____ un cuarto con vista al mar en el hotel Calinda? ¿Ochenta dólares por noche?
   recordar   —(Yo) no _____.

4. *poder*   —¿Uds. _____ ir a la farmacia ahora?
                —No, no _____. ¿Tú _____ ir más tarde?
                —Sí, yo _____ ir más tarde con Daniel.

5. *dormir /*   —¿Tú _____ cuando _____?
   volar   —No, porque tengo miedo.

B. Ask a classmate the following questions, then switch roles.

1. Cuando viajas, ¿vuelas o vas en ómnibus?
2. ¿Cuánto cuestan tus libros para la universidad?
3. ¿A qué hora vuelves a tu casa?
4. ¿Cuántas horas duermes?
5. ¿Puedes venir a clase la semana que viene?
6. ¿Recuerdas el número de teléfono de tu mejor amigo o amiga? (¿Cuál es?)
7. ¿A qué hora almuerzan Uds. en su casa?

2. Affirmative and negative expressions

Expresiones afirmativas y negativas

Affirmative		Negative	
algo	something, anything	nada	nothing
alguien	someone, anyone	nadie	nobody, no one
alguno(a)		ninguno(a)	
algún	any, some	ningún	none, not any
algunos(as)			
siempre	always	nunca	
alguna vez	ever	jamás	never
algunas veces	sometimes		
también	also, too	tampoco	neither
o... o	either . . . or	ni... ni	neither . . . nor

—¿Hay **algo** en la cama? *"Is there anything on the bed?"*
—No, no hay **nada.** *"No, there is nothing. (No, there isn't anything.)"*

—¿Hay **alguien** con el guía? *"Is there anyone with the guide?"*
—No, no hay **nadie.** *"No, there is no one. (No, there isn't anyone.)"*

—¿Va Ud. **siempre** a la playa? *"Do you always go to the beach?"*
—No, no voy **nunca.** No me gusta. *"No, I never go. I don't like to."*

—¿Quieren venir Uds. **también?** *"Do you want to come, too?"*
—No, Juan no quiere ir, **ni** yo tampoco. *"No, Juan doesn't want to go and neither do I."*

—¿Qué quiere Ud., vino o champán? *"What do you want, wine or champagne?"*
—Yo no bebo **ni** vino **ni** champán. No tomo bebidas alcohólicas. *"I don't drink (either) wine or champagne. I don't drink alcoholic beverages."*

♦ **Alguno** and **ninguno** drop the **-o** before a masculine singular noun, but **alguna** and **ninguna** keep the final **-a.**

—¿Hay **algún** mercado o **alguna** tienda cerca de aquí? *"Is there any market or store near here?"*
—No, no hay **ningún** mercado ni **ninguna** tienda. *"No, there isn't any market or store."*

♦ **Alguno(a)** is used in the plural form to agree with a plural noun, but **ninguno(a)** must be used in the singular form.

—¿Hay **algunos** lugares de interés en este pueblo? *"Are there any places of interest in this town?"*
—No, no hay **ninguno.** *"No, there aren't any."*

—¿Vienen **algunas** chicas hoy? *"Are some girls coming today?"*
—No, no viene **ninguna** chica. *"No, no girls are coming (not one girl)."*

◆ A double negative is frequently used in Spanish. In this construction, the adverb **no** is placed immediately before the verb. The second negative word may either precede the verb, follow the verb, or come at the end of the sentence. If the negative word precedes the verb, **no** is not used.

—¿Uds. van al teatro   *"Do you go to the theater*
  algunas veces?   *sometimes?"*
—No, **no** vamos **nunca.**   *"No, we never go."*
  (**Nunca** vamos.)

—¿Compra Ud. **algo** aquí?   *"Do you buy anything here?"*
—No, aquí **no** compro   *"No, I never buy anything here."*
  nada nunca. (**Nunca**
  compro **nada** aquí.)

Práctica

A. Answer the following questions in the negative.

1. ¿Necesita Ud. algo?
2. ¿Hay alguien aquí?
3. ¿Estudia Ud. siempre por la noche?
4. ¿Quiere té o café?
5. ¿Hay algunos lugares de interés cerca de aquí?
6. Su amigo no va a la excursión. ¿Va Ud.?
7. ¿Va Ud. a la playa algunas veces?

B. With a partner, act out the following dialogues in Spanish.

1. "Are you going to travel by bus?"
   "No, I never travel by bus. I always travel by car."
2. "Do you want to go to the movies or to the theater?"
   "I do not want to go to the movies or the theater."
   "Neither do I."
3. "Is there anybody with the students now?"
   "No, there isn't anybody . . . Oh, yes! The guide is with the students."

3. Pronouns as object of a preposition
Pronombres usados como objetos de preposición

Preposition a word that introduces a noun, pronoun, adverb, or verb and indicates its function in the sentence. They were **with** us. She is **from** Lima.

Prepositional Pronouns			
Singular		*Plural*	
mí	me	nosotros(as)	us
ti	you (*familiar*)		
Ud.	you (*formal*)	Uds.	you (*formal, plural*)
él	him	ellos	them (*masc.*)
ella	her	ellas	them (*fem.*)

◆ Notice that only the first and the second persons singular (**mí, ti**) have special forms. The other persons use the forms of the subject pronouns.

◆ When used with the preposition **con,** the first and second person singular forms become **conmigo** and **contigo.**

—¿Vas a casa **conmigo?**	*"Are you going home with me?"*
—No, no voy **contigo.** Voy **con** ellos.	*"No, I'm not going with you. I'm going with them."*
—¿Es **para nosotros** el regalo?	*"Is the present for us?"*
—Sí, es **para Uds.**	*"Yes, it's for you."*
—¿Hablan **de ti?**	*"Are they talking about you?"*
—No, no hablan **de mí.**	*"No, they're not talking about me."*

Práctica

A. Complete the following sentences with the correct form of the pronoun.

1. Mi hermana va a la playa con _____. (*us*)
2. El regalo es para _____. (*him*)
3. Ellos siempre hablan de _____, no de _____. (*you, fam./me*)
4. La cama es para _____ y el colchón es para _____, señor. (*her/you*)
5. Ellos vienen con _____; no vienen con _____. (*you, fam./me*)

B. Interview a classmate, using the following questions and two questions of your own. When you have finished, switch roles. Use the appropriate prepositions and pronouns in your responses.

1. ¿Hablas con tus amigos en la clase?
2. ¿Puedes estudiar español conmigo?
3. ¿Trabajas para tus padres?
4. ¿Vives cerca de tus abuelos?
5. ¿Hablas mucho con tus amigos por teléfono?
6. ¿Vas de vacaciones con tu familia?

4. Uses of se
Usos de se

In Spanish, the pronoun **se** is used before the third person of the verb (either singular or plural, depending on the subject) when the person performing the action is not mentioned or is not known.

La librería **se abre** a las ocho.	*The bookstore opens (is opened) at eight.*
Las oficinas **se cierran** a las cinco.	*The offices close (are closed) at five.*

◆ Notice the use of **se** in the following impersonal constructions, announcements, and general directions.

—Necesito estampillas. ¿A qué hora **se abre** la oficina de correos?	*"I need stamps. What time does the post office open?"*
—**Se abre** a las ocho.	*"It opens at eight."*
—¿A qué hora **se cierran** los bancos?	*"What time do banks close?"*
—Los bancos **se cierran** a las tres de la tarde.	*"Banks close at 3 P.M."*
—¿Allí **se habla** inglés?	*"Is English spoken there?"*
—No, **se habla** sólo francés.	*"No, only French is spoken (there)."*

◆ **Se** is also used with the third person singular of the verb as the equivalent of *one, they,* or *people,* when the subject of the verb is not definite.

—¿Cómo **se dice** "blanket" en español?	*"How does one say 'blanket' in Spanish?"*
—**Se dice** "frazada".	*"One says frazada."*

Práctica

Luis Otero, a student from Chile, is visiting your home town and needs some information. Can you answer his questions?

1. ¿A qué hora se abre la librería de la universidad?
2. ¿Se habla español aquí?
3. ¿Cómo se dice "estampilla" en inglés?
4. ¿A qué hora se cierra la cafetería?
5. ¿Se abren las oficinas de la universidad los sábados?
6. ¿A qué hora se cierra la oficina de correos?
7. ¿Se abren los bancos los sábabos en este pueblo?
8. ¿A qué hora se abre la biblioteca?

5. The present progressive
El presente progresivo

The present progressive describes an action that is in process at the moment we are talking. In Spanish, it is formed with the present tense of **estar** and the Spanish equivalent of the present participle (-*ing* form)[1] of the main verb.

-*ing* Form Endings		
-ar: **hablar**	-er: **comer**	-ir: **escribir**
habl- **ando**	com- **iendo**	escrib- **iendo**

◆ Some irregular -*ing* forms:

pedir	**pidiendo**	servir	**sirviendo**
decir	**diciendo**	leer	**leyendo**[2]
dormir	**durmiendo**	traer	**trayendo**[2]

—¿Qué **están haciendo** tus hermanos? — "*What are your brothers doing?*"

—**Están estudiando.** — "*They are studying.*"

—¿Qué **estás comiendo?** — "*What are you eating?*"
—**Estoy comiendo** pollo. — "*I'm eating chicken.*"

—¿Qué **está leyendo** Ud.? — "*What are you reading?*"
—**Estoy leyendo** el periódico. — "*I'm reading the newspaper.*"

---

[1] The equivalent of the -*ing* form of the verb is called **el gerundio** in Spanish.
[2] Notice that the **-i** of **-iendo** becomes **y** between vowels.

ATENCIÓN: Unlike in English the present progressive is never used in Spanish to refer to a future action. Instead, the present indicative is used for actions that will occur in the near future.

Salgo mañana.   *I'm leaving tomorrow.*

Verbs such as **ser, estar, ir (yendo),** and **venir (viniendo)** are rarely used in the progressive construction.

Práctica

A. Imagine what these people are doing according to where they are.

Modelo: Yo / en el hotel
Yo estoy hablando con el gerente.

1. Julia / en su cuarto
2. el mozo / en el restaurante
3. nosotros / en la biblioteca
4. Ud. / en la oficina de correos
5. mis padres / en el restaurante
6. los estudiantes / en la clase de español

B. With a partner, act out the following dialogues in Spanish.

1. "Is he serving wine?"
   "No, they don't drink alcoholic beverages."
2. "What's María doing there?"
   "She is asking (for) a blanket."
3. "What are they saying?"
   "Nothing. They are reading the newspaper."

En el laboratorio

The following material is to be used with the tape in the language laboratory.

I. Vocabulario

Repeat each word after the speaker. When repeating words that are cognates, notice the difference in pronunciation between English and Spanish.

COGNADOS: alcohólico   el banco   la excursión
                 la farmacia

NOMBRES:	la cama el colchón la estampilla
	el sello el timbre la frazada
	la manta la cobija el guía la librería
	los lugares de interés el mar
	la oficina de correos el periódico
	el diario la playa el pueblo
	el regalo el teatro
VERBOS:	almorzar costar decir dormir
	pedir poder recordar servir traer
	volar volver
ADJETIVOS:	este
OTRAS PALABRAS Y EXPRESIONES:	allí cerca de ¿cómo se dice?
	con vista al mar mañana por noche
	que viene se dice

II. Práctica

A. Answer the questions, using the cue provided. Repeat the correct answer after the speaker's confirmation. Listen to the model.

Modelo: —¿Cuándo puede volver Ud.? (mañana)
—**Puedo volver mañana.**

1. (a las dos y cuarto)
2. (el lunes)
3. (ocho horas)
4. (los sábados)
5. (con (Raúl)

B. Change the following negative statements to the affirmative. Repeat the correct answer after the speaker's confirmation. Listen to the model.

Modelo: Ellos nunca van al teatro.
Ellos siempre van al teatro.

C. Answer the questions, using the cue provided. Repeat the correct answer after the speaker's confirmation. Listen to the model.

Modelo: ¿A qué hora se abre el banco? (a las diez)
El banco se abre a las diez.

1. (a las nueve)
2. (español)
3. (playa)
4. (no)
5. (a las doce)

D. Change the verbs in each sentence to the present progressive. Repeat the correct answer after the speaker's confirmation. Listen to the model.

Modelo: —Yo tomo café.
           —Yo **estoy tomando** café.

III. Para escuchar y entender

1. Listen carefully to the narration. It will be read twice.

(Narración)

Now the speaker will make statements about the narration you just heard. Tell whether each statement is true (**verdadero**) or false (**falso**). The speaker will confirm the correct answer.

2. Listen carefully to the dialogue. It will be read twice.

(Diálogo)

Now the speaker will ask some questions about the dialogue you just heard. Answer each question, omitting the subject. The speaker will confirm the correct answer. Repeat the correct answer.

Lección

7

Vocabulario

COGNADOS

la información information	**el poema** poem
la novela novel	**la reservación** reservation
el pasaporte passport	

NOMBRES
la agencia de viajes travel agency
el (la) agente de viajes travel agent
la avenida avenue
el avión plane
la carne meat
la carta letter
la embajada embassy
la ensalada salad
los folletos turísticos tourist brochures
la oficina de turismo tourist office
el pasaje, el billete ticket
el postre dessert
la sopa soup
la verdad truth

VERBOS
conducir to drive
confirmar to confirm
conocer to know, to be familiar with

conseguir (e:i) to obtain, to get
hacer to do; to make
nadar to swim
poner to put, to place
quedar to be located
saber to know how, to know a fact
salir to go out, to leave
seguir (e:i) to follow, to continue
traducir to translate
ver to see

ADJETIVOS
helado(a) iced
ocupado(a) busy

OTRAS PALABRAS Y EXPRESIONES
de memoria by heart
entonces then, in that case

1. Stem-changing verbs (e:i)
Verbos que cambian en la raíz (e:i)

Some **-ir** verbs undergo a special stem change in the present indicative. For these verbs, when **e** is the last stem vowel and it is stressed, it changes to **i**.

servir *(to serve)*		
sirvo	servimos	
sirves		
sirve	sirven	

♦ Notice that the stem vowel is not stressed in the verb form corresponding to **nosotros**; therefore, the **e** does not change to **i**.

—¿Qué **sirven** Uds.?   *"What do you serve?"*
—**Servimos** té helado.   *"We serve iced tea."*

—¿Qué **sirven** en la   *"What do they serve at the*
    cafetería?   *cafeteria?"*
—**Sirven** sopa, ensalada,   *"They serve soup, salad, meat,*
    carne y postre.   *and dessert."*

♦ Some other common verbs that undergo the same **e** to **i** change in the stem are **pedir** *(to ask for, to request, to order)*, **seguir** *(to follow, to continue)*, and **repetir** *(to repeat)*. Verbs like **seguir** (such as **conseguir**, *to obtain*) contain a **u** to preserve the hard **g** sound before an **e** or an **i**. Verbs that follow this pattern drop the **u** before an **a** or an **o: yo sigo, yo consigo.**

—¿Qué **pide** Enrique en   *"What is Enrique requesting at*
    la agencia de viajes?   *the travel agency?"*
—**Pide** información.   *"He is requesting information."*

—¿A quién **siguen** Uds.?   *"Whom are you following?"*
—**Seguimos** al guía.   *"We are following the guide."*

—¿Dónde **consiguen**   *"Where do you get tourist*
    Uds. folletos turísticos?   *brochures?"*
—En la oficina de   *"At the tourist office."*
    turismo.

♦ The verb **decir** *(to say, to tell)* undergoes the same **e** to **i** stem change, but in addition it is irregular in the first person singular: **yo digo.**

—¿**Dice** Ud. la verdad   *"Do you always tell the truth?"*
    siempre?
—Sí, yo siempre **digo** la   *"Yes, I always tell the truth."*
    verdad.

Práctica

A. Complete the following dialogues with the correct verb forms. Then act them out with a partner.

1. —En este restaurante mexicano _____ una sopa muy buena. (servir)
   —Cuando yo vengo aquí, siempre _____ tacos. (pedir)
   —Yo siempre _____ que los tacos de aquí son los mejores. (decir)

2. —Carlos, ¿dónde _____ tú folletos en español? (conseguir)
   —Yo _____ algunos en Los Ángeles y algunos en la oficina de turismo. (conseguir)
   —¿Tú _____ en la clase de la Dra. Peña? (seguir)
   —Sí, y ella siempre _____ que yo soy su mejor estudiante. (decir)

3. —Los chicos _____ que tú sólo _____ carne y ensalada. (decir/servir)
   —No es verdad; algunas veces también _____ sopa y postre. (servir)

B. Tell about yourself by answering the following questions.

1. ¿Dónde consigue Ud. libros de español?
2. ¿Sigue Ud. en la clase de español?
3. En un restaurante mexicano, ¿qué pide Ud.?
4. ¿A qué hora sirven Uds. la cena?
5. ¿Sirve Ud. té helado con la comida?
6. ¿Dice Ud. siempre la verdad?

The three types of stem-changing verbs

Here is a list of stem-changing verbs studied up to now. Every time you learn a new one, add it to the list.

e:ie	o:ue	e:i
cerrar	almorzar	conseguir
comenzar	costar	decir
empezar	dormir	pedir
entender	poder	repetir
perder	recordar	seguir
preferir	volar	servir
querer	volver	

2. Irregular first-person forms
Verbos irregulares en la primera persona

Some common verbs are irregular in the present indicative only in the first person singular. The other persons are regular.

Verb	First-person (yo) form	Regular forms
salir (*to go out, to leave*)	**salgo**	sales, sale, salimos, salen
hacer (*to do, to make*)	**hago**	haces, hace, hacemos, hacen
poner (*to put, to place*)	**pongo**	pones, pone, ponemos, ponen
traer (*to bring*)	**traigo**	traes, trae, traemos, traen
conducir (*to drive*)	**conduzco**	conduces, conduce, conducimos, conducen
traducir (*to translate*)	**traduzco**	traduces, traduce, traducimos, traducen
conocer (*to know*)	**conozco**	conoces, conoce, conocemos, conocen
ver (*to see*)	**veo**	ves, ve, vemos, ven
saber (*to know*)	**sé**	sabes, sabe, sabemos, saben

—¿Tú **sabes** conducir?
—Sí, yo **sé** conducir. **Conduzco** el coche de mi hermano.

"Do you know how to drive?"
"Yes, I know how to drive. I drive my brother's car."

—¿A qué hora **sales** de tu casa por la mañana?
—**Salgo** a las siete.

"What time do you leave your house in the morning?"
"I leave at seven."

—¿Qué **haces** los domingos?
—No **hago** nada.
—Entonces, ¿no **ves** a tus amigos?
—No, no **veo** a nadie.

"What do you do on Sundays?"
"I don't do anything."
"Then, you don't see your friends?"
"No, I don't see anybody."

Práctica

Interview a classmate, using the following questions. When you have finished, switch roles.

1. ¿Sales a menudo?
2. ¿Ves a tus amigos los sábados?

3. ¿Haces algo los domingos?
4. ¿Conoces la ciudad de Nueva York?
5. ¿Conduces bien?
6. ¿Sabes francés?
7. ¿Traduces del español al inglés?
8. ¿Traes tus libros a clase?
9. ¿Dónde pones tus libros?
10. ¿Conoces a alguien de Venezuela?

3. Saber **contrasted with** conocer
Saber **vs.** conocer

There are two verbs in Spanish that mean *to know:* **saber** and **conocer.** These verbs are not interchangeable.

◆ **Saber** means to know something by heart, to know how to do something, or to know a fact.

—¿**Sabe** Ud. algunos poemas de memoria?	*"Do you know any poems by heart?"*
—No, no **sé** ninguno.	*"No, I don't know any."*
—¿**Saben** ellos nadar?	*"Do they know how to swim?"*
—Sí, ellos **saben** nadar.	*"Yes, they know how to swim."*
—¿**Sabes** dónde queda la embajada norteamericana?	*"Do you know where the American Embassy is located?"*
—Sí, queda en la avenida Juárez.	*"Yes, it's located on Juárez Avenue."*

◆ **Conocer** means to be familiar or acquainted with a person, a thing, or a place.

—¿**Conoces** al agente de viajes?	*"Do you know the travel agent?"*
—¿Al Sr. Paz? Sí.	*"Mr. Paz? Yes."*
—¿**Conocen** Uds. las novelas de Cervantes?	*"Are you familiar with Cervantes's novels?"*
—Sí, **conocemos** algunas.	*"Yes, we are familiar with some (of them)."*
—¿**Conoces** Puerto Rico?	*"Are you familiar with Puerto Rico?"*
—No, yo no **conozco** Puerto Rico.	*"No, I'm not familiar with Puerto Rico."*

Práctica

Tell what these people know or don't know, using **saber** or **conocer.**

1. Ellos / California
2. Ud. / a mi madre
3. Tú / el poema de memoria
4. Él / al supervisor
5. Yo no / nadar
6. ¿Uds. / los poemas de Neruda?
7. Yo no / qué día es hoy
8. Yo no / la Ciudad de México
9. Nosotras no / dónde queda la embajada
10. Ellas / al hijo del profesor

4. Direct object pronouns
Los pronombres de complemento directo

> **Direct Object** generally a noun or a pronoun that is the receiver of a verb's action and answers the question *"what?"* or *"whom?".* Take **it.** We know **her.** I call **Mary.**

The forms of the direct object pronouns are as follows.

Subject	Direct Object	
yo	**me** (*me*)	Ella **me** visita.
tú	**te** (*you, familiar*)	Yo **te** sigo.
Ud.	{ **lo** (*you, masc., formal*) { **la** (*you, fem., formal*)	Yo **lo** conozco. (a Ud.)[1] Yo **la** conozco. (a Ud.)[1]
él	**lo** (*him, it*)	Él **lo** ve. (a él)[1]
ella	**la** (*her, it*)	Él **la** ve. (a ella)[1]
nosotros } nosotras }	**nos** (*us, masc. and fem.*)	Tú **nos** llamas.
Uds.	{ **los** (*you, masc., pl., formal*) { **las** (*you, fem., pl., formal*)	Nosotros **los** llevamos. (a Uds.)[1] Nosotros **las** llevamos. (a Uds.)[1]
ellos	**los** (*them, masc.*)	Él **los** trae. (a ellos)[1]
ellas	**las** (*them, fem.*)	Él **las** trae. (a ellas)[1]

---

[1] Use for clarification to avoid confusion between **Ud.** and **él** or **ella,** or between **Uds.** and **ellos** or **ellas.**

The direct object pronoun replaces the direct object noun and is placed *before* the conjugated verb.

Yo espero **al Sr. Lima.**
Yo   **lo**   espero.

Ella escribe **la carta.**
Ella   **la**   escribe.

Nosotros llevamos **a nuestros amigos.**
Nosotros   **los**   llevamos.

—¿**Me** ves ahora?	*"Do you see me now?"*
—Sí, ahora **te** veo.	*"Yes, now I see you."*
—¿Conduce Ud. el coche?	*"Do you drive the car?"*
—Sí, yo **lo** conduzco.	*"Yes, I drive it."*
—¿Pides los pasaportes?	*"Are you asking for the passports?"*
—Sí, **los** pido.	*"Yes, I am asking for them."*

◆ In a negative sentence, the **no** must precede the object pronoun.

Yo traduzco **las lecciones.**
Yo   **las**   traduzco.
Yo   **no**   **las**   traduzco.

—¿Confirma Ud. la reservación hoy?	*"Are you confirming the reservation today?"*
—No, you **no la** confirmo hoy. Estoy muy ocupada. **La** confirmo mañana.	*"No, I'm not confirming it today. I'm very busy. I'm confirming it tomorrow."*

◆ If a conjugated verb and an infinitive appear together, the direct object pronoun may be placed before the conjugated verb or attached to the infinitive.

Te quiero ver. ⎫
   Quiero ver**te.** ⎬   *I want to see you.*

—¿Vas a traer los pasajes?   *"Are you going to bring the tickets?"*

—Sí, **los** voy a traer. ⎫
   Sí,   voy a traer**los.** ⎬   *"Yes, I am going to bring them."*

◆ In the present progressive, the direct object pronoun can be placed either before the verb **estar** or after the present participle.

Lo está leyendo. ⎫
  Está leyéndo**lo**. ⎬ *He's reading **it**.*
        ⎭

Note that when the direct object pronoun is attached to the present participle, a written accent is added to preserve the original stress.

Práctica

A. Tell the person asking you these questions that you have to do everything. Follow the model.

Modelo: —¿Quién trae los pasajes?
      —Yo **los** traigo.

1. ¿Quién pide la información?
2. ¿Quién hace las reservaciones?
3. ¿Quién consigue los folletos turísticos?
4. ¿Quién llama al agente de viajes?
5. ¿Quién compra los billetes para el avión?
6. ¿Quién lleva los pasaportes a la agencia?
7. ¿Quién confirma la reservación?
8. ¿Quién escribe las cartas?

B. You are planning a trip to Spain. How are you getting ready for it? What is going to happen there? Answer the following questions, always using direct object pronouns.

1. ¿Tiene Ud. su pasaporte?
2. ¿Sabe Ud. hablar bien el español?
3. ¿Sus amigos van a esperarlo (esperarla)?
4. ¿Va a ver a sus profesores allí?
5. ¿Va a visitar los museos?
6. ¿Va a conducir su coche?
7. ¿Ud. va a llamarnos?
8. ¿Va a llevarme a España con Ud.?

C. With a partner, act out the following dialogues in Spanish.

1. "Can you call me tomorrow, Anita?"
   "Yes, I can call you in the morning, Paco."
2. "Are you going to take us to the travel agency, Miss Soto?"
   "No, I can't take you today. I'm very busy."
3. "Do you know Delia, Mr. Vega?"
   "Yes, I know her."
   "Do you have her phone number?"
   "No, I don't have it."

En el laboratorio

The following material is to be used with the tape in the language laboratory.

I. Vocabulario

Repeat each word after the speaker. When repeating words that are cognates, notice the difference in pronunciation between English and Spanish.

COGNADOS:	la información la novela el pasaporte el poema la reservación
NOMBRES:	la agencia de viajes el agente de viajes la avenida el avión la carne la carta la embajada la ensalada los folletos turísticos la oficina de turismo el pasaje el billete el postre la sopa la verdad
VERBOS:	conducir confirmar conocer conseguir hacer nadar poner quedar saber salir seguir traducir ver
ADJETIVOS:	helado ocupado
OTRAS PALABRAS Y EXPRESIONES:	de memoria entonces

II. Práctica

A. Change each sentence, using the verb provided. Repeat the correct answer after the speaker's confirmation. Listen to the model.

Modelo: Yo quiero carne. (pedir)
    Yo pido carne.

B. Answer the questions, always using the first choice. Omit the subject. Repeat the correct answer after the speaker's confirmation. Listen to the model.

Modelo: —¿Conduces un Ford o un Chevrolet?
    —Conduzco un Ford.

C. Answer the following questions in the negative. Replace the direct objects with the appropriate pronouns. Repeat the correct answer after the speaker's confirmation. Listen to the model.

Modelo: —¿Ud. conoce a Carlos?
—**No, no lo conozco.**

III. Para escuchar y entender

1. Listen carefully to the dialogue. It will be read twice.

(*Diálogo 1*)

Now the speaker will make statements about the dialogue you just heard. Tell whether each statement is true (**verdadero**) or false (**falso**). The speaker will confirm the correct answer.

2. Listen carefully to the narration. It will be read twice.

(*Narración*)

Now the speaker will ask questions about the narration you just heard. Answer each question, omitting the subject. The speaker will confirm the correct answer. Repeat the correct answer.

3. Listen carefully to the dialogue. It will be read twice.

(*Diálogo 2*)

Now the speaker will ask some questions about the dialogue you just heard. Answer each question, omitting the subject. The speaker will confirm the correct answer. Repeat the correct answer.

Lección

8

1. **Demonstrative adjectives and pronouns**
2. **Indirect object pronouns**
3. *Pedir* **contrasted with** *preguntar*
4. **Direct and indirect object pronouns used together**

Vocabulario

COGNADOS

el básquetbol basketball
la bicicleta bicycle
el club club
el parque park

el (la) presidente(a)
president
la raqueta racket
el tenis tennis

NOMBRES
la bolsa de dormir sleeping
bag
el caballo horse
la entrada ticket (*for an
event*)
el (la) entrenador(a)
trainer, coach
los esquíes skis
la mochila backpack
el (la) niño(a) child, kid
la página deportiva sports
page
el partido game, match
los patines skates
la pelota ball
la raqueta de tenis tennis
racket
la tía aunt
la tienda de campaña tent
el tío uncle

VERBOS
esquiar to ski
jugar[1] to play (*e.g. a
game*)
mandar to send
preguntar to ask (*a
question*)
prestar to lend
regalar to give (*a present*)

OTRAS PALABRAS Y
EXPRESIONES
allá over there
ir a esquiar to go skiing
¿para quién? for whom?
que that, which
si if

1. Demonstrative adjectives and pronouns
Los adjetivos y pronombres demostrativos

Demonstrative   a word that points out a definite person
or object: **this, that, these, those**

---

[1] Present tense: **juego, juegas, juega, jugamos, juegan**

Demonstrative adjectives

Demonstrative adjectives point out persons or things. They agree in gender and number with the nouns they modify or point out. The forms of the demonstrative adjectives are as follows.

Masculine		Feminine		
Singular	*Plural*	*Singular*	*Plural*	
este	**estos**	**esta**	**estas**	this, these
ese	**esos**	**esa**	**esas**	that, those
aquel	**aquellos**	**aquella**	**aquellas**	that, those *(at a distance)*

—¿Para quién es **esta** raqueta de tenis?

—**Esta** raqueta es para Marta y **esa** pelota es para Rita.

"Whom is this tennis racket for?"

"This racket is for Marta and that ball is for Rita."

—¿Te gusta **este** caballo?

—No, me gusta **aquel** caballo blanco que está allá.

"Do you like this horse?"

"No, I like that white horse over there."

Práctica

Change the demonstrative adjectives so that they agree with the new nouns.

1. Este caballo, _____ raqueta, _____ revistas, _____ programas.
2. Esas ciudades, _____ teatros, _____ biblioteca, _____ museo.
3. Aquella mesa, _____ sillas, _____ hombre, _____ restaurantes.
4. Esta lección, _____ idioma, _____ problemas, _____ universidades.
5. Ese jabón, _____ frazadas, _____ cuartos, _____ toalla.

Demonstrative pronouns

The demonstrative pronouns are the same as the demonstrative adjectives, except that the pronouns have a written accent mark. The forms of the demonstrative pronouns are as follows.

Masculine		Feminine		Neuter	
Singular	*Plural*	*Singular*	*Plural*		
éste	éstos	ésta	éstas	esto	this (*one*), these
ése	ésos	ésa	ésas	eso	that (*one*), those
aquél	aquéllos	aquélla	aquéllas	aquello	that (*one*), those (*at a distance*)

—¿Qué patines quiere Ud.? ¿**Éstos** o **aquéllos?**   "*Which skates do you want? These or those* (over there)*?*"

—Quiero **aquéllos.**   "*I want those* (over there)*.*"

—¿Qué mochilas van a llevar los niños, **éstas** o **ésas?**   "*Which backpacks are the children going to take, these or those?*"

—**Éstas.**   "*These.*"

◆ Each demonstrative pronoun has a neuter form. The neuter pronoun has no accent, because there are no corresponding demonstrative adjectives.

◆ The neuter forms are used to refer to situations, ideas, or things that are abstract, general or unidentified. The neuter pronouns are equivalent to the English *this* or *that* (*matter, business; thing, stuff*).

—¿Qué crees de **eso?**	*"What do you think about that* (matter, issue)*?"*
—Creo que es un problema para el presidente del club.	*"I think it is a problem for the president of the club."*
—¿Qué es **esto?**	*"What is this* (thing, stuff)*?"*
—No sé.	*"I don't know."*

Práctica

Complete the following sentences with the Spanish equivalent of the pronouns in parentheses.

1. El presidente del club quiere este coche y _____ (*that one*).
2. Necesitamos esa pelota y _____ (*that one [over there]*).
3. Compramos esos patines y _____ (*these*).
4. Recibimos este periódico y _____ (*those*).
5. ¿Estudia Ud. esta lección o _____ (*that one*)?
6. ¿Habla Ud. con este señor o con _____ (*that one [over there]*)?
7. ¿Prefieren ellos estas mesas de madera o _____ (*those [over there]*)?
8. ¿Va Ud. a leer este libro o _____ (*those*)?
9. Deseo aquellas mochilas y _____ (*these*).
10. ¿Van Uds. a comprar esa raqueta o _____ (*this one*)?
11. Ellas no saben qué es _____ (*this*).
12. ¿Para quién es _____ (*that*)?

2. Indirect object pronouns
Los pronombres de complemento indirecto

Indirect object   a word or phrase that tells *to whom*, or *for whom* something is done. An indirect object pronoun can be used in place of the indirect object. In Spanish, the indirect object pronoun includes the meaning *to* or *for*: Yo **les** mando los libros (*a los estudiantes*). I send the books **to them** (*to the students*).

The forms of the indirect object pronouns are as follows.

Subject	Indirect Object	
yo	**me** (*to / for me*)	Él **me** da las revistas.
tú	**te** (*to / for you, familiar*)	Yo **te** doy la pelota.
Ud.	**le** (*to / for you, formal, masc. and fem.*)	Ella **le** compra una entrada.
él ⎱ ella ⎰	**le** (*to / for him / her*)	Yo **le** hablo en inglés.
nosotros ⎱ nosotras ⎰	**nos** (*to / for us, masc. and fem.*)	Ella **nos** da la lección.
Uds. ⎱ ellos ⎬ ellas ⎰	**les** (*to / for you, formal pl., masc. and fem.*) **les** (*to / for them, masc. and fem.*)	Yo **les** digo la verdad. El presidente **les** da el dinero.

The forms of the indirect object pronouns are the same as the forms of the direct object pronouns, except in the third person. Indirect object pronouns are usually placed *in front* of a conjugated verb.

—¿Quién **les** compra a Uds. las entradas?　　*"Who buys you the tickets?"*

—Mi padre **nos** compra las entradas.　　*"My father buys us the tickets."*

—¿En qué idioma **le** hablas?　　*"In which language do you speak to him?"*

—**Le** hablo en español.　　*"I speak to him in Spanish."*

◆ When an infinitive follows the conjugated verb, the indirect object pronoun may be placed in front of the conjugated verb or attached to the infinitive.

Te voy a comprar　　una bolsa de dormir.
Voy a comprar**te**　　una bolsa de dormir.

◆ With the present progressive forms, the indirect object pronoun can be placed in front of the conjugated verb or it can be attached to the end of the progressive construction.[1]

Le estoy escribiendo　　al entrenador.
Estoy escribiéndo**le**[2]　　al entrenador.

[1] This is also true of direct object pronouns.
[2] See Appendix A, part 7, number 3 (p. 282) for rules governing the use of accent marks in Spanish.

ATENCIÓN: The indirect object pronouns **le** and **les** require clarification when the person to whom they refer is not specified. Spanish provides clarification by using the preposition **a** + *noun or personal (subject) pronoun.*

Le doy la información.	*I give the information . . .* (to whom? to him? to her? to you?)
but: **Le** doy la información **a ella** (a Rosa).	*I give the information **to her*** (to Rosa).

This prepositional form is also used to express emphasis.

Me da la bicicleta **a mí.**	*He gives the bicycle to me* (and to nobody else).

Although the prepositional form provides clarification, it is not a substitute for the indirect object pronoun. The prepositional form may be omitted, but the indirect object pronoun must always be used.

—¿Qué **le** vas a traer (a Roberto)?
—**Le** voy a traer una tienda de campaña.

Práctica

A. Add the missing indirect object pronouns to express for whom the following are being done.

Modelo: Ella trae las entradas. (**para él**)
Ella **le** trae las entradas.

1. Yo compro la mochila. (**para ti**)
2. Nosotros vamos a traer los caballos. (**para Uds.;** *both ways*)
3. Ada compra la bicicleta. (**para mí**)
4. Ellos están escribiendo una carta (**para ella;** *both ways*)
5. Yo voy a traer los pasajes. (**para Ud.;** *both ways*)
6. Fernando compra los patines. (**para nosotros**)

B. Answer the following questions, using the information in parentheses.

1. ¿Qué vas a comprarle a tu hermano? (una bicicleta; *both ways*)
2. ¿Qué les da a Uds. el entrenador? (unas entradas)
3. ¿Quién te escribe? (mi novio / mi novia)
4. ¿Qué vas a traerme? (una pelota; *both ways*)
5. ¿Qué les vas a mandar a los niños? (unas raquetas; *both ways*)
6. ¿Cuándo nos va a escribir Ud.? (mañana; *both ways*)

C. Answer the following questions.

1. ¿Ud. les pide dinero a sus padres?
2. ¿El profesor le va a dar a Ud. una «A» en español?
3. ¿Puede Ud. darme el periódico?
4. ¿Uds. pueden traernos unos refrescos?
5. ¿El profesor les trae a Uds. revistas en español?

D. With a partner, act out the following dialogues in Spanish.

1. "Can he bring me the tickets tomorrow, Luis?"
   "Yes, but you have to give him the money tonight."
2. "Do your parents speak to you in Spanish?"
   "No, they speak to us in English."
3. "Does he write to you, Anita?"
   "Yes, he writes to me very often."

3. Pedir **contrasted with** preguntar
Pedir **contrastado con** preguntar

♦ **Pedir** means *to ask for* or *to request something.*

—¿Qué te **piden** los muchachos?	*"What do the boys ask you for?"*
—Me **piden** entradas para el partido de básquetbol.	*"They ask me for tickets for the basketball game."*
—¿Vas a **pedir**le dinero a tu tío?	*"Are you going to ask your uncle for money?"*
—Sí, le voy a **pedir** veinte dólares.	*"Yes, I am going to ask him for twenty dollars."*

♦ **Preguntar** means *to ask a question.*

—¿Qué vas a **preguntar**le a René?	*"What are you going to ask René?"*
—Voy a **preguntar**le si quiere ir a esquiar.	*"I'm going to ask him if he wants to go skiing."*
—¿Qué le vas a **preguntar** a Ana?	*"What are you going to ask Ana?"*
—Si quiere jugar al tenis.	*"If she wants to play tennis."*

Práctica

Complete the following dialogues, using **pedir** and **preguntar** as appropriate. Then act them out with a partner.

1. —¿Qué le vas a _____ al entrenador?
   —Si vamos a jugar al básquetbol mañana.

2. —¿Cuánto dinero le vas a _____ a tu tía?
   —Cien dólares.
3. —¿Qué te está _____ Elsa?
   —Me está _____ adónde voy a ir a esquiar.
4. —¿Qué están haciendo los niños?
   —Están _____ información sobre (*about*) el partido.
5. —¿Tú siempre les _____ consejo (*advice*) a tus padres?
   —No, nunca les _____ consejo.
6. —¿Qué le quiere _____ a Ester?
   —Le quiero _____ si vamos al parque hoy.

4. Direct and indirect object pronouns used together
Pronombres de complemento directo e indirecto usados juntos

When both an indirect object pronoun and a direct object pronoun are used in the same sentence, the indirect object pronoun always appears first.

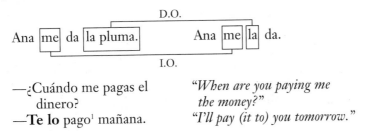

| —¿Cuándo me pagas el dinero? | "When are you paying me the money?" |
| —**Te lo** pago[1] mañana. | "I'll pay (it to) you tomorrow." |

◆ With an infinitive, the pronouns may be placed either before the main verb or attached to the infinitive.

I.O. D.O.
Ana me la va a dar.
Ana   va a dármela.[2]
                 I.O. D.O.

| —Necesito la página deportiva. ¿Puedes prestár**mela**?[2] | "I need the sports page. Can you lend it to me?" |
| —Sí, **te la** puedo prestar. | "Yes, I can lend it to you." |

---

[1] Remember that the present indicative is frequently used in Spanish to express future time.
[2] See Appendix A, part 7, number 3 (p. 282) for rules governing the use of accent marks in Spanish.

♦ With the present progressive, the pronouns can be placed either before the conjugated verb or attached to the present participle.

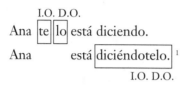

Ana te lo está diciendo.
Ana está diciéndotelo. [1]

♦ If both pronouns begin with l, the indirect object pronoun (**le** or **les**) is changed to **se.**

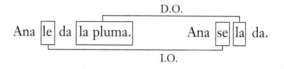

Ana le da la pluma.   Ana se la da.

♦ For clarification, it is sometimes necessary to specify the person(s) to whom the indirect object pronoun refers: **a él, a ella, a Ud., a Uds., a ellos, a ellas, a José,** etc.

—¿**Le** vas a regalar los esquíes **a él** o **a ella?**   *"Are you going to give the skis to him or to her?"*
—**Se los** voy a regalar **a ella.**   *"I'm going to give them to her."*

—¿Uds. **les** mandan las cartas **a ellas** o **a ellos?**   *"Do you send the letters to them (fem.) or to them (masc.)?"*
—**Se las** mandamos **a ellos.**   *"We send them to them (masc.)."*

Práctica

A. Mom is always doing things for the family. Explain what she does, using the information provided.

Modelo: **Yo** quiero **una mochila.** (comprar)
Mamá **me la** compra.

1. **Papá** quiere **café.** (servir)
2. **Nosotros** necesitamos **dinero.** (dar)
3. **Tú** quieres **los periódicos.** (traer)
4. **Yo** quiero **una raqueta.** (prestar)
5. **Mis hijos** necesitan **toallas.** (comprar)
6. **Papá** quiere **la página deportiva.** (traer)
7. **Uds.** necesitan **la bolsa de dormir.** (dar)
8. **Ud.** quiere comer **comida mexicana.** (hacer)

---

[1] See Appendix A, part 7, number 3 (p. 282) for rules governing the use of accent marks in Spanish.

B. You keep changing your mind when someone asks you a question. First you say "yes" and then you say "no." Substitute pronouns for the boldface nouns.

Modelo: —¿Me compra Ud. **el jabón?**
—**Sí, se lo compro.**
—**No, no se lo compro.**

1. ¿Me presta Ud. **sus patines?**
2. ¿Me compra Ud. **la tienda de campaña?**
3. ¿Les paga Ud. **los pasajes** a ellos?
4. ¿Está Ud. pidiéndole **el periódico** a Inés?
5. ¿Nos va a traer Ud. **los esquíes?**
6. ¿Le vas a regalar **la raqueta de tenis** a tu tía?

C. With a partner act out the following dialogues in Spanish.

1. "I need the tent. Can you bring it to me, Paquito?"
"Yes, I can bring it to you this afternoon, sir."
2. "I need the skates."
"I can give them to you (*as a gift*), Anita. I don't need them."
3. "Where do you get the tickets, Mario?"
"My father sends them to me."
4. "Can you lend me the sleeping bag, Mr. Peña?"
"No, Paquito, I can't lend it to you, because I'm going to need it."

📼 *En el laboratorio*

The following material is to used with the tape in the language laboratory.

I. Vocabulario

Repeat each word after the speaker. When repeating words that are cognates, notice the difference in pronunciation between English and Spanish.

COGNADOS:	el básquetbol la bicicleta el club el parque el presidente la raqueta el tenis
NOMBRES:	la bolsa de dormir el caballo la entrada el entrenador los esquíes la mochila el niño la página deportiva el partido los patines la pelota la raqueta de tenis la tía la tienda de campaña el tío

VERBOS: esquiar jugar mandar preguntar
                           prestar regalar

OTRAS PALABRAS
Y EXPRESIONES: allá ir a esquiar ¿para quién? que si

II. Práctica

A. Give the Spanish equivalent of the demonstrative adjectives that agrees with each noun mentioned by the speaker. Repeat the correct answer after the speaker's confirmation. Listen to the model.

Modelo: this / raqueta
           esta raqueta

1. this / these
2. that / those
3. that (*over there*) / those (*over there*)

B. Repeat each sentence, then substitute the new indirect object pronouns in the sentence. Repeat the correct answer after the speaker's confirmation. Listen to the model.

Modelo: Carmen **me da** el dinero. (les)
           Carmen les da el dinero.

1. Pedro me trae los patines. (nos / les / te / le)
2. Van a pedirte la mochila. (me / nos / les / le)
3. Está escribiéndote una carta. (nos / le / me / les)

C. Answer the questions, using the cue provided. Repeat the correct answer after the speaker's confirmation. Listen to the model.

Modelo: —¿Qué te pide Jorge? (la pelota)
           —Me pide la pelota.

1. (mi dirección)
2. (500 dólares)
3. (no, a mi papá)
4. (si pueden ir al cine)
5. (la sección deportiva)

D. Repeat each sentence, changing the direct object to the corresponding direct object pronoun. Make all the necessary changes in the sentence. Repeat the correct answer after the speaker's confirmation. Listen to the model.

Modelo: **Le** traen **el periódico.**
           Se lo traen.

III. Para escuchar y entender

1. Listen carefully to the dialogue. It will be read twice.

   (Diálogo 1)

   Now the speaker will make statements about the dialogue you just heard. Tell whether each statement is true (**verdadero**) or false (**falso**). The speaker will confirm the correct answer.

2. Listen carefully to the dialogue. It will be read twice.

   (Diálogo 2)

   Now the speaker will ask some questions about the dialogue you just heard. Answer each question, omitting the subject. The speaker will confirm the correct answer. Repeat the correct answer.

Lección

9

Vocabulario

COGNADOS

el champú shampoo
generalmente generally
impaciente impatient

el momento moment
el perfume perfume
la terraza terrace

NOMBRES
el baño bathroom
el botiquín medicine cabinet
el cepillo brush
el dormitorio bedroom
el espejo mirror
la máquina de afeitar razor
la medianoche midnight
el pantalón, los pantalones pants
el peine comb
el pelo hair
la peluquería beauty salon, beauty parlor
el (la) peluquero(a) hair dresser
la tarjeta card
la tarjeta de crédito credit card
la tintorería dry cleaners
la ventana window
el vestido dress

VERBOS
acordarse (o:ue) (de) to remember
acostarse (o:ue) to go to bed

atender (e:ie) to wait on, to attend to
bañar(se) to bathe (oneself)
cortar(se) to cut (oneself)
doblar to turn
lavar(se) to wash (oneself)
levantarse to get up
llamarse to be named
probarse (o:ue) to try on
sentarse (e:ie) to sit down

ADJETIVOS
corto(a) short
querido(a) dear

OTRAS PALABRAS Y EXPRESIONES
a la derecha to the right
a la izquierda to the left
ahora mismo right now
antes de before
lavarse la cabeza to wash one's hair
seguir derecho to continue straight ahead
todavía yet

1. Possessive pronouns

Los pronombres posesivos

Singular		Plural		
Masculine	*Feminine*	*Masculine*	*Feminine*	
el mío	la mía	los míos	las mías	mine
el tuyo	la tuya	los tuyos	las tuyas	yours (*familiar*)
el suyo	la suya	los suyos	las suyas	his / hers / yours (*formal*)
el nuestro	la nuestra	los nuestros	las nuestras	ours
el suyo	la suya	los suyos	las suyas	theirs / yours (*formal*)

The possessive pronouns in Spanish agree in gender and number with the thing possessed. They are generally used with the definite article.

—Aquí están las máquinas de afeitar de ellos. ¿Dónde están **las nuestras?**   *"Here are their razors. Where are ours?"*

—**Las nuestras** están en el dormitorio.   *"Ours are in the bedroom."*

—Tus pantalones están aquí. ¿Donde están **los míos?**   *"Your trousers are here. Where are mine?"*

—**Los tuyos** están en la tintorería.   *"Yours are at the cleaners."*

—**Mi** peine está aquí. ¿Dónde está **el suyo?**   *"My comb is here. Where is yours?"*

—**El mío** está en el baño.   *"Mine is in the bathroom."*

◆ After the verb **ser**, the definite article is frequently omitted.

—¿Es **tuyo** este perfume?   *"Is this perfume yours?"*

—Sí, este perfume es **mío,** pero ése es **tuyo.**   *"Yes, this perfume is mine, but that one is yours."*

—¿Esta tarjeta de crédito **es suya,** Sr. Muñoz?   *"Is this credit card yours, Mr. Muñoz?"*

—Sí, **es mía,** gracias.   *"Yes, it's mine, thanks."*

◆ Since the third-person forms of the possessive pronouns (**el suyo, la suya, los suyos, las suyas**) could be ambiguous, they may be replaced for clarification by the following

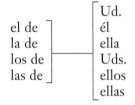

—Estos cepillos y estos peines son de Marta y de Arturo, ¿no?
—Bueno, los cepillos son **de ella,** pero los peines son **de él.**

"These brushes and these combs are Marta's and Arturo's, right?"
"Well, the brushes are hers, but the combs are his."

Práctica

A. Supply the correct possessive pronouns and read the sentences aloud. Follow the models.

Modelos: Yo tengo una tarjeta. Es _____.
Yo tengo una tarjeta. Es **mía.**

Juan tiene una tarjeta. Es _____. (Es _____.)
Juan tiene una tarjeta. Es **suya.** (Es **de él.**)

1. Tú tienes un cepillo. Es _____.
2. Juan tiene una entrada. Es _____. (Es _____.)
3. Nosotros tenemos una tarjeta de crédito. Es _____.
4. Ud. tiene unos peines. Son _____. (Son _____.)
5. Yo tengo un coche. Es _____.
6. Uds. tienen dos bicicletas. Son _____. (Son _____.)
7. Yo tengo unos pantalones. Son _____.
8. Lucía tiene tres hijos. Son _____. (Son _____.)

B. Interview a classmate, using the following questions. When you have finished, switch roles.

1. Mi mejor amigo vive en _____. ¿Dónde vive el tuyo?
2. Mis padres son de _____. ¿De dónde son los tuyos?
3. Nuestros abuelos son de _____. ¿De dónde son los de Uds.?
4. Yo tengo mis tarjetas de crédito en el dormitorio. ¿Tú tienes las tuyas?

5. Mis libros de español están aquí. ¿Dónde están los del profesor? ¿Dónde están los tuyos?
6. Tu pantalón (vestido) es _____ . ¿De qué color es el mío?

2. Reflexive constructions
Las construcciones reflexivas

Reflexive pronouns

A **reflexive construction**, such as *I introduce myself*, consists of a reflexive pronoun and a verb. Reflexive pronouns refer to the same person who is the subject of the sentence.

Subjects	Reflexive Pronouns	
yo	**me**	*myself, to / for myself*
tú	**te**	*yourself, to / for yourself* (**tú** form)
nosotros	**nos**	*ourselves, to / for ourselves*
Ud.		*yourself, to / for yourself*
Uds.		*yourselves, to / for yourselves*
él	**se**	*himself, to / for himself*
ella		*herself, to / for herself*
		itself, to / for itself
ellos, ellas		*themselves, to / for themselves*

◆ Note that, with the exception of **se**, reflexive pronouns have the same forms as the direct and indirect object pronouns.

◆ The third-person singular and plural **se** is invariable.

◆ Reflexive pronouns are positioned in the sentence in the same manner as object pronouns. They are placed in front of a conjugated verb.

Yo **me** baño a las ocho.   *I bathe at eight.*

They may be attached to an infinitive or to a present participle.

Yo voy a bañar**me** a las ocho.   *I'm going to bathe at eight.*
Yo estoy bañándo**me**.   *I'm bathing.*

◆ In Spanish most verbs can be made reflexive with the aid of a reflexive pronoun to indicate that they act upon the subject.

Julia le prueba el
vestido a su hija.

Julia se prueba
el vestido.

Reflexive verbs

◆   Reflexive verbs are conjugated in the following manner.

lavarse *(to wash oneself, to wash up)*	
Yo **me lavo**	*I wash (myself)*
Tú **te lavas**	*You wash (yourself—fam.)*
Ud. **se lava**	*You wash (yourself—formal)*
Él **se lava**	*He washes (himself)*
Ella **se lava**	*She washes (herself)*
Nosotros **nos lavamos**	*We wash (ourselves)*
Uds. **se lavan**	*You wash (yourselves)*
Ellos **se lavan**	*They (masc.) wash (themselves)*
Ellas **se lavan**	*They (fem.) wash (themselves)*

◆   Some commonly used reflexive verbs.

acostarse (o:ue)   *to go to bed, to lie down*
afeitarse   *to shave*
bañarse   *to bathe*
despertarse (e:ie)   *to wake up*
levantarse   *to get up*
sentarse (e:i)   *to sit down*
vestirse (e:i)   *to get dressed*

—¿A qué hora **se levanta**   *"At what time do you get*
  Ud., Señorita López?   *up, Miss Lopez?"*
—Generalmente **me levanto**   *"I generally get up at eight*
  a las ocho, pero no **me**   *o'clock, but I don't go to*
  acuesto hasta la   *bed until midnight."*
  medianoche.

◆ Some verbs change their meaning when they are used with reflexive pronouns.

acostar (o:ue)	*to put to bed*	**acostarse**	*to go to bed*
dormir (o:ue)	*to sleep*	**dormirse**	*to fall asleep*
ir	*to go*	**irse**	*to leave, to go away*
levantar	*to lift, to raise*	**levantarse**	*to get up*
llamar	*to call*	**llamarse**	*to be named*
probar (o:ue)	*to try, to taste*	**probarse**	*to try on*
poner	*to put*	**ponerse**	*to put on* (e.g. clothing)
quitar	*to take away, to remove*	**quitarse**	*to take off* (e.g. clothing)

◆ Notice the use of the reflexive in the following sentences.

—¿Por qué no **te acuestas**, querido?   *"Why don't you go to bed, dear?"*

—Primero voy a **acostar** a los chicos.   *"First I'm going to put the children to bed."*

—Voy a **llamar** al hermano de Teresa antes de salir.[1]   *"I'm going to call Teresa's brother before going out."*

—¿Cómo **se llama** él?   *"What's his name?"*

—**Se llama** Alberto.   *"His name is Alberto."*

◆ Some verbs are *always* used with reflexive pronouns in Spanish.

acordarse (o:ue) (de)   *to remember*
quejarse (de)   *to complain*

Notice that the use of a reflexive pronoun does not necessarily imply a reflexive action.

—¿**Se acuerda** Ud. de Rosita?   *"Do you remember Rosita?"*

—Sí, **me acuerdo** de ella.   *"Yes, I remember her."*

Práctica

A. Describe what these people do, using the present indicative or the infinitive of the verbs in parentheses.

1. Elena _____ (probarse) el vestido.
2. Ella _____ (acostarse) y Ud. _____ (acostar) a los niños.
3. Carlos _____ (bañarse) y Luis _____ (vestirse).

[1] The infinitive, not the *-ing* form is used after a preposition in Spanish.

4. Tú siempre _____ (dormirse) en la clase.
5. Nosotros nunca _____ (quejarse) de nada.
6. Yo voy a _____ (probarse) los pantalones.
7. Debes _____ (bañarse) antes de _____ (vestirse).
8. Nosotros vamos a _____ (sentarse) aquí.
9. ¿Por qué no _____ (afeitarse), querido?
10. Pepito, tienes que _____ (lavarse) las manos.

B. Interview a classmate, using the following questions. When you are finished, switch roles.

1. ¿A qué hora te acuestas generalmente?
2. ¿Te duermes en la clase?
3. ¿A qué hora te levantas?
4. ¿Siempre te despiertas temprano?
5. ¿Qué te vas a poner para salir mañana?
6. ¿Te acuerdas del número de teléfono de tus amigos?
7. ¿Siempre pruebas la comida antes de servirla?
8. ¿Uds. se quejan de sus profesores?

C. Describe what you do during a typical day from the time you wake up to the time you go to bed.

Summary of Personal Pronouns

Subject	Direct object	Indirect object	Reflexive	Object of prepositions
yo	me	me	me	mí
tú	te	te	te	ti
Ud. (f.)	la			Ud.
Ud. (m.)	lo	le	se	Ud.
él	lo			él
ella	la			ella
nosotros	nos	nos	nos	nosotros
Uds. (f.)	las			Uds.
Uds. (m.)	los	les	se	Uds.
ellos	los			ellos
ellas	las			ellas

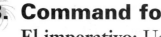

3. Command forms: Ud. and Uds.
El imperativo: Ud. y Uds.

Command form   the form of a verb used to give an order or a direction: **Go! Come back! Turn to the right.**

To form the command for **Ud.** and **Uds.**,[1] drop the **-o** of the first person singular of the present indicative and add the following endings to the stem.

-ar verbs: **-e** (Ud.) and **-en** (Uds.)
-er verbs: **-a** (Ud.) and **-an** (Uds.)
-ir verbs: **-a** (Ud.) and **-an** (Uds.)

ATENCIÓN: Notice that the endings for the **-er** and **-ir** verbs are the same.

Infinitive	First Person Present Ind.	Stem	Commands	
			Ud.	Uds.
hablar	Yo hablo	habl-	hable	hablen
comer	Yo como	com-	coma	coman
abrir	Yo abro	abr-	abra	abran
cerrar	Yo cierro	cierr-	cierre	cierren
volver	Yo vuelvo	vuelv-	vuelva	vuelvan
pedir	Yo pido	pid-	pida	pidan
decir	Yo digo	dig-	diga	digan
hacer	Yo hago	hag-	haga	hagan
traducir	Yo traduzco	traduzc-	traduzca	traduzcan

—¿Con quién debo hablar?
—**Hable** con el peluquero.

"With whom must I speak?"
"Speak with the hairdresser."

—¿Vengo por la mañana o por la tarde?
—**Venga** por la mañana y **traiga** a su hija.

"Shall I come in the morning or in the afternoon?"
"Come in the morning and bring your daughter."

—¿Cierro la puerta?
—No, no **cierre** la puerta. **Cierre** la ventana, por favor.

"Shall I close the door?"
"No, don't close the door. Close the window, please."

—Para ir a la peluquería, ¿sigo derecho o doblo a la derecha?
—**Doble** a la izquierda.

"To go to the beauty parlor shall I continue straight ahead or shall I turn right?"
"Turn left."

[1] The **tú** form will be studied in **Lección 11**.

◆   The command forms of the following verbs are irregular.

	dar	estar	ser	ir
Ud.	dé	esté	sea	vaya
Uds.	den	estén	sean	vayan

—¿Podemos ir solas al parque?	*"Can we go to the park alone?"*
—No, no **vayan** solas. **Vayan** con sus padres.	*"No, don't go alone. Go with your parents."*
—¡Tiene que atenderme ahora mismo!	*"You must wait on me right now!"*
—Un momento, señora. ¡No **sea** impaciente!	*"One moment, madam. Don't be impatient!"*

Práctica

A. Answer the questions in the negative, using the cues provided.

> *Modelos:* —¿Hablo con el peluquero? (dueño)
> —No, **hable** con el dueño.
>
> —¿Tenemos que hablar con el peluquero? (dueño)
> —No, **hablen** con el dueño.

1. ¿Vamos a la peluquería mañana? (hoy)
2. ¿Tenemos que estar allí a las diez? (a las nueve)
3. Para ir a la peluquería, ¿tengo que seguir derecho? (doblar en la calle Lima)
4. ¿Doblo a la derecha? (izquierda)
5. ¿Desayunamos antes de salir? (en la cafetería)
6. ¿Qué perfume compro para Estela? (Chanel número cinco)
7. ¿Qué traemos para la cena? (pollo frito)
8. ¿A qué hora volvemos? (a las tres)
9. ¿Cerramos las ventanas antes de salir? (la puerta)

B. With a partner, prepare a list of ten commands (five affirmative and five negative) that a professor would give to students.

4. Uses of object pronouns with command forms
Uso de los pronombres con el imperativo

Affirmative commands

With all direct *affirmative* commands, the object pronouns are placed *after* the verb and are attached to it, forming a single word.

—¿Dónde pongo el champú?	*"Where shall I put the shampoo?"*
—**Póngalo**[1] en el botiquín.	*"Put it in the medicine cabinet."*
—¿Dónde sirvo el café?	*"Where shall I serve (the) coffee?"*
—**Sírvalo** en la terraza.	*"Serve it on the terrace."*
—¿Qué le doy a la chica?	*"What shall I give the girl?"*
—**Dele** el espejo.	*"Give her the mirror."*
—¿Abrimos la puerta?	*"Shall we open the door?"*
—Sí, **ábranla.**	*"Yes, open it."*
—¿Se lo digo a Ana?	*"Shall I tell (it to) Ana?"*
—Sí, **dígaselo** a Ana.	*"Yes, tell (it to) Ana."*
—¿Dónde me siento?	*"Where shall I sit?"*
—**Siéntese** aquí.	*"Sit here."*
—¿Le corto el pelo?	*"Shall I cut your hair (for you)?"*
—Sí, **córtemelo**, por favor.	*"Yes, cut it (for me), please."*

Práctica

A. Answer the following questions, using affirmative commands.

> *Modelo:* —El peluquero necesita el champú. ¿Lo traigo ahora?
> —Sí, **tráigalo**.

1. Mi amiga quiere ir a la peluquería. ¿La llevo?
2. Las ventanas están abiertas (*open*). ¿Las cierro?
3. Tienen un disco compacto que me gusta. ¿Lo compro?
4. Los niños están durmiendo. ¿Los despierto?
5. La señora quiere el espejo. ¿Se lo doy?
6. Mi hermana quiere un perfume. ¿Se lo compro?
7. La peluquera necesita los peines. ¿Se los traigo?
8. Mis amigos necesitan mis cintas. ¿Se las presto?

B. Answer the following questions, using the appropriate pronouns and the cues provided.

> *Modelo:* —¿Cuándo traemos las maletas? (ahora mismo)
> —**Tráiganlas** ahora mismo.

1. ¿Dónde servimos el desayuno? (en la terraza)
2. ¿Compramos pescado para el almuerzo? (sí)

---

[1] See Appendix A, part 7, number 3 (p. 282) for rules governing the use of accent marks in Spanish.

3. ¿Cuándo llamamos a nuestros amigos? (esta tarde)
4. ¿A qué hora nos levantamos? (a las siete)
5. ¿Dónde nos bañamos? (en este baño)
6. ¿Nos ponemos los pantalones blancos? (sí)
7. ¿Nos lavamos las manos antes de comer? (sí)
8. ¿A qué hora nos acostamos hoy? (a la medianoche)

Negative commands

With all *negative* commands, the object pronouns are placed in front of the verb.

—¿Nos levantamos ahora?	*"Shall we get up now?"*
—No, **no se levanten** todavía.	*"No, don't get up yet."*
—¿Sirvo los refrescos?	*"Shall I serve the sodas?"*
—No, **no los sirva** todavía.	*"No, don't serve them yet."*
—¿Me lavo la cabeza con este champú?	*"Shall I wash my hair with this shampoo?"*
—No, no **se la lave** con ese champú. No es muy bueno.	*"No, don't wash it with that shampoo. It's not very good."*
—¿Le corto el pelo?	*"Shall I cut your hair (for you)?"*
—No, **no me lo corte**. No me gusta el pelo corto.	*"No, don't cut it (for me). I don't like short hair."*

Práctica

A. Answer the following questions with negative commands. Use the appropriate pronouns.

Modelo: —¿Atiendo **a la señora** ahora?
—No, no **la atienda** todavía.

1. ¿Traemos **el champú**?
2. ¿Llevamos **a Mirta** a la peluquería?
3. ¿**Me** lavo **la cabeza** ahora?
4. ¿Pongo **el perfume** en el botiquín?
5. ¿Le traigo **el espejo** a Ud.?
6. ¿Le doy **el peine** a Roberto?
7. ¿Llevamos **los pantalones** a la tintorería?
8. ¿Esperamos **a Rosa** un momento?
9. ¿**Les** decimos que son muy impacientes?
10. ¿**Nos** acostamos ahora?

B. Say what Mrs. Rodríguez asked her hairdresser to do by transforming the infinitives in the following instructions to command forms.

Lavarle la cabeza, pero **no usar** el champú que usa siempre. **Cortarle** el pelo, pero **no cortárselo** muy corto. **Traerle** una revista y **darle** una taza (*cup*) de café pero **no ponerle** leche al café.

C. You and a partner have a group of teenagers coming to stay with you for a few days. Use **Uds.** commands to prepare a list of ten to fifteen things they should and shouldn't do.

En el laboratorio

The following material is to be used with the tape in the language laboratory.

I. Vocabulario

Repeat each word after the speaker. When repeating words that are cognates, notice the difference in pronunciation between English and Spanish.

COGNADOS:	el champú generalmente impaciente el momento el perfume la terraza
NOMBRES:	el baño el botiquín el cepillo el dormitorio el espejo la máquina de afeitar la medianoche el pantalón los pantalones el peine el pelo la peluquería el peluquero la tarjeta la tarjeta de crédito la tintorería la ventana el vestido
VERBOS:	acordarse acostarse atender bañarse cortarse doblar lavarse levantarse llamarse probarse sentarse
ADJETIVOS:	corto querido
OTRAS PALABRAS Y EXPRESIONES:	a la derecha a la izquierda ahora mismo antes de lavarse la cabeza seguir derecho todavía

II. Práctica

A. Answer the questions, using the cue provided. Repeat the correct answer after the speaker's confirmation. Listen to the model.

Modelo: —Mi maleta es verde. ¿Y la de Eva? (blanca)
     —**La suya es blanca.**

1. (grande)   4. (también)
2. (aquí)   5. (en Honduras)
3. (azules)   6. (de Guatemala)

B. Answer the questions, using the cue provided. Repeat the correct answer after the speaker's confirmation. Listen to the model.

Modelo: —¿A qué hora te levantas tú? (a las seis)
     —**Me levanto a las seis.**

1. (no, tarde)   4. (aquí)
2. (en el dormitorio)   5. (no, de nada)
3. (no, por la noche)   6. (sí)

C. Change the following statements to commands. Repeat the correct answer after the speaker's confirmation. Listen to the model.

Modelo: **Debe hablar** con el peluquero.
     Hable con el peluquero.

III. Para escuchar y entender

1. Listen carefully to the narration. It will be read twice.

(Narración)

Now the speaker will make statements about the narration you just heard. Tell whether each statement is true (**verdadero**) or false (**falso**). The speaker will confirm the correct answer.

2. Listen carefully to the dialogue. It will be read twice.

(Diálogo 1)

Now the speaker will make statements about the dialogue you just heard. Tell whether each statement is true (**verdadero**) or false (**falso**). The speaker will confirm the correct answer.

3. Listen carefully to the dialogue. It will be read twice.

(Diálogo 2)

Now the speaker will ask questions about the dialogue you just heard. Answer each question, omitting the subject. The speaker will confirm the correct answer. Repeat the correct answer.

Lección

10

1. **The preterit of regular verbs**
2. **The preterit of** ser, ir, **and** dar
3. **Uses of** por **and** para
4. **Weather expressions**

Vocabulario

COGNADOS

el límite limit
la milla mile
el suéter sweater

el tomate tomato
la velocidad velocity, speed

NOMBRES
el abrigo coat
la aspiradora vacuum
  cleaner
la cocina kitchen
el (la) criado(a) servant
la escoba broom
el impermeable raincoat
la lata, el bote (*Méx.*) can
la lavadora washing
  machine
la lluvia rain
la niebla fog
el paraguas umbrella
la puerta de atrás back
  door
la ropa clothes, clothing
la salsa sauce
la suegra mother-in-law
el suegro father-in-law
el supermercado
  supermarket
**los tallarines, los
  espaguetis** spaghetti
el vuelo flight

VERBOS
ayudar to help

barrer to sweep
cocinar to cook
entrar to enter, to
  come in
limpiar to clean
llover (o:ue) to rain
nevar (e:ie) to snow
pasar (por) to go by
preparar to prepare

ADJETIVOS
nublado(a) cloudy
pasado(a) past, last

**OTRAS PALABRAS Y
EXPRESIONES**
anoche last night
ayer yesterday
**¿Cuál es el límite de
  velocidad?** What's the
  speed limit?
por hora per hour
los (las) dos both
¿Qué tiempo hace hoy?
  What's the weather like
  today?

1. The preterit of regular verbs
El pretérito de los verbos regulares

Spanish has two simple past tenses: the preterit and the imperfect.
(The imperfect will be studied in Lesson 11.) The preterit of regular verbs is formed by dropping the infinitive ending and adding the
appropriate preterit ending to the verb stem, as follows. Note that
the endings for **-er** and **-ir** verbs are identical.

-ar *Verbs*	-er *Verbs*	-ir *Verbs*
entrar *(to enter)*	comer *(to eat)*	escribir *(to write)*
stem: entr-	com-	escrib-
entré	comí	escribí
entraste	comiste	escribiste
entró	comió	escribió
entramos	comimos	escribimos
entraron	comieron	escribieron

yo **entré**   *I entered; I did enter*
Ud. **comió**   *you ate; you did eat*
ellos **escribieron**   *they wrote; they did write*

◆ The preterit tense is used to refer to actions or states that the speaker views as completed in the past. Note that Spanish has no equivalent for the English auxiliary verb *did* in questions and negative sentences.

—¿Quién **cocinó** ayer?   *"Who cooked yesterday?"*
—Yo **cociné** y Pablo me   *"I cooked and Pablo helped me."*
   ayudó.

—¿Qué **comieron?**   *"What did you eat?"*
—**Comimos** tallarines.   *"We ate spaghetti."*

—¿Uds. **prepararon** la salsa?   *"Did you prepare the sauce?"*
—No, **abrimos** dos latas de   *"No, we opened two cans of*
   salsa de tomate.   *tomato sauce."*

—¿A qué hora **volvieron** tus   *"What time did your parents*
   padres anoche?   *come back last night?"*
—**Volvieron** a las once.   *"They came back at eleven."*

—¿A qué hora **llegaste** a la   *"What time did you arrive*
   universidad hoy?   *at the university today?"*
—**Llegué** a las ocho.   *"I arrived at eight."*

ATENCIÓN: **-ar** and **-er** stem-changing verbs do not change stems in the preterit: **Yo** *volví* **anoche y** *cerré* **la puerta.** Verbs ending in **-gar** change **g** to **gu** before **e** in the first person singular preterit: **llegué.**[1]

---

[1] For other verbs with orthographic changes, see Appendix B, p. 291.

Práctica

A. Change the following description of Carmen's daily routine to say what happened yesterday, changing all verbs to the preterit.

Yo me <u>levanto</u> a las seis y me <u>baño</u>. <u>Salgo</u> de casa a las siete. Mi hermano y yo <u>desayunamos</u> en la cafetería. <u>Comemos</u> huevos y <u>bebemos</u> café. Mi hermano <u>trabaja</u> en la oficina y yo <u>estudio</u> en la biblioteca. Mis amigos <u>estudian</u> conmigo. Yo <u>vuelvo</u> a casa a las cinco y mi hermano <u>vuelve</u> a las seis. Yo me <u>acuesto</u> a las diez.

B. Complete the following sentences with the preterit of the verbs in parentheses.

1. ¿Dónde _____ (aprender) Ud. a hablar español?
2. ¿Qué _____ (decidir) Uds. anoche? ¿Ir al supermercado?
3. Yo no _____ (entender) su carta.
4. ¿Dónde _____ (comprar) tú ese impermeable?
5. ¿_____ (Abrir) Ud. las puertas?
6. ¿Qué le _____ (preguntar) Ud. a su suegra?
7. ¿A qué hora _____ (pasar) tú por mi casa ayer?
8. Carmen y yo _____ (ayudar) a preparar la cena.
9. ¿Cuántas horas lo _____ (esperar) Uds.?

C. Interview a classmate, using the following questions. When you have finished, switch roles.

1. ¿A qué hora te levantaste hoy?
2. ¿Desayunaste en tu casa?
3. ¿Quién preparó el desayuno?
4. ¿Qué bebiste en el desayuno?
5. ¿Viste a tus amigos ayer?
6. ¿Tus amigos almorzaron contigo?
7. ¿Quién cocinó anoche en tu casa?
8. ¿Le escribiste a alguien ayer?
9. ¿A qué hora volviste a tu casa?
10. ¿A qué hora cenaron Uds.?
11. ¿Comieron tallarines con salsa de tomate?
12. ¿A qué hora te acostaste?

2. The preterit of ser, ir, and dar
El pretérito de los verbos ser, ir y dar

The preterit forms of **ser, ir,** and **dar** are irregular. Note that **ser** and **ir** have the same forms.

ser *(to be)*	ir *(to go)*	dar *(to give)*
fui	fui	di
fuiste	fuiste	diste
fue	fue	dio
fuimos	fuimos	dimos
fueron	fueron	dieron

—¿Uds. **fueron** estudiantes del profesor Vargas el año pasado?	*"Were you professor Vargas's students last year?"*
—Yo **fui** estudiante suyo pero mi hermano **fue** estudiante de la profesora Rojas.	*"I was his student, but my brother was professor Rojas's student."*
—¿Tú **fuiste** a la biblioteca anoche?	*"Did you go to the library last night?"*
—No, Teresa y yo **fuimos** al supermercado.	*"No, Teresa and I went to the supermarket."*
—¡Ah, **viste** a Teresa! ¿Le **diste** la ropa para su hija?	*"Oh, you saw Teresa! Did you give her the clothing for her daughter?"*
—Sí, se la **di.**	*"Yes, I gave it to her."*

Práctica

A. Complete the following dialogues, using the preterit of **ser, ir,** or **dar** as appropriate. Then act them out with a partner.

1. —¿Adónde _____ tú ayer?
   —Por la tarde _____ a una tienda con mi suegro. Él me _____ dinero para comprar ropa.
   —¿_____ Uds. a casa de tía Eva por la noche?
   —Sí, _____ y le _____ el regalo que tú le mandaste.
2. —¿Adónde _____ Uds. anoche?
   —_____ a un concierto. Los padres de Dora nos _____ las entradas.
3. —¿Tú _____ estudiante del profesor Vega el año pasado?
   —No, yo _____ estudiante de la profesora Soto.

B. Answer the following questions.

1. ¿Dieron Ud. y sus amigos una fiesta el viernes pasado?
2. ¿Dio Ud. dinero para la fiesta?
3. ¿Adónde fue Ud. el sábado pasado?

4. ¿Sus amigos fueron con Ud.?
5. ¿Fue Ud. al supermercado la semana pasada?
6. ¿Fue Ud. estudiante en esta universidad el año pasado?

C. Write a short paragraph describing what you did yesterday. Give as many details as possible.

3. Uses of por and para
Usos de por y para

◆ The preposition **por** is used to express the following concepts.

1. Motion (*through, along, by*)

—¿**Por** dónde entró la criada?   *"How (through where) did the maid come in?"*

—Entró **por** la puerta de atrás.   *"She came in through the back door."*

—¿A qué hora pasaste **por** mi casa ayer?   *"At what time did you go by my house yesterday?"*

—Pasé **por** tu casa a las tres.   *"I went by your house at three o'clock."*

2. Cause or motive of an action (*because of, on account of, on behalf of*)

—¿Por qué no fueron Uds. a la playa ayer?   *"Why didn't you go to the beach yesterday?"*

—No fuimos **por** la lluvia.   *"We didn't go because of the rain."*

3. Agency, means, manner, unit of measure (*by, for, per*)

—¿Vas a San Francisco **por** avión?   *"Are you going to San Francisco by plane?"*

—No, llevo el coche.   *"No, I'm taking the car."*

—¿Cuál es el límite de velocidad en California?   *"What's the speed limit in California?"*

—Cincuenta y cinco millas **por** hora.   *"Fifty-five miles per hour."*

4. *In exchange for*

—¿Cuánto pagaste **por** el abrigo y **por** el suéter?   *"How much did you pay for the coat and sweater?"*

—Pagué cien dólares **por** los dos.   *"I paid one hundred dollars for both."*

5. Period of time during which an action takes place (*during, in, for*)

—¿**Por** cuánto tiempo vas a estar en Puerto Rico?	*"How long are you going to be in Puerto Rico?"*
—Voy a estar allí **por** un mes.	*"I'm going to be there for a month."*

◆ The preposition **para** is used to express the following concepts.

1. Destination in space (*to*)

—¿A qué hora hay vuelos **para** México?	*"What time are there flights to Mexico?"*
—A las diez y a las doce de la noche.	*"At ten and twelve P.M."*

2. Goal for a point in the future (*by, for*)

—¿Cuándo necesita Ud. la aspiradora?	*"When do you need the vacuum cleaner?"*
—La necesito **para** mañana.	*"I need it by tomorrow."*

3. Whom or what something is for

—¿**Para** quién es la lavadora?	*"Whom is the washing machine for?"*
—Es **para** mi suegra.	*"It's for my mother-in-law."*

4. Purpose (*in order to*)

—¿**Para** qué necesita la criada la escoba?	*"What does the maid need the broom for?"*
—La necesita **para** barrer la cocina.	*"She needs it (in order) to sweep the kitchen."*

Práctica

A. Complete the following paragraph, using **por** or **para** as appropriate.

Mañana _____ la mañana salimos _____ Chile. Vamos _____ avión y pensamos estar allí _____ tres semanas. Pagamos quinientos dólares _____ el pasaje y vamos a viajar _____ todo el país (*country*). En Santiago voy a comprar regalos _____ todos mis amigos. Tengo que estar aquí _____ el veinte de agosto _____ poder comenzar las clases en septiembre.

B. With a partner, act out the following dialogues in Spanish.

1. "How did you enter, Paquito?"
   "I came in through the back door."
   "Why didn't you take the children to the park?"
   "We didn't go because of the rain."

2. "Did you buy the washing machine and the vacuum cleaner for Mom?"
"Yes, and I paid seven hundred dollars for both!"
3. "I'm going to Costa Rica to visit my mother-in-law. I'm going to be there for a month."
"Are you going by plane?"
"No, I'm going by bus."
4. "What is the speed limit here?"
"I don't know...Fifty-five miles per hour?"
5. "We are leaving for Madrid tomorrow."
"When are you coming back?"
"We have to be here by December tenth."
6. "I need the broom to sweep the kitchen and the terrace."
"I can help you, Anita."

4. Weather expressions
Expresiones para describir el tiempo

In the following expressions, the verb **hacer** (*to make*) followed by a noun is used in Spanish, whereas the verb *to be* followed by an adjective is used in English

Hace (mucho) **frío**.	*It is (very) cold.*
Hace (mucho) **calor**.	*It is (very) hot.*
Hace (mucho) **viento**[1].	*It is (very) windy.*
Hace sol.[1]	*It is sunny.*
Hace buen (mal) tiempo.[2]	*The weather is good (bad).*

◆ **Hacer** is not used in weather expressions with **llover (o:ue)** (*to rain*) or **nevar (e:ie)** (*to snow*).

Llueve.	*It rains (It's raining).*
Está lloviendo.	*It's raining.*
Nieva.	*It snows (It's snowing).*
Está nevando.	*It's snowing.*

◆ Other words and expressions related to the weather are

la **lluvia**	*rain*
la **niebla**	*fog*
Está nublado.	*It's cloudy.*

[1] It is also correct to say **hay viento, hay sol.**
[2] **Bueno** and **malo** drop the **o** before a masculine singular noun.

◆ As in English, the Spanish impersonal verbs use third person singular forms only.

—¿Vas a limpiar la terraza?   *"Are you going to clean the terrace?"*

—No, porque **hace** mucho   *"No, because it's very windy* **viento** y **va** a **llover.**   *and it's going to rain."*

Práctica

A. Complete the following sentences, using a word from the list or an appropriate weather expression.

el paraguas   **el suéter**
el impermeable   **el abrigo**

1. ¿Necesitas un paraguas? Sí, porque _____.
2. ¿No necesitas un abrigo? No, porque _____.
3. ¿Quieres un impermeable? No, no está _____.
4. ¿Necesitas un suéter? No, hoy _____.
5. Está nevando. Lleve el _____.
6. Va a llover. Está _____.

B. ¿Qué tiempo hace? (How is the weather?)

1.

2.

3.

4.

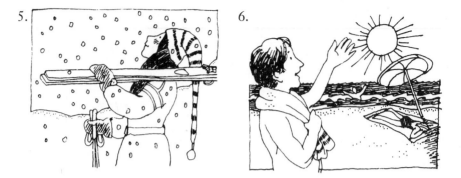

C. With a partner, act out the following dialogues in Spanish.

1. "There are no flights . . . ?"
   "No, because there is fog."
2. "Are you going to clean the terrace, Juanita?"
   "No, because it's going to rain."
3. "Does it snow here?"
   "No, it's very cold in the winter, but it never snows."

🎧 *En el laboratorio*

The following material is to be used with the tape in the language laboratory.

I. Vocabulario

Repeat each word after the speaker. When repeating words that are cognates, notice the difference in pronunciation between English and Spanish.

COGNADOS:	el límite la milla el suéter el tomate la velocidad
NOMBRES:	el abrigo la aspiradora la cocina el criado la escoba el impermeable la lata el bote la lavadora la lluvia la niebla el paraguas la puerta de atrás la ropa la salsa la suegra el suegro el supermercado los tallarines los espaguetis el vuelo
VERBOS:	ayudar barrer cocinar entrar limpiar llover nevar pasar preparar

ADJETIVOS:	nublado pasado
OTRAS PALABRAS Y EXPRESIONES:	anoche ayer ¿Cuál es el límite de velocidad? por hora los dos ¿Qué tiempo hace hoy?

II. Práctica

A. Answer the following questions, using the cues provided. Repeat the correct answer after the speaker's confirmation. Listen to the model.

> *Modelo:* —¿Quién te ayudó ayer? (Roberto)
> —**Me ayudó Roberto.**

B. Answer the questions, always using the first choice. Omit the subject. Repeat the correct answer after the speaker's confirmation. Listen to the model.

> *Modelo:* —¿Entraron Uds. por la ventana o por la puerta?
> —**Entramos por la ventana.**

C. Answer the following questions, using the cues provided. Repeat the correct answer following the speaker's confirmation. Listen to the model.

> *Modelo:* —¿Dónde hace mucho frío? (Alaska)
> —**Hace mucho frío en Alaska.**

III. Para escuchar y entender

1. Listen carefully to the dialogue. It will be read twice.

(*Diálogo 1*)

Now the speaker will make statements about the dialogue you just heard. Tell whether each statement is true (**verdadero**) or false (**falso**). The speaker will confirm the correct answer.

2. Listen carefully to the dialogue. It will be read twice.

(*Diálogo 2*)

Now the speaker will ask you some questions about the dialogue you just heard. Answer each question, omitting the subject. The speaker will confirm the correct answer. Repeat the correct answer.

¿Cuánto sabe usted ahora?

LECCIONES 6–10

Lección 6

A. Stem-changing verbs (**o:ue**)

Answer the following questions.

1. ¿A qué hora vuelve Ud. a casa?
2. Cuando Uds. van a México, ¿vuelan o van en auto?
3. ¿Recuerdan Uds. los verbos irregulares?
4. ¿Cuántas horas duerme Ud.?
5. ¿Pueden Uds. ir a la fiesta?

B. Affirmative and negative expressions

Change the following sentences to the affirmative.

1. Ellos no recuerdan nada.
2. No hay nadie en el cuarto.
3. Yo no quiero volar tampoco.
4. No recibimos ningún regalo.
5. Nunca tiene fiestas en su casa.

C. Pronouns as object of a preposition

How would you say the following in Spanish?

1. Can you come with me?
2. Are you going to work with them?
3. The money is for you, Anita.
4. The gift is not for me; it is for her.
5. No, Paco, I can't go with you.

D. The impersonal **se**

Answer the following questions

1. ¿Qué idioma se habla en los Estados Unidos?
2. ¿Cómo se dice *mattress* en español?
3. ¿A qué hora se cierra la oficina de correos?
4. ¿Cómo se escribe su nombre?
5. ¿A qué hora se abren las bibliotecas?

E. The present progressive

Complete the following sentences with the present progressive of **leer, decir, estudiar, beber,** or **comer,** as appropriate. Use each verb once.

1. Él _____ la lección.
2. Ella _____ en la cafetería.

3. Nosotros _____ el periódico.
4. Tú no _____ la verdad.
5. Yo _____ café.

F. Vocabulary

Complete the following sentences using words learned in **Lección 6.**

1. Una habitación con _____ al _____ cuesta más.
2. Ellos _____ dos días a la semana en la cafetería.
3. El _____ de esta cama es muy malo.
4. ¿Cuánto _____ el libro de español?
5. Los Ángeles tiene muchos _____ de interés.
6. No quiero ni vino ni cerveza. No tomo bebidas _____.
7. Él _____ siete horas todas las noches.
8. ¿Dónde está la _____ de _____? Necesito comprar estampillas.

A. Stem-changing verbs (**e:i**)   **Lección 7**

Answer the following questions.

1. ¿Qué sirven Uds., sopa o ensalada?
2. ¿Qué pide Ud. para beber cuando va a un restaurante?
3. ¿Dice Ud. su edad?
4. ¿Sigue Ud. en la universidad?
5. ¿Uds. siempre piden postre?

B. Irregular first persons

Complete the sentences with the present indicative of the verbs in the following list. Use each verb once.

traer   conocer   traducir   hacer   saber
ver   salir   poner   conducir

1. Yo _____ mi coche.
2. Yo siempre _____ con ella.
3. Yo _____ la carne en la mesa.
4. Yo _____ del inglés al español.
5. Yo no _____ al maestro de mi hijo.
6. Yo _____ los folletos turísticos.
7. Yo _____ el postre.
8. Yo no _____ el regalo. ¿Dónde está?
9. Yo no _____ nadar.

C. **Saber** contrasted with **conocer**

How would you say the following in Spanish?

1. I know your son.
2. He doesn't know French.

3. Do you know how to swim, Miss Vera?
4. Do you know the travel agent?
5. Are the students familiar with Cervantes's novels?

D. Direct object pronouns

Complete the following sentences with the Spanish equivalent of the direct object pronouns in parentheses. Follow the models.

Modelos: Yo veo (*him*)
Yo lo veo.
Yo quiero ver (*him*)
Yo quiero verlo.

1. Yo conozco (*them*, fem.)
2. Uds. van a comprar (*it*, masc.)
3. Nosotros no queremos ver (*you*, familiar)
4. Ella sirve (*it*, fem.)
5. ¿Ud. no conoce... ? (*me*)
6. Él escribe (*them*, masc.)
7. Carlos va a visitar (*us*)
8. Nosotros no vemos (*you*, formal, sing., masc.)

E. Vocabulary

Complete the following sentences, using the words learned in **Lección 7.**

1. Compré el pasaje en la _____ de viajes.
2. Ellos van a _____ en la piscina.
3. Mi hijo sabe de _____ todos los verbos.
4. Necesita confirmar la _____ hoy.
5. ¿Necesitamos los _____ para entrar en México?
6. Tengo mucho trabajo. Estoy muy _____.
7. «*The Raven*» es un _____ muy famoso de Poe.

Lección 8   **A.** Demonstrative adjectives and pronouns

How would you say the following in Spanish?

1. I need these balls and those (*over there*).
2. Do you want this horse or that one?
3. I prefer these skates, not those (*over there*).
4. Do you want to buy this racket or that one, Dad?
5. I don't want to eat at this restaurant. I prefer that one (*over there*).
6. I don't understand that. (*neuter form*)

B. Indirect object pronouns

Answer the following questions according to the model.

Modelo: —¿Qué me vas a traer de México? (una frazada)
—**Te voy a traer una frazada.**

1. ¿Qué te va a comprar Carlos? (unos patines)
2. ¿Qué le das tú a Luis? (la bicicleta)
3. ¿En qué idioma les habla a Uds. el profesor? (en español)
4. ¿Qué va a decirles Ud. a los niños? (la verdad)
5. ¿Qué nos pregunta Ud.? (la dirección de la oficina)
6. ¿A quién están escribiéndole Uds.? (a nuestro padre)
7. ¿Cuándo le escribe Ud. a su abuelo? (los lunes)
8. ¿A quién le da Ud. la información? (al entrenador)
9. ¿En qué idioma me hablas tú? (en inglés)
10. ¿Qué te compran tus hijos? (nada)

C. Pedir contrasted with **preguntar**

How would you say the following in Spanish?

1. I'm going to ask her where she lives.
2. I always ask my aunt for money.
3. She always asks how you are, Mrs. Nieto.
4. They are going to ask me for the tent.
5. I want to ask him how old he is.

D. Direct and indirect object pronouns used together.

How would you say the following in Spanish?

1. The money? I'll give it to you tomorrow, Mr. Peña.
2. I know you need the dictionary, Anita, but I can't lend it to you.
3. I need my backpack. Can you bring it to me, Miss López?
4. The pens? She is bringing them to us.
5. When he needs skates, his mother buys them for him.

E. Vocabulary

Complete the following sentences, using words learned in **Lección 8.**

1. Quiero leer la página _____.
2. ¿Para _____ son esos patines? ¿Para tu hijo?
3. Para jugar al tenis, los niños necesitan una _____ y una _____ de tenis.
4. Tenemos dos _____ de dormir. Te presto una.
5. Voy a comprar las _____ para el partido del domingo.
6. El hermano de mi madre es mi _____.
7. Necesito la tienda de _____ este fin de semana.
8. Los niños están jugando en el _____.

Lección 9   **A.** Possessive pronouns

Answer the following questions in the negative, according to the model.

Modelo: —¿Estos pantalones son **de Juan?**
            —No, no son **de él.**

1. ¿Son **tuyas** estas tarjetas?
2. ¿Estos cepillos son **de Julia?**
3. ¿El vestido es **suyo,** señora?
4. ¿Es **de Uds.** esta cama?
5. ¿Esta tarjeta de crédito es **de tus padres?**
6. ¿Son **tuyos** estos espejos?
7. ¿Es **de Uds.** esta máquina de afeitar?
8. ¿Es **nuestro** este dormitorio?

B. Reflexive constructions

How would you say the following in Spanish?

1. I get up at seven, I bathe, I get dressed, and I leave at seven-thirty.
2. What time do the children wake up?
3. She doesn't want to sit down.
4. He shaves every day.
5. Do you remember your teachers, Carlitos?
6. They are always complaining.
7. First she puts the children to bed, and then she goes to bed.
8. Do you want to try on these pants, Miss?
9. Where are you going to put the money, ladies?
10. The students always fall asleep in this class.

C. Command forms **Ud.** and **Uds.**

Complete the sentences with the command forms of the verbs in the following list, as appropriate, and read each sentence aloud. Use each verb once.

escribir	venir	dar	hablar	doblar
servir	cerrar	volver	seguir	ser
estar	poner	ir	abrir	traer

1. _____ la puerta, Sr. Benítez.
2. _____ español, señores.
3. _____ a su hija, señora.
4. _____ mañana por la mañana, señoras.
5. No _____ la ventana, señorita. Tengo calor.
6. _____ a la izquierda, señores.
7. _____ derecho, señorita.

8. _____ su nombre y dirección, señores.
9. _____ en la oficina mañana por la tarde, señores.
10. ¡No _____ tan impacientes, señoritas!
11. Sr. Vega, _____ a la casa del director.
12. _____ el martes, señora. El doctor no está hoy.
13. _____ el café en la terraza, señorita.
14. _____ los libros aquí, señores.
15. _____ las cartas mañana, señoras.

D. Uses of object pronouns with command forms

How would you say the following in Spanish?

1. Tell them the truth, Mr. Mena.
2. The dress? Don't bring it to me now, Miss Ruiz.
3. Don't tell (it to) my hairdresser, please.
4. Bring the drinks, gentlemen. Bring them to the terrace.
5. Don't get up, Mrs. Miño.
6. The tea? Bring it to her at four o'clock in the afternoon, Mr. Vargas.

E. Vocabulary

Complete the following sentences, using words learned in **Lección 9.**

1. No tengo máquina de _____.
2. Mañana voy a la _____. Necesito lavarme la _____ y cortarme el _____.
3. Lleve los pantalones a la _____, señorita.
4. No tengo dinero; voy a pagar con la _____.
5. No está a la derecha; está a la _____.
6. Ponga el botiquín en el baño ahora _____.
7. Voy a _____ a los niños; ya son las nueve de la noche.
8. Para llegar a la universidad, siga Ud. _____.

A. Preterit of regular verbs / Preterit of **ser, ir,** and **dar**   **Lección 10**

Rewrite the following sentences according to the new beginnings. Follow the model.

Modelo: Voy al cine. (Ayer...)
   Ayer fui al cine.

1. Ella entra en la cafetería y come tallarines. (Ayer...)
2. María le escribe a su suegra. (Ayer...)
3. Ella me presta su abrigo. (El viernes pasado...)
4. Ellos son los mejores estudiantes. (El año pasado...)
5. Ellos te esperan cerca del supermercado. (El sábado pasado...)
6. Mi hijo va a Buenos Aires. (El verano pasado...)
7. Le doy el impermeable. (Ayer por la mañana...)
8. Nosotros decidimos comprar la aspiradora. (El lunes pasado...)

9. Le pregunto la hora. (Anoche...)
10. Tú no pagas por la ropa. (Anoche...)
11. Somos los primeros. (El jueves pasado...)
12. Me dan muchos problemas. (Ayer...)
13. Mi suegro no bebe café. (Anoche...)
14. Yo no voy a esquiar. (Ayer...)
15. Te damos el suéter. (La semana pasada...)

B. Uses of **por** and **para**

How would you say the following in Spanish?

1. The maid went in through the back door.
2. She went by my house.
3. She didn't come because of the rain.
4. There are flights to Mexico on Saturdays.
5. We are going by plane.
6. The speed limit is fifty-five miles per hour.
7. I need the washing machine by tomorrow.
8. Whom is the umbrella for?
9. I need the money to pay for the raincoat.
10. She paid two hundred dollars for that vacuum cleaner.

C. Weather expressions

How would you say the following in Spanish?

1. It is very windy today.
2. It is very cold, and it is also snowing.
3. It is very hot in Cuba.
4. How is the weather today?
5. Is it sunny or is it cloudy?
6. There are no flights because of the fog.

D. Vocabulary

Complete the following sentences, using words learned in **Lección 10.**

1. Necesito el _____ porque hace frío.
2. ¿Cuál es el _____ de velocidad?
3. Ella quiere ponerse el _____ porque va a llover.
4. ¿Dónde compraste la _____ de tomate? ¿En el mercado?
5. Ponga el vestido en la _____, señorita.
6. Adela siempre _____ unos tallarines muy buenos.
7. ¿Quién barrió la cocina? ¿La _____?
8. ¿Qué _____ hace hoy? ¿Hace frío?

Lección

11

1. **Time expressions with** *hacer*
2. **Irregular preterits**
3. **The imperfect tense**
4. **Command forms** (*tú*)

Vocabulario

COGNADOS

el favor favor	**la paciencia** patience

NOMBRES
el arroz rice
la basura trash
el (la) cocinero(a) cook
el fregadero sink
la liquidación, la venta sale
el piso floor
el postre dessert
la secadora dryer
la tostadora toaster
los trabajos de la casa
    household chores

VERBOS
apagar to turn off
caminar to walk
enseñar to teach

ADJETIVOS
todo(a) all
todos(as) every

OTRAS PALABRAS Y
EXPRESIONES
arroz con pollo chicken
    with rice
casi nunca hardly ever
¿cuánto tiempo? how
    long?
de vez en cuando once
    in a while
debajo (de) underneath
en esa época in those
    days
ir de compras to go
    shopping
media hora half an hour
otra vez again
¡Rápido! Quick!
Ten paciencia. Be
    patient.

1. Time expressions with hacer
Expresiones de tiempo con hacer

Spanish uses the following formula to express how long something has been going on.

Hace + length of time + **que** + verb (in present tense)
Hace   quince años   que   vivo en esta ciudad.
I have been living in this city for fifteen years.

—¿Cuánto tiempo **hace que**
    Ud. enseña aquí?
—**Hace** tres años **que** enseño
    aquí.

"*How long have you been
    teaching here?*"
"*I have been teaching here
    for three years.*"

—¿Cuánto tiempo **hace que**
    Uds. caminan?
—**Hace** media hora **que**
    caminamos.

"*How long have you been
    walking?*"
"*We have been walking for
    half an hour.*"

—¿Tienes hambre?   *"Are you hungry?"*
—Sí, **hace** ocho horas **que**   *"Yes, I haven't eaten for*
    no como.   *eight hours."*

Práctica

A. Use the expression **hace... que** to say how long each action has been taking place.

> *Modelo:* Estamos en enero. / Él empezó a trabajar en octubre.
> **Hace** tres meses **que** él trabaja.

1. Son las tres de la tarde. / Ellos están aquí desde (*since*) las dos y media.
2. Estamos en 1996. / Raquel empezó a enseñar en 1993.
3. Hoy es viernes. / Empezamos a trabajar el lunes.
4. Son las cuatro. / Graciela empezó a hablar por teléfono a las cuatro menos cuarto.
5. Son las cinco. / Empezaste a cocinar a las tres.

B. Interview a classmate, using the following questions. When you have finished, switch roles.

1. ¿Cuánto tiempo hace que estudias español?
2. ¿Cuánto tiempo hace que conoces a tu mejor amigo o amiga?
3. ¿Cuánto tiempo hace que no comes?
4. ¿Cuánto tiempo hace que vives en esta ciudad?
5. ¿Cuánto tiempo hace que no ves a tus padres?
6. ¿Cuánto tiempo hace que Uds. no van de vacaciones?
7. ¿Cuánto tiempo hace que no llueve aquí?

2. Irregular preterits
Pretéritos irregulares

The following Spanish verbs are irregular in the preterit.

tener:	tuve, tuviste, tuvo, tuvimos, tuvieron
estar:	estuve estuviste, estuvo, estuvimos, estuvieron
poder:	pude, pudiste, pudo, pudimos, pudieron
poner:	puse, pusiste, puso, pusimos, pusieron
saber:	supe, supiste, supo, supimos, supieron
hacer:	hice, hiciste, hizo, hicimos, hicieron
venir:	vine, viniste, vino, vinimos, vinieron
querer:	quise, quisiste, quiso, quisimos, quisieron
decir:	dije, dijiste, dijo, dijimos, dijeron[1]
traer:	traje, trajiste, trajo, trajimos, trajeron[1]
conducir:	conduje, condujiste, condujo, condujimos, condujeron[1]
traducir:	traduje, tradujiste, tradujo, tradujimos, tradujeron[1]

[1] Note that the **-i** is omitted in the third person plural ending of these verbs.

—¿Dónde **pusieron** Uds. la lata de la basura?	*"Where did you put the garbage can?"*
—Debajo del fregadero.	*"Underneath the sink."*
—¿**Hizo** el postre la cocinera?	*"Did the cook make the dessert?"*
—No, no **pudo** hacerlo porque **tuvo** que limpiar el piso de la cocina.	*"No, she wasn't able to do it because she had to clean the kitchen floor."*
—¿No **vino** la criada?	*"Didn't the maid come?"*
—Sí, pero **trajo** a su hijo y no **pudo** hacer los trabajos de la casa.	*"Yes, but she brought her son and she couldn't do the household chores."*

ATENCIÓN: Notice that the third person singular form of the verb **hacer** changes the **c** to **z** in order to maintain the soft sound of the **c** in the infinitive.

◆ The preterit of **hay** (from the verb **haber**) is **hubo**.

Ayer **hubo** una fiesta en casa de Eva.	*Yesterday there was a party at Eva's house.*

Práctica

A. Complete the following paragraph with the preterit of the verbs in parentheses.

Isabel le escribe una carta a Teresa.

Toledo, 15 de julio de 19..

Querida Teresa:

Ayer yo _____ (estar) en Madrid, pero no _____ (poder) ir a verte. Salí de Toledo por la mañana y _____ (conducir) por tres horas hasta llegar a Madrid. Allí _____ (tener) que ir al hospital para ver a Gustavo. Caminé por la ciudad y _____ (querer) llamarte por teléfono, pero no _____ (poder) encontrar uno. Como siempre, ayer _____ (hacer) mucho calor. _____ (Venir) de Madrid muy cansada. Esta mañana hablé por teléfono con Ramón. Él me _____ (decir) muchas cosas interesantes. ¡Ah...! Me _____ (poner) el vestido que compré en Madrid y salí con Jorge. El sábado vuelvo a Madrid para verte.

Tu amiga,

Isabel

B. Complete the following dialogue, using appropriate irregular verbs in the preterit. Then act it out with a partner.

—¿Dónde _____ Uds. anoche? ¿Adónde fueron?

—_____ en casa de Julio. _____ una cena en su casa.

—¿Tú _____ tu coche o fueron caminando?

—Yo _____ mi coche.

—¿Tus primos fueron a la cena?

—No, ellos no _____ ir porque _____ que trabajar.

—¿Quién _____ la comida?

—La _____ Julio y su esposa.

—¿Qué vestido te _____ para ir a la cena?

—Me _____ el vestido negro.

C. Answer the following questions, using complete sentences.

1. ¿A qué hora vino Ud. a la universidad hoy?
2. ¿Condujo su coche o caminó?
3. ¿Trajo sus libros de español?
4. ¿Pudo Ud. venir a clase la semana pasada?
5. ¿Tuvo que trabajar ayer?
6. ¿Dónde estuvo Ud. anoche?
7. ¿Qué hizo anoche para la cena?
8. ¿En qué banco puso Ud. su dinero?

D. Using the **tú** form, ask a classmate all the questions in **Práctica C.** When you have finished, switch roles.

3. The imperfect tense
El imperfecto de indicativo

There are two simple past tenses in Spanish: the preterit, which you have studied in **Lecciones 10** and **11,** and the imperfect.

Regular imperfect forms

To form the imperfect tense, add these endings to the verb stem.

The Imperfect Tense		
-ar *Verbs*	-er *and* -ir *Verbs*	
hablar	**comer**	**vivir**
habl**aba**	com**ía**	viv**ía**
habl**abas**	com**ías**	viv**ías**
habl**aba**	com**ía**	viv**ía**
habl**ábamos**	com**íamos**	viv**íamos**
habl**aban**	com**ían**	viv**ían**

◆ Notice that the endings of **-er** and **-ir** verbs are the same. Notice also that there is a written accent mark on the final **í** of **-er** and **-ir** verbs.

◆ The imperfect tense in Spanish is equivalent to three forms in English.

Yo **vivía** en Chicago.
$\left\{\begin{array}{l}\textit{\textbf{I used to live}} \textit{ in Chicago.} \\ \textit{\textbf{I was living}} \textit{ in Chicago.} \\ \textit{\textbf{I lived}} \textit{ in Chicago.}\end{array}\right.$

◆ The imperfect is use to refer to habitual or repeated actions in the past, with no reference to when they began or ended.

—¿**Comían** ellos arroz con pollo? — *"Did they used to eat chicken and rice?"*
—Sí, lo **comían** de vez en cuando. — *"Yes, they used to eat it once in a while."*

—¿Dónde **vivía** Ud. en esa época? — *"Where did you live in those days?*
—Yo **vivía** en La Habana. — *"I lived (was living) in Havana."*

◆ The imperfect is also used to describe actions or events that the speaker views as in the process of happening in the past, again with no reference to when they began or ended.

Empezábamos a barrer la cocina cuando él vino. — *We were beginning to sweep the kitchen when he came.*

◆ The imperfect is also used to describe physical, mental, or emotional conditions in the past.

Mi casa **era** muy grande. — *My house was very big.*
Ella **estaba** enferma. — *She was sick.*

Irregular imperfect forms

There are only three irregular verbs in the imperfect tense: **ser, ir,** and **ver.**

ser	ir	ver
era	iba	veía
eras	ibas	veías
era	iba	veía
éramos	íbamos	veíamos
eran	iban	veían

—¿Dónde vivían Uds.
cuando **eran** niños?

*"Where did you live when you
were children?"*

—En Quito, pero **íbamos**
a Guayaquil todos los
meses a visitar a
nuestros abuelos.

*"In Quito, but we went to
Guayaquil every month to visit
our grandparents."*

—Yo casi nunca **veía** a
mis abuelos cuando
era niña.

*"I hardly ever saw my
grandparents when I was a
child."*

Práctica

A. Complete the following dialogues using the imperfect tense of
the verbs in parentheses. Then act them out with a partner.

1. —¿Tú _____ (trabajar) cuando _____ (estar) en la
   universidad?
   —No, pero de vez en cuando _____ (ayudar) a mi mamá
   con los trabajos de la casa. ¡Y _____ (ser) muy buena
   cocinera! _____ (Preparar) unos postres muy buenos.
2. —Mamá y yo siempre _____ (ir) al supermercado los
   sábados, y después _____ (limpiar) la casa.
   —Cuando yo _____ (ser) niño, generalmente no _____
   (hacer) nada los sábados.
3. —¿Tú _____ (ver) a tus primos cuando _____ (ser)
   niño?
   —No, casi nunca, pero les _____ (escribir) a menudo.

B. Interview a classmate, using the following questions. When you
have finished, switch roles.

1. ¿Dónde vivías cuando eras niño(a)?
2. ¿A qué escuela ibas?
3. ¿Iban Uds. al cine a veces?
4. ¿Veías a tus abuelos en esa época?
5. ¿Cocinaban tú y tus hermanos cuando eran niños? (¿Qué
   preparaban?)
6. Cuando eras chico(a), ¿qué hacías los domingos?

4. Command forms (tú)
Las formas imperativas (tú)

The affirmative command

The affirmative command for **tú** has exactly the same form as the
third person singular of the present indicative.

Verb	*Present Indicative Third Person Singular*	*Familiar Command (tú Form)*
hablar	él habla	**habla**
comer	él come	**come**
abrir	él abre	**abre**
cerrar	él cierra	**cierra**
volver	él vuelve	**vuelve**
pedir	él pide	**pide**
traer	él trae	**trae**

—**Cierra** las ventanas y **apaga** las luces antes de salir.[1]

"Close the windows and turn off the lights before going out."

—Muy bien. **Espérame** en el coche. ¿Vamos a llevarle la tostadora a Inés?

"Very well. Wait for me in the car. Are we going to take the toaster to Ines?"

—Sí, **tráela,** por favor.

"Yes, bring it, please."

ATENCIÓN: Remember that direct, indirect, and reflexive pronouns are always attached to an affirmative command.

◆ Eight Spanish verbs have irregular affirmative familiar command forms.

decir:	**di** (*say, tell*)	salir:	**sal** (*go out, leave*)
hacer:	**haz** (*do, make*)	ser:	**sé** (*be*)
ir:	**ve** (*go*)	tener:	**ten** (*have*)
poner:	**pon** (*put*)	venir:	**ven** (*come*)

—Carlitos, **ven** aquí. **Haz**me un favor. **Ve** y **di**le a tu mamá que necesito la escoba. ¡Rápido!

"Carlitos, come here. Do me a favor. Go and tell your mom that I need the broom. Quick!"

—¡**Ten** paciencia!

"Be patient!"

The negative command

The negative command for **tú** is formed by adding **-s** to the command form for **Ud.**

---

[1] The infinitive, not the *-ing* form, is used after a preposition in Spanish.

hable	no hable**s**	*don't talk*
vuelva	no vuelva**s**	*don't return*
venga	no venga**s**	*don't come*
salga	no salga**s**	*don't leave*

—Voy a la tienda porque
  tienen una liquidación.
      "I'm going to the store because
      they are having a sale."
—**No** me **digas** que quieres
  ir de compras otra vez.
      "Don't tell me (that) you
      want to go shopping again."
—Sí, porque necesito una
  secadora.
      "Yes, because I need a dryer."
—Bueno, pero **no vayas** hoy;
  ve mañana.
      "Okay, but don't go today;
      go tomorrow."

ATENCIÓN: Remember that all object pronouns are placed *before* a negative comand: **No *me lo* traigas hoy.**

Práctica

A. You and a partner are doing household chores. Take turns asking each other what to do, answering in the affirmative. Follow the model.

> *Modelo:* —¿Traigo la escoba?
> —Sí, **tráela,** por favor.

1. ¿Pongo el pan (*bread*) en la tostadora?
2. ¿Hago el postre?
3. ¿Lo pongo en la mesa?
4. ¿Limpio el piso?
5. ¿Pongo la lata de la basura debajo del fregadero?
6. ¿Preparo el arroz con pollo?
7. ¿Lavo el mantel?
8. ¿Lo pongo en la secadora después (*afterwards*)?
9. ¿Llamo a Estrella otra vez?
10. ¿Cierro las ventanas?
11. ¿Apago la luz?
12. ¿Me voy?

B. Now answer the questions in **Práctica A** in the negative. Follow the model.

> *Modelo:* —¿Traigo la escoba?
> —No, **no la traigas** ahora.

C. You are leaving a child home alone for a few hours. Using the **tú** form, tell the child what to do and what not to do. Give at least ten commands.

 # En el laboratorio

The following material is to be used with the tape in the language laboratory.

I. Vocabulario

Repeat each word after the speaker. When repeating words that are cognates, notice the difference in pronunciation between English and Spanish.

COGNADOS:	el favor la paciencia
NOMBRES:	el arroz la basura el cocinero el fregadero la liquidación la venta el piso el postre la secadora la tostadora los trabajos de la casa
VERBOS:	apagar caminar enseñar
ADJETIVOS:	todo todos
OTRAS PALABRAS Y EXPRESIONES:	arroz con pollo casi nunca ¿cuánto tiempo? de vez en cuando debajo en esa época ir de compras media hora otra vez ¡Rápido! Ten paciencia.

II. Práctica

A. Answer the following questions, using the cues provided. Repeat the correct answer after the speaker's confirmation. Listen to the model.

Modelo: —¿Cuánto tiempo hace que vives en La Habana?
(tres años)
—**Hace tres años que vivo en La Habana.**

B. Answer the following questions, using the cues provided. Repeat the correct answer after the speaker's confirmation. Listen to the model.

Modelo: —¿Qué tuviste que hacer ayer? (estudiar español)
—**Tuve que estudiar español.**

1. (una secadora)
2. (anoche)
3. (los estudiantes)
4. (a las siete)
5. (debajo del fregadero)
6. (nada)
7. (el postre)
8. (sí, otra vez)

C. Explain what these people used to do by changing the following sentences to the imperfect. Listen to the model.

Modelo: Mis abuelos **hablan** en español.
Mis abuelos hablaban en español.

D. Change the following commands from the negative to the affirmative. Repeat the correct answer after the speaker's confirmation. Listen to the model.

Modelo: **No hables** inglés.
Habla inglés.

E. Change the following commands from the affirmative to the negative. Repeat the correct answer after the speaker's confirmation. Listen to the model.

Modelo: **Ponlo** en la mesa.
No lo pongas en la mesa.

III. Para escuchar y entender

1. Listen carefully to the dialogue. It will be read twice.

(Diálogo 1)

Now the speaker will make statements about the dialogue you just heard. Tell whether each statement is true (**verdadero**) or false (**falso**). The speaker will confirm the correct answer.

2. Listen carefully to the dialogue. It will be read twice.

(Diálogo 2)

Now the speaker will make statements about the dialogue you just heard. Tell whether each statement is true (**verdadero**) or false (**falso**). The speaker will confirm the correct answer.

3. Listen carefully to the narration. It will be read twice.

(Narración)

Now the speaker will ask you some questions about the narration you just heard. Answer each question, omitting the subject. The speaker will confirm the correct answer. Repeat the correct answer.

Lección

12

1. **The past progressive**
2. **The preterit contrasted with the imperfect**
3. **Changes in meaning with the imperfect and preterit of** *conocer, saber,* **and** *querer*
4. *En* **and** *a* **as equivalents of at**

Vocabulario

COGNADOS

el aeropuerto airport	**el catálogo** catalogue

NOMBRES
la cartera purse
el centro comercial mall
la cuñada sister-in-law
el cuñado brother-in-law
la joyería jewelry store
la máquina de escribir
 typewriter
el sombrero hat
el traje de baño bathing suit
la vidriera, el escaparate
 store window
la zapatería shoe store

VERBOS
 conocer to meet (for the
 first time)
 encontrarse (con) (o:ue)
 to meet (i.e., for an
 appointment)

mirar to look at
quedarse to stay, to remain
sentir(se) (e:ie) to feel

ADJETIVO
 nuevo(a) new

OTRAS PALABRAS Y
EXPRESIONES
 anteayer the day before
 yesterday
 en casa at home
 escribir a máquina to type
 ir de vacaciones to go on
 vacation
 juntos(as) together
 mirar vidrieras to window
 shop
 todo el día   all day long

1. The past progressive
El pasado progresivo

The past progressive indicates an action in progress in the past. It is formed with the imperfect tense of the verb **estar** and the Spanish equivalent of the present participle (the **gerundio**).

—¿Qué **estabas haciendo**
 cuando te llamé?
—**Estaba escribiendo** a
 máquina. Tengo una
 máquina de escribir
 nueva.

*"What were you doing when I
 called you?"*
*"I was typing. I have a new
 typewriter."*

—¿Qué **estaban haciendo**
 los chicos?
—**Estaban mirando** un
 catálogo. Ana **me
 estaba diciendo** que
 quería un traje de
 baño nuevo.

"What were the kids doing?"
*"They were looking at a
 catalogue. Ana was telling me
 that she wanted a new bathing
 suit."*

Práctica

Tell what the following people were doing when a friend came to visit. Use the cues provided.

Modelo: Elsa / hablar con Jorge.
            Elsa **estaba hablando** con Jorge.

1. yo / beber un refresco
2. Uds. / mirar un catálogo
3. tu mamá / limpiar la máquina de escribir
4. Isabel / probarse el traje de baño nuevo
5. los niños / dormir
6. la cocinera / barrer la cocina
7. Carlos y papá / jugar al tenis
8. tu hermana / escribir a máquina

2. The preterit contrasted with the imperfect

El pretérito contrastado con el imperfecto

There are two simple past tenses in Spanish: the imperfect and the preterit. The difference between the two can be visualized this way.

The continuous moving line of the imperfect represents an action or state that was taking place in the past. We don't know when the action started or ended. The vertical line of the preterit represents a completed or finished event in the past.

The following table summarizes the uses of the preterit and the imperfect.

Preterit	Imperfect
1. Records, narrates, and reports an independent past act or event as a completed and undivided whole, regardless of its duration. 2. Sums up a past condition or state viewed as a whole.	1. Describes an action in progress in the past. 2. Indicates a continuous and habitual action: *used to . . .*[1] 3. Describes a physical, mental, or emotional state or condition in the past. 4. Expresses time in the past. 5. Indicates age in the past.

The preterit

—¿Qué **compró** Ud. ayer?   *"What did you buy yesterday?"*

—**Compré** un sombrero y una cartera.   *"I bought a hat and a purse."*

—¿Su esposo **fue** a la tienda también?   *"Did your husband go to the store too?"*

—No él **estuvo** enfermo todo el día.   *"No, he was sick all day long."*

The imperfect

—Anteayer cuando **íbamos** a la joyería, vimos a María Ortiz mirando vidrieras.   *"The day before yesterday as (when) we were going to the jewelry store, we saw María Ortiz window shopping."*

—¿Sí? Ella y yo siempre **íbamos** juntas de vacaciones.   *"Really? She and I always used to go on vacation together."*

—¿Cuantos años **tenías** tú cuando viniste a los Estados Unidos?   *"How old were you when you came to the United States?"*

—**Tenía** quince años.   *"I was fifteen years old."*

---

[1] Note that this use of the imperfect also corresponds to the English *would*, when used to describe a repeated action in the past: **Cuando yo era niña,** *comía* **pollo** *todos los domingos.* When I was a child, I used to eat *chicken every Sunday.* (When I was a child, I would eat *chicken every Sunday.*)

—¿Por qué te fuiste tan
   temprano? **Eran** sólo
   las ocho de la noche.
—Me fui porque no **me**
   sentía muy bien.

"Why did you leave so early?"
It was only eight o'clock in
the evening."
"I left because I wasn't feeling
very well."

ATENCIÓN: In the first exchange, **íbamos** describes an action in
progress, while in the third exchange, **me sentía** describes a
physical state. These verbs in the imperfect act as background
for completed actions in the past, which are expressed by the
preterit verbs **vimos** and **me fui**.

Práctica

A. Complete the following paragraph with the preterit or the
imperfect of the verbs in parentheses, as appropriate.

_____ (Ser) las cuatro de la tarde cuando yo _____ (llegar)
a casa ayer. _____ (Preparar) la cena y _____ (escribir) a
máquina hasta las ocho. Roberto _____ (venir) a comer conmigo y después (*afterwards*) _____ (mirar) la televisión juntos.
Roberto y yo _____ (vivir) en Lima cuando _____ (ser)
niños, pero él _____ (irse) a Colombia cuando _____
(tener) quince años. A las diez Roberto _____ (decidir) irse y
yo _____ (acostarse) porque no _____ (sentirse) muy bien.

B. With a partner, act out the following dialogues in Spanish.

1. "How old were you when you started to study at the
   university?"
   "I was seventeen years old."
2. "What time was it when you saw Maribel the day before
   yesterday?"
   "It was ten o'clock. She was going to the store."
3. "Where did you and your family go on vacation when you
   were a child?"
   "We used to go to the beach together."
4. "Why did you leave, Anita?"
   "Because I wasn't feeling well."
5. "What did you buy yesterday?"
   "I bought a purse and a hat."

C. Interview a classmate, using the following questions. When you
have finished, switch roles.

1. ¿Dónde vivías cuando tenías diez años?
2. ¿Hablabas inglés o español con tus amigos?
3. ¿Adónde ibas de vacaciones?
4. ¿Veías a tus abuelos a menudo?

5. ¿Adónde fuiste anoche?
6. ¿A quién viste?
7. ¿Qué hora era cuando volviste a tu casa ayer?
8. ¿Estuviste enfermo(a) ayer?
9. ¿Cómo te sentías hoy cuando saliste de tu casa?
10. ¿Te dijo tu profesor(a) hoy que hablabas bien el español?

D. With a partner, prepare a list of ten questions you would like to ask your teacher about his or her childhood and youth.

3. Changes in meaning with the imperfect and preterit of conocer, saber, **and** querer
Cambios de significado del imperfecto y del pretérito de conocer, saber y querer

In Spanish, a few verbs have different meanings when used in the preterit or the imperfect.

Preterit		Imperfect	
conocer		conocer	
conocí	*I met*	conocía	*I knew, I was acquainted with*
saber		saber	
supe	*found out, I learned*	sabía	*I knew (a fact, how to)*
querer		querer	
no quise	*I refused*	no quería	*I didn't want to*

—Mario, ¿**conocías** a la cuñada de Luisa?
—No, la **conocí** ayer.

"Mario, did you know Luisa's sister-in-law?"
"No, I met her yesterday."

—Rita, ¿**sabías** que había una liquidación hoy?
—No, lo **supe** esta mañana.

"Rita, did you know that there was a sale today?"
"No, I found out this morning."

—¿Por qué no fuiste a la zapatería?
—Porque mi hermano **no quiso** llevarme. Tuve que quedarme en casa.

"Why didn't you go to the shoe store?"

"Because my brother refused to take me. I had to stay home."

Práctica

A. Complete the following dialogue, using the preterit or the imperfect of **saber, conocer,** or **querer,** as appropriate. Then act it out with a partner.

—¿Tú _____ a Graciela?
—No, la _____ anteayer.
—¿Tú _____ que ella era la esposa de Roberto?
—No, lo _____ anoche. Me lo dijo Raquel.
—¿Alberto fue a la fiesta anoche?
—Sí, fue. Él no _____ ir, pero su hermano lo llevó.
—¿Y Rosa? ¿Por qué no fue?
—Rosa no fue porque no _____.

B. With a partner, act out the following dialogues in Spanish.

1. "Why didn't Mario go to the shoe store?"
   "Because he didn't know that they were having a sale."
   "I found out about it this morning when I talked with Carmen."
2. "Did Laura's brother-in-law go to the party?"
   "No, he refused to go. He stayed home."
   "I didn't want to go either. But I had to go with my husband."
3. "Did you know Mrs. Vega?"
   "No, I met her last night."

4. En **and** a **as equivalents of** *at*
En y a **como equivalentes de** *at*

◆ **En** is used in Spanish as the equivalent of *at* to indicate a certain place or location.

—¿Dónde están los chicos? ¿No están **en** casa?	*"Where are the boys? Aren't they at home?"*
—No, están **en** el centro comercial.	*"No, they're at the mall."*

◆ **A** is used in Spanish as the equivalent of *at*

1. to refer to a specific moment in time.

—¿Cuándo se encontraron Uds.?	*"When did you meet?"*
—Ayer **a** las once.	*"Yesterday at eleven."*

2. to indicate direction towards a point after the verb **llegar**.

—¿A qué hora llegaron   *"What time did they arrive at*
  al aeropuerto?   *the airport?"*
—**A** las cinco.   *"At five."*

Práctica

Complete the following dialogues, using **en** or **a**, as appropriate. Then act them out with a partner.

1. —¿ _____ qué hora llegaron Uds. _____ California?
   —Llegamos _____ las seis.
   —¿Dónde comieron?
   —_____ un restaurante mexicano que había _____ el aeropuerto.
2. —¿Dónde está tu esposa ahora? ¿ _____ casa?
   —No, está _____ el centro comercial mirando vidrieras.
3. —¿Carlos está _____ la joyería?
   —Sí, él trabaja allí todo el día.
   —¿ _____ qué hora te vas a encontrar con él _____ el restaurante?
   —_____ las ocho y media.

📼 *En el laboratorio*

The following material is to be used with the tape in the language laboratory.

I. *Vocabulario*

Repeat each word after the speaker. When repeating words that are cognates, notice the difference in pronunciation between English and Spanish.

COGNADOS:	el aeropuerto el catálogo
NOMBRES:	la cartera el centro comercial la cuñada el cuñado la joyería la máquina de escribir el sombrero el traje de baño la vidriera el escaparate la zapatería
VERBOS:	conocer encontrarse con mirar quedarse sentirse

ADJETIVO:	nuevo
OTRAS PALABRAS Y EXPRESIONES:	anteayer en casa escribir a máquina ir de vacaciones juntos mirar vidrieras todo el día

II. Práctica

A. Change the following sentences from the imperfect to the past progressive. Repeat the correct answer after the speaker's confirmation. Listen to the model.

Modelo: Yo **comía** en la cafetería.
Yo **estaba comiendo** en la cafetería.

B. Answer the following questions, using the cues provided. Notice the use of the preterit or the imperfect. Repeat the correct answer after the speaker's confirmation. Listen to the model.

Modelo: —¿Qué hora era cuando él llegó? (las nueve)
—**Eran** las nueve cuando él llegó.

1. (en casa)
2. (en México)
3. (esta mañana)
4. (en una fiesta)
5. (sí)
6. (que no podían venir)
7. (sí)
8. (no, pero vine)
9. (no)
10. (a Luisa)

III. Para escuchar y entender

1. Listen carefully to the dialogue. It will be read twice.

(*Diálogo 1*)

Now the speaker will make statements about the dialogue you just heard. Tell whether each statement is true (**verdadero**) or false (**falso**). The speaker will confirm the correct answer.

2. Listen carefully to the dialogue. It will be read twice.

(*Diálogo 2*)

Now the speaker will ask you some questions about the dialogue you just heard. Answer each question, omitting the subject. The speaker will confirm the correct answer. Repeat the correct answer.

Lección

13

1. **The preterit of stem-changing verbs** (*e:i* **and** *o:u*)
2. **The expression** *acabar de*
3. **Special construction with** *gustar, doler,* **and** *hacer falta*
4. **¿Qué?** **and** *¿cuál?* **used with** *ser*

Vocabulario

COGNADOS

el accidente accident	**la persona** person
la aspirina aspirin	**el tipo** type

NOMBRES
el anillo, la sortija ring
los aretes earrings
la cabeza head
el camisón nightgown
el collar necklace
la corbata tie
la chaqueta jacket
la escalera stairs
la escalera mecánica
   escalator
el lugar place
la moda fashion
el oro gold
el traje suit, outfit

VERBOS
   arreglar to fix
   despedirse (e:i) to say
   good-bye
   divertirse (e:ie) to have
   a good time
   doler (o:ue) to hurt, to
   ache

elegir (e:i) to choose, to
   select
funcionar to work
gustar to like, to be
   pleasing
mentir (e:ie) to lie
morir (o:ue) to die
vender to sell

ADJETIVOS
aburrido(a) boring,
   bored
varios(as) several, various

**OTRAS PALABRAS Y
EXPRESIONES**
acabar de (+ *inf.*) to have
   just (done something)
hacer falta to need, to
   lack
por suerte luckily
según according to
sobre about
ya already

1. The preterit of stem-changing verbs (e:i and o:u)

El pretérito de verbos de cambio radical
e:i y o:u

e:i verbs

Stem-changing verbs of the **-ir** conjugation, whether they change **e**
to **ie** or **e** to **i** in the present indicative, change **e** to **i** in the third person singular and plural of the preterit.

sentir		pedir	
sentí	sentimos	pedí	pedimos
sentiste		pediste	
sintió	sintieron	pidió	pidieron

◆ The following verbs follow the same **e** to **i** pattern.

conseguir	**preferir**
despedirse (*to say good-bye*)	**repetir**
divertirse (*to have a good time*)	**seguir**
elegir (*to choose*)	**servir**
mentir (*to lie*)	

—¿Daniel compró el traje marrón?

"*Did Daniel buy the brown suit?*"

—No, **prefirió** comprar el pantalón gris y la chaqueta azul.

"*No, he preferred to buy the gray pants and the blue jacket.*"

—¿Qué corbata **eligió**?

"*What tie did he choose?*"

—La corbata roja.

"*The red tie.*"

—Según Juan, todos **se divirtieron** mucho en la fiesta.

"*According to Juan, everybody had a good time at the party.*"

—¡Te **mintió**! La fiesta estuvo muy aburrida y no **sirvieron** nada para comer.

"*He lied to you! The party was very boring and they didn't serve anything to eat.*"

o:u verbs

Stem-changing verbs of the **-ir** conjugation that change **o** to **ue** in the present indicative change **o** to **u** in the third person singular and plural of the preterit.

dormir	
dormí	dormimos
dormiste	
durmió	durmieron

◆ Another verb that follows the same **o** to **u** pattern is **morir** (*to die*).

—¿Cuántas horas **durmió** Ud. anoche?

"*How many hours did you sleep last night?*"

—Yo dormí seis horas, pero Ana y Luis sólo **durmieron** tres.

"*I slept six hours, but Ana and Luis slept only three.*"

—¿Cuántas personas **murieron**   *"How many people died in*
    en el accidente?   *the accident?"*
—Por suerte, no **murió** nadie.   *"Luckily, nobody died."*

Práctica

Complete the following dialogues, using the preterit of the verbs in parentheses. Then act them out with a partner.

1. —¿Doblaron?
   —No, _____ (seguir) derecho (*straight ahead*).
2. —¿Dónde _____ (dormir) Uds. anoche?
   —Yo _____ (dormir) en la casa de Ana, pero Carlos
     _____ (dormir) en un hotel.
3. —¿_____ (Conseguir) Uds. la chaqueta que querían?
   —Sí, por suerte la _____ (conseguir) en El Corte Inglés.
     También _____ (elegir) dos corbatas muy bonitas.
4. —¿Uds. _____ (despedirse) de los chicos?
   —No, porque no se fueron. No _____ (conseguir) pasaje.
   —¿Entonces fueron a la fiesta?
   —Sí, y _____ (divertirse) mucho.
5. —¿Qué te dijo Gerardo?
   —Me _____ (repetir) que no quería salir contigo.
   —¡Te _____ (mentir)!
6. —¿Hubo un accidente aquí ayer?
   —Sí, y _____ (morir) dos personas.

Now create two original exchanges using stem-changing verbs in the preterit.

2. **The expression** acabar de
La expresión acabar de

Acabar de means *to have just*. The following formula is used in Spanish.

subject +	**acabar** (present tense) +	**de** +	*infinitive*
Pedro	**acaba**	**de**	**llegar.**

—Elena tiene un anillo de oro   *"Elena has a very pretty gold*
    muy bonito.   *ring."*
—Sí, **acaba de** comprarlo.   *"Yes, she has just bought it."*

—¿Funciona ya la escalera   *"Is the escalator working*
    mecánica?   *(already)?"*
—Sí, **acaban de** arreglarla.   *"Yes, they have just fixed it."*

—¿Vendieron Uds. la casa?   *"Did you sell the house?"*
—Sí, **acabamos de** venderla.   *"Yes, we (have) just sold it."*

Práctica

Company is coming. Say what the people named have just done, using the correct form of **acabar de** + *infinitive*.

1. Teresa _____ la cocina. (*has just swept*)
2. Yo _____ mi cuarto. (*have just cleaned*)
3. Uds. _____ un postre. (*have just prepared*)
4. Tú _____ la ropa en la lavadora. (*have just put*)
5. Nosotros _____ arroz con pollo. (*have just made*)
6. Roberto _____ una corbata. (*has just bought*)
7. Ana y yo _____ una ensalada. (*have just made*)
8. Nosotros _____ el coche y ya funciona. (*have just fixed*)

3. Special construction with gustar, doler, **and** hacer falta
Construcción especial con gustar, doler y hacer falta

The verb **gustar** means *to like*. A special construction is required in Spanish to translate the English structure *to like*. This is done by making the English direct object the subject of the Spanish sentence. The English subject then becomes the indirect object of the Spanish sentence.

English:	*I like **your suit.***
	subj. d.o.
Spanish:	**Me** gusta **tu traje.**
	i.o. subj.
Literally:	*Your suit appeals to me.*

The two most commonly used forms of **gustar** are: (1) the third person singular **gusta** if the subject is singular or if **gustar** is followed by one or more infinitives; and (2) the third person plural **gustan** if the subject is plural.

Indirect Object Pronouns

Me
Te
Le   gusta ⟶   ese collar.
Nos   comer y beber.
Les   gustan ⟶   esos aretes.

◆ Note that the verb **gustar** agrees with the subject of the sentence, that is, the person or thing *being liked*.

Me gust**a el café.**   Le gust**an los aretes.**

◆ Note that the person who does the liking is the *indirect object*.

Me gusta el café.   **Le** gustan las chicas inteligentes.
I.O.   I.O.

—¿**Les gusta** el café?   *"Do you (pl.) like coffee?"*
—Sí, **nos gusta** mucho   *"Yes, we like coffee very much, but*
  el café, pero **nos gusta**   *we like tea better."*
  más el té.

ATENCIÓN: Note that the words **más** (*better*) and **mucho** immediately follow **gustar.**

◆ The preposition **a** + *noun or pronoun* is used to clarify meaning or to emphasize the indirect object.

A Aurora (A ella) le gusta   *Aurora likes that place, but*
  ese lugar, pero **a mí** no me   *I don't like it.*
  gusta.
A Roberto y **a Rosa** les   *Roberto and Rosa like that*
  gusta esa tienda.   *store.*

◆ The verb **doler** (*to hurt, to ache*) and the expression **hacer falta** (*to need*) use the same construction as **gustar.**

—¿Qué **les hace falta,**   *"What do you need, ladies?"*
  señoras?
—**Nos hacen falta**   *"We need nightgowns."*
  camisones.

—¿Por qué estás tomando   *"Why are you taking aspirin?"*
  aspirinas?
—Porque **me duele** la cabeza. *"Because my head hurts."*

ATENCIÓN: In Spanish, the definite article is generally used instead of the possessive adjective with parts of the body.

Práctica

A. Use **gustar** to say what you and the people named like.

Modelo: José / el café
        (A José) **Le gusta** el café.

1. Elsa / ese anillo   4. ellos / comer y beber
2. nosotros / la chaqueta azul   5. tú / las corbatas rojas
3. yo / ese traje   6. Uds. / ese camisón

B. With a partner, act out the following dialogues in Spanish.

1. "Do you like this book, Paquito?"
   "No, it's very boring."
2. "Do you want to go shopping, Mr. Alba?"
   "Yes, I need a gray suit."
3. "My head hurts!"
   "Take two aspirins."
4. "Do you want the red tie, sir?"
   "No, I like the blue tie better."
5. "According to Raquel, we need gold earrings."
   "And necklaces . . ."

C. Ask a classmate the following questions, then switch roles.

1. ¿Cuándo tomas aspirinas?
2. ¿Te duele la cabeza a menudo?
3. ¿Qué te duele hoy?
4. ¿Qué te hace falta?
5. ¿Les hace falta más dinero a tu familia y a ti?
6. ¿Les gusta a tus amigos y a ti el español?
7. ¿Te gusta caminar?
8. ¿Qué te gusta más, el café o el té?

4. ¿Qué? **and** ¿cuál[1]? **used with** ser
¿Qué? y ¿cuál? **usados con el verbo** ser

◆ When asking for a definition, use **¿qué?** to translate *what*.

—¿**Qué** es un centro comercial?	*"What is a mall?"*
—Es un lugar donde hay varios tipos de tiendas.	*"It's a place where there are various types of stores."*

◆ When asking for a choice, use **¿cuál?** (**¿cuáles?**) to translate *what (which)*. ¿**Cuál?** implies selection from among many objects or ideas.

—¿**Cuál** es su número de seguro social?	*"What is your social security number?"*
—Mi número de seguro social es 243-50-8139.	*"My social security number is 243-50-8139."*
—¿**Cuáles** son sus ideas sobre la moda?	*"What are your ideas about fashion?"*
—Yo no sé nada de la moda.	*"I don't know anything about fashion."*

[1] Plural : **cuáles**

Práctica

Write the questions that correspond to the following answers, using **qué** or **cuál**.

1. —¿_____?
   —348-5490.
2. —¿_____?
   —Calle Victoria, número 1542.
3. —¿_____?
   —Es un metal amarillo.
4. —¿_____?
   —Una enchilada es un tipo de comida mexicana.
5. —¿_____?
   —¿Mis ideas sobre la educación? ¡Creo que es muy impor-
     tante y necesaria!
6. —¿_____?
   —Rodríguez.
7. —¿_____?
   —Una residencia universitaria (*dorm*) es un lugar donde
     viven estudiantes.

🔘 *En el laboratorio*

The following material is to be used with the tape in the language laboratory.

I. Vocabulario

Repeat each word after the speaker. When repeating words that are cognates, notice the difference in pronunciation between English and Spanish.

COGNADOS:	el accidente la aspirina la persona el tipo
NOMBRES:	el anillo la sortija los aretes la cabeza el camisón el collar la corbata la chaqueta la escalera la escalera mecánica el lugar la moda el oro el traje
VERBOS:	arreglar despedirse divertirse doler elegir funcionar gustar mentir morir vender
ADJETIVOS:	aburrido varios
OTRAS PALABRAS Y EXPRESIONES:	acabar de hacer falta por suerte según sobre ya

II. Práctica

A. The speaker will read some sentences in the present tense. Restate each one, changing the verb to the preterit. Repeat the correct answer after the speaker's confirmation. Listen to the model.

> *Modelo:* Ellos piden café.
> **Ellos pidieron café.**

B. Repeat each statement or question, replacing **preferir** with **gusta más** or **gustan más** and the appropriate indirect object pronoun. Repeat the correct answer after the speaker's confirmation. Listen to the model.

> *Modelo:* Yo prefiero la corbata gris.
> **Me gusta más la corbata gris.**

C. Answer the following questions, always using the first choice. Omit the subject. Repeat the correct answer after the speaker's confirmation. Listen to the model.

> *Modelo* —¿Te gusta el traje marrón o el traje gris?
> **—Me gusta el traje marrón.**

III. Para escuchar y entender

1. Listen carefully to the dialogue. It will be read twice.

(Diálogo 1)

Now the speaker will make statements about the dialogue you just heard. Tell whether each statement is true (**verdadero**) or false (**falso**). The speaker will confirm the correct answer.

2. Listen carefully to the dialogue. It will be read twice.

(Diálogo 2)

Now the speaker will ask you some questions about the dialogue you just heard. Answer each question, omitting the subject. The speaker will confirm the correct answer. Repeat the correct answer.

3. Listen carefully to the dialogue. It will be read twice.

(Diálogo 3)

Now the speaker will make statements about the dialogue you just heard. Tell whether each statement is true (**verdadero**) or false (**falso**). The speaker will confirm the correct answer.

Lección

14

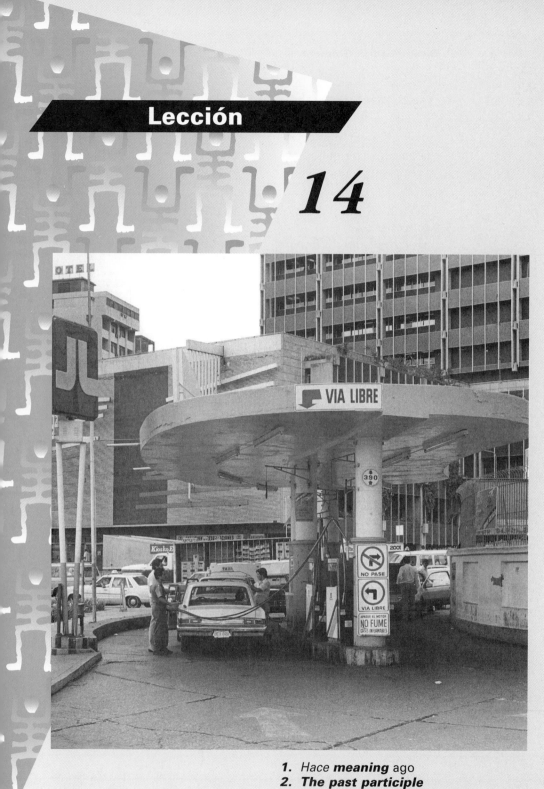

1. *Hace **meaning** ago*
2. *The past participle*
3. *The present perfect tense*
4. *The past perfect (pluperfect) tense*

Vocabulario

COGNADOS

la gasolina gasoline	**el mecánico** mechanic
imposible impossible	**el tanque** tank

NOMBRES
el aceite oil
el acumulador, la batería battery
el club automovilístico auto club
el (la) empleado(a) clerk, attendant
el freno brake
la gasolinera, la estación de servicio gas station
la goma, la llanta, el neumático tire
la goma pinchada flat tire
el limpiaparabrisas windshield wiper
la marca brand
el parabrisas windshield
la pieza de repuesto spare part
el remolcador, la grúa tow truck

VERBOS
cambiar to change
cubrir to cover
llenar to fill
romper to break
usar to use

ADJETIVOS
listo(a) ready
vacío(a) empty

OTRAS PALABRAS Y EXPRESIONES
casi almost
¿Cuánto tiempo hace que... ? How long ago . . . ?
en seguida right away

1. Hace meaning *ago*
Hace **como equivalente de** *ago*

In sentences in the preterit and in some cases the imperfect, **hace** + *period of time* is equivalent to the English *ago*.[1]

Llegué **hace dos años.**   *I arrived two years ago.*

---

[1] The imperfect is used with **hacer** to mean *ago* in sentences such as *Hace dos años,* **yo vivía en Buenos Aires** (*Two years ago, I lived in Buenos Aires*) in which the action or condition described is not viewed as complete or finished.

When **hace** is placed at the beginning of the sentence, the construction is as follows.

Hace + *period of time* +	**que** +	*verb (preterit)*
Hace dos años	que	llegué.

—¿Cuánto tiempo **hace
que** el mecánico arregló
los frenos?

*"How long ago did the
mechanic fix the brakes?"*

—**Hace dos meses que** los
arregló.

*"He fixed them two months
ago."*

—¿Cuánto tiempo **hace que**
compraste las llantas?

*"How long ago did you buy
the tires?"*

—**Hace tres semanas que**
las compré.

*"I bought them three weeks
ago."*

Práctica

A. Interview a classmate, using the following questions. When you have finished, switch roles.

1. ¿Cuánto tiempo hace que empezaste a estudiar en esta universidad?
2. ¿Cuánto tiempo hace que comiste?
3. ¿Cuánto tiempo hace que tomaste un examen en una de tus clases?
4. ¿Cuánto tiempo hace que conociste a tu mejor amigo o amiga?
5. ¿Cuánto tiempo hace que fuiste a una fiesta?
6. ¿Cuánto tiempo hace que aprendiste a conducir?

B. With a partner, prepare six questions to ask your instructor. Use **hace** to mean *ago* in each question.

2. The past participle
El participio pasado

Past participle   a past form of a verb that may be used in conjunction with another (auxiliary) verb in certain past tenses. The past participle may also be used as an adjective: *gone, worked, written*

The past participle of regular verbs is formed by adding the following endings to the stem of the verb.

Past Participle Endings		
-ar *Verbs*	**-er** *Verbs*	**-ir** *Verbs*
habl- **ado**	ten- **ido**	ven- **ido**

◆ The following verbs have irregular past participles in Spanish.

abrir	**abierto**	hacer	**hecho**	ver	**visto**
cubrir	**cubierto**	morir	**muerto**	volver	**vuelto**
decir	**dicho**	poner	**puesto**	romper	**roto**
escribir	**escrito**				

◆ In Spanish, most past participles may be used as adjectives. As such, they agree in number and gender with the nouns they modify.

—¿La gasolinera está **abierta**?   *"Is the gas station open?"*
—No, está **cerrada**.   *"No, it's closed. Do you*
  ¿Necesitas gasolina?   *need gas?"*
—No, tengo una goma   *"No, I have a flat tire and*
  pinchada y el parabrisas   *the windshield is broken."*
  está **roto**.

Práctica

A. What are the past participles of the following verbs?

1. dormir	6. cubrir	11. caminar	16. abrir
2. romper	7. recibir	12. pedir	17. ver
3. estar	8. hacer	13. decir	18. volver
4. comer	9. cerrar	14. comprar	19. aprender
5. poner	10. ser	15. morir	20. escribir

B. Using the elements from the two columns and the verb **estar**, create ten descriptive sentences. You may use a verb more than once.

Modelo: ventanas / cerrar
         Las ventanas **están cerradas.**

los hombres	pinchar
Pedro	arreglar
la gasolinera	cerrar
la carta	morir
los frenos	dormir
las puertas	escribir (en español)
el neumático	hacer (de madera)
la mesa	abrir
el parabrisas	romper

3. The present perfect tense
El pretérito perfecto

The present perfect tense is formed by using the present tense of the auxiliary verb **haber** and the past participle of the verb to be conjugated.

This tense is equivalent to the use in English of the auxiliary verb *have* + past participle, as in *I have spoken.*

Present of **haber**[1] *(to have)*	
he	hemos
has	
ha	han

The Present Perfect Tense

	hablar	tener	venir
yo	**he** hablado	**he** tenido	**he** venido
tú	**has** hablado	**has** tenido	**has** venido
Ud. él ella	**ha** hablado	**ha** tenido	**ha** venido
nosotros	**hemos** hablado	**hemos** tenido	**hemos** venido
Uds. ellos ellas	**han** hablado	**han** tenido	**han** venido

—¿Está listo el coche?
—No, porque el mecánico todavía no **ha conseguido** las piezas de repuesto.
—¿Le **ha puesto** un acumulador nuevo?
—Sí, y también **ha cambiado** los limpiaparabrisas.

"Is the car ready?"
"No, because the mechanic still hasn't obtained the spare parts."
"Has he put a new battery in it?"
"Yes, and he has also changed the windshield wipers."

—¿**Han llamado** al club automovilístico?
—Sí, y el empleado **dice** que el remolcador viene en seguida.

"Have you called the auto club?"
"Yes, and the clerk says that the tow truck is coming right away."

---

[1] Note that the English verb *to have* has two equivalents in Spanish: **haber** (used only as an auxiliary verb) and **tener.**

—¿**Han comprado** alguna vez   *"Have you ever bought this*
esta marca de aceite?   *brand of oil?"*

—No, nunca la **hemos**   *"No, we have never bought*
comprado.   *it."*

ATENCIÓN: Note that when the past participle is part of a perfect
tense, it is invariable and cannot be separated from the auxiliary
verb **haber.**

Práctica

A. Say what the subjects given have or haven't done.

1. yo / comprar / un limpiaparabrisas nuevo
2. el mecánico / arreglar / los frenos
3. tú / no llamar / al club automovilístico
4. ellos / venir / en seguida
5. nosotros / no ver / al empleado
6. Uds. / cambiar / las llantas

B. Interview a classmate, using the following questions. When you
have finished, switch roles.

1. ¿Has comprado un coche alguna vez? (¿Cuánto te ha
   costado?)
2. ¿Cuántas veces (*times*) has cambiado el aceite de tu coche
   este año?
3. ¿Has tenido una goma pinchada alguna vez?
4. ¿Has cambiado una llanta alguna vez?
5. ¿Has cambiado los frenos de tu coche últimamente (*lately*)?
6. ¿Han tenido tú y tus amigos un accidente alguna vez?
7. ¿Han llamado una grúa alguna vez?
8. ¿Has tenido que comprar un acumulador últimamente?
9. ¿Has llevado tu coche al mecánico recientemente?

4. The past perfect (pluperfect) tense
El pluscuamperfecto

The past perfect tense is formed by using the imperfect tense of
the auxiliary verb **haber** and the past participle of the verb to be
conjugated.

This tense is equivalent to the use, in English, of the auxiliary
verb *had* + past participle, as in *I had spoken.* As in English, the past
perfect tense in Spanish describes an action or event completed
before some other past action or event.

	Imperfect of haber	
	había	habíamos
	habías	
	había	habían

The Past Perfect Tense

	estudiar	beber	ir
yo	**había** estudi**ado**	**había** beb**ido**	**había** ido
tú	**habías** estudi**ado**	**habías** beb**ido**	**habías** ido
Ud. ⎫ él ⎬ ella ⎭	**había** estudi**ado**	**había** beb**ido**	**había** ido
nosotros	**habíamos** estudi**ado**	**habíamos** beb**ido**	**habíamos** ido
Uds. ⎫ ellos ⎬ ellas ⎭	**habían** estudi**ado**	**habían** beb**ido**	**habían** ido

—El tanque está casi vacío.   *"The tank is almost empty."*
—Eso es imposible. Carlos   *"That's impossible. Carlos told*
  me dijo que lo **había**   *me that he had filled it."*
  llenado.

—Nosotros nunca **habíamos**   *"We had never used that brand*
  usado esa marca de aceite.   *of oil."*
—¿Por qué la compraron?   *"Why did you buy it?"*

—Porque el mecánico nos   *"Because the mechanic had*
  había dicho que era muy   *told us that it was very good."*
  buena.

Práctica

A. Complete the following dialogues, using the pluperfect of the
verbs in parentheses. Then act them out with a partner.

1. —¿Por qué no le pusiste gasolina al coche?
   —Porque Javier ya _____ (llenar) el tanque.
2. —¿Hablaste con los empleados?
   —No, porque cuando yo llegué, (ellos) ya _____ (irse).
3. —¿Uds. _____ (viajar) a México en coche antes?
   —No, siempre _____ (ir) en avión.
4. —¿Tú _____ (usar) esta marca de gasolina?
   —No, nunca la _____ (usar).

5. —¿Cuando tú llegaste a casa, tus padres ya _____
(venir)?
—No, no _____ (llegar) todavía.
6. —¿Ya estaba listo el coche cuando llegaste?
—No, porque ellos no _____ (traer) las piezas de repuesto.
—¿Por qué _____ (ir) ellos a la gasolinera?
—Porque el tanque estaba casi vacío.

B. Say what the subjects given had done to prepare for a car trip across the country.

1. el mecánico / los frenos
2. tú / el tanque
3. yo / la goma pinchada
4. mis padres / una batería nueva
5. mi hermano y yo / el coche

C. Tell a partner five things you had already done today by the time you arrived at Spanish class.

Cuando llegué a la clase de español, ya (*already*) **había tomado** cuatro tazas de café...

En el laboratorio

The following material is to be used with the tape in the language laboratory.

I. Vocabulario

Repeat each word after the speaker. When repeating words that are cognates, notice the difference in pronunciation between English and Spanish.

COGNADOS:	la gasolina imposible el mecánico el tanque
NOMBRES:	el aceite el acumulador la batería el club automovilístico el empleado el freno la gasolinera la estación de servicio la goma la llanta el neumático la goma pinchada el limpiaparabrisas la marca el parabrisas la pieza de repuesto el remolcador la grúa
VERBOS:	cambiar cubrir llenar romper usar

ADJETIVOS: listo   vacío

OTRAS PALABRAS   casi   ¿Cuánto tiempo hace que... ?
Y EXPRESIONES: en seguida

II. Práctica

A. Answer the following questions, using the cues provided. Repeat the correct answer after the speaker's confirmation. Listen to the model.

Modelo: —¿Cuánto tiempo hace que tú llamaste la grúa? (casi veinte minutos)
     —**Hace casi veinte minutos que yo llamé la grúa.**

1. (tres meses)   4. (ocho años)
2. (quince minutos)   5. (cuatro horas)
3. (cinco años)

B. Answer each question in the affirmative, using the past participle of the verb in the question as an adjective in your response. Repeat the correct answer after the speaker's confirmation. Listen to the model.

Modelo: —Terminaste la carta?
     —Sí, ya **está terminada.**

C. Change each sentence to the present perfect tense. Repeat the correct answer after the speaker's confirmation. Listen to the model.

Modelo: Yo llamo al club automovilístico.
     Yo he llamado al club automovilístico.

D. Restate the model sentence according to the new subjects. Repeat the correct answer after the speaker's confirmation. Listen to the model.

Modelo: Yo no lo había hecho todavía.

1. (Uds.)   4. (Eva)
2. (nosotras)   5. (ellos)
3. (tú)   6. (Ud.)

III. Para escuchar y entender

1. Listen carefully to the narration. It will be read twice.

   (Narración)

   Now the speaker will make statements about the narration you just heard. Tell whether each statement is true (**verdadero**) or false (**falso**). The speaker will confirm the correct answer.

2. Listen carefully to the dialogue. It will be read twice.

   (Diálogo)

   Now the speaker will ask you some questions about the dialogue you just heard. Answer each question, omitting the subject. The speaker will confirm the correct answer. Repeat the correct answer.

Lección

15

1. **The future tense**
2. **The conditional tense**
3. **Some uses of the prepositions** *a,* *de,* **and** *en*

Vocabulario

automático(a) automatic	**probablemente** probably
el examen exam	**el (la) veterinario(a)** veterinarian

NOMBRES
la agencia de alquiler de automóviles car rental agency
el (la) cajero(a) cashier
la cuenta account
la motocicleta, la moto motorcycle
el motor engine
el perro dog
la plata silver
el precio price
el tren train

VERBOS
alquilar to rent
cobrar to charge
depositar to deposit

manejar to drive
revisar, chequear to check

ADJETIVOS
hermoso(a) beautiful
peligroso(a) dangerous

OTRAS PALABRAS Y EXPRESIONES
cambiar un cheque to cash a check
de cambios mecánicos with a standard shift
después afterwards, later
hasta until
sin falta without fail

1. The future tense
El futuro

The English equivalent of the Spanish future is *will* or *shall* + *verb*. As you have already learned, Spanish also uses the construction **ir a** + *infinitive* or the present tense with a time expression to express future actions or states, very much like the English present tense or the expression *going to*.

Vamos a ir al cine esta noche.
or: **Iremos** al cine esta noche. } *We're going (We'll go) to the movies tonight.*

Anita **toma** el examen mañana.
or: Anita **tomará** el examen mañana. } *Anita is taking (will take) the exam tomorrow.*

ATENCIÓN: The Spanish future is *not* used to make requests, as is the English future. In Spanish, requests are expressed with the verb **querer**.
¿Quieres llamar a Tomás? *Will you call Tomás?*

Regular future forms

Most Spanish verbs are regular in the future. The infinitive serves as the stem of almost all Spanish verbs. The endings are the same for all three conjugations.

The Future Tense			
Infinitive		*Stem*	*Endings*
trabajar	yo	trabajar-	**é**
aprender	tú	aprender-	**ás**
escribir	Ud.	escribir-	**á**
hablar	él	hablar-	**á**
decidir	ella	decidir-	**á**
entender	nosotros	entender-	**emos**
caminar	Uds.	caminar-	**án**
perder	ellos	perder-	**án**
recibir	ellas	recibir-	**án**

ATENCIÓN: Notice that all the endings, except the one for the **nosotros** form, have written accent marks.

—¿Cómo **viajarán** Uds. de Los Ángeles a San Francisco?

—**Alquilaremos** un coche o **viajaremos** en tren.

—¿Cuánto tiempo **estarán** en San Francisco?

—Ana y yo **estaremos** allí por una semana y Jorge se quedará un mes. ¿Y adónde **irás** tú?

—Probablemente **iré** a San Diego. Dicen que es una hermosa ciudad.

"How will you travel from Los Angeles to San Francisco?"

"We will rent a car or we will travel by train."

"How long will you be in San Francisco?"

"Ana and I will be there for a week and Jorge will stay for a month. And where will you go?"

"I'll probably go to San Diego. They say it's a beautiful city."

Práctica

The following sentences say what everybody did. Rephrase them using the future tense to say what everyone will do.

1. Nosotros viajamos en tren.
2. Tú alquilaste un coche.
3. Yo fui a México.

4. Juan compró gasolina.
5. El empleado cambió el aceite.
6. Mis padres llamaron al club automovilístico.
7. Ud. consiguió las piezas de repuesto.
8. Estela cubrió el coche.
9. El mecánico volvió a la gasolinera.
10. Uds. llenaron el tanque.

Irregular future forms

A few verbs are irregular in the future tense. These verbs use a modified form of the infinitive as a stem. The endings are the same as the ones for regular verbs.

Infinitive	Stem		Future Tense	
decir	dir-	yo	**dir-**	é
hacer	har-	tú	**har-**	ás
saber	sabr-	Ud.	**sabr-**	á
poder	podr-	ella	**podr-**	á
poner	pondr-	nosotros	**pondr-**	emos
venir	vendr-	Uds.	**vendr-**	án
tener	tendr-	ellos	**tendr-**	án
salir	saldr-	ellas	**saldr-**	án

◆ The future of **hay** (from the verb **haber**) is **habrá**.

—Mañana **tendré** que ir al banco para depositar un cheque. ¿Tú **podrás** llevarme?

"*Tomorrow I'll have to go to the bank to deposit a check. Will you be able to take me?*"

—Sí, pero no **vendré** por ti hasta las once porque tengo que trabajar.

"*Yes, but I won't come for you until eleven because I have to work.*"

—¿Qué le **dirán** Uds. a Roberto?

"*What will you tell Roberto?*"

—Le **diremos** que **saldremos** de la agencia de alquiler de automóviles a las once.

"*We will tell him that we'll be leaving the car rental agency at eleven.*"

—¿Qué **harán** después?

"*What will you do afterwards?*"

—Iremos al banco para cambiar un cheque.

"*We will go to the bank to cash a check.*"

Práctica

A. Complete the following dialogues, using the future tense of the verbs in parentheses. Then act them out with a partner.

1. —¿Qué le _____ (decir) Uds. al empleado?
   —Le _____ (decir) que (nosotros) _____ (tener) que venir mañana.
   —¿Cuándo _____ (estar) listo el coche?
   —Nosotros lo _____ (saber) esta tarde.
2. —¿_____ (Poder) el mecánico traer el coche?
   —Sí, él me ha dicho que _____ (venir) mañana.
   —Muy bien, porque nosotros _____ (salir) para San José por la noche.
3. —¿Cuándo _____ (poder) Uds. depositar el cheque?
   —Lo _____ (hacer) esta tarde después de salir de la agencia de alquiler de automóviles.
4. —¿Qué _____ (hacer) Uds. el domingo?
   —_____ (Ir) a la fiesta que _____ (haber) en el club.
   —¿Qué te _____ (poner) para ir a la fiesta?
   —El traje azul.

B. Interview a classmate, using the following questions. When you have finished, switch roles.

1. ¿A qué hora llegarás a tu casa hoy?
2. ¿Vendrán tú y tus amigos a una fiesta en la universidad esta noche? (¿A cuál?)
3. ¿Habrá mucha gente (*people*)?
4. ¿A qué hora llegarás a tu casa hoy?
5. ¿Podrás venir a clase mañana?
6. ¿Qué más tendrás que hacer mañana?
7. ¿Qué harán tú y tus amigos el domingo?
8. ¿Adónde irás el verano próximo?

2. The conditional tense
El condicional

The conditional tense in Spanish is equivalent to the conditional in English, expressed by *would* + *verb*.[1] Like the future tense, the conditional uses the infinitive as the stem and has only one set of endings for all three conjugations.

---

[1] The imperfect, not the conditional, is used in Spanish as an equivalent of *used to:* **Cuando era pequeño siempre *iba* a la playa.** *When I was little **I would always go** to the beach.*

Regular conditional forms

The Conditional Tense			
Infinitive		*Stem*	*Endings*
trabajar	yo	trabajar-	**ía**
aprender	tú	aprender-	**ías**
escribir	Ud.	escribir-	**ía**
ir	él	ir-	**ía**
ser	ella	ser-	**ía**
dar	nosotros	dar-	**íamos**
servir	Uds.	servir-	**ían**
estar	ellos	estar-	**ían**
preferir	ellas	preferir-	**ían**

—¿**Vendería** Ud. su coche por cinco mil dólares?
—No, yo no lo **vendería** por ese precio. **Preferiría** regalárselo a mi hijo.

"Would you sell your car for five thousand dollars?"
"No, I wouldn't sell it at that price. I would prefer to give it (as a gift) to my son."

◆ The conditional is also used to express the future of a past action; that is, the conditional describes an event that in the past was perceived as occurring in the future.

—¿Qué te dijo el mecánico ayer?
—Me dijo que **revisaría** el motor.
—¿Te dijo cuánto te **cobraría?**
—No, pero me dijo que no **costaría** mucho.

"What did the mechanic tell you yesterday?"
"He told me that he would check the motor."
"Did he tell you how much he would charge you?"
"No, but he told me it wouldn't cost very much."

Práctica

Most people don't agree with Eduardo's ideas. Use the cues in parentheses to explain what the people named wouldn't do.

Modelo: Eduardo va a vender su coche. (yo)
   Yo no lo vendería.

1. Eduardo va a revisar el motor del coche. (tú)
2. Eduardo va a ponerle una batería nueva al coche (ellos)
3. Eduardo va a cobrar diez mil dólares por su coche. (Elsa)

4. Eduardo no va a regalarle el coche a su hija. (yo)
5. Eduardo va a comprar un coche nuevo por veinte mil dólares. (nosotros)
6. Eduardo va a trabajar en la agencia de alquiler de automóviles. (Uds.)

Irregular conditional forms

The same verbs that are irregular in the future are also irregular in the conditional. The conditional endings are added to the modified form of the infinitive.

Infinitive	Stem	Conditional Tense		
decir	dir–	yo	**dir–**	ía
hacer	har–	tú	**har–**	ías
saber	sabr–	Ud.	**sabr–**	ía
poder	podr–	ella	**podr–**	ía
poner	pondr–	nosotros	**pondr–**	íamos
venir	vendr–	Uds.	**vendr–**	ían
tener	tendr–	ellos	**tendr–**	ían
salir	saldr–	ellas	**saldr–**	ían

ATENCIÓN: The conditional of **hay** (from the verb **haber**) is **habría.**

—Mi coche no es automático. ¿Tú **podrías** manejarlo?

"My car is not automatic. Would you be able to drive it?"

—Sí, pero primero **tendría** que aprender a manejar coches de cambios mecánicos.

"Yes, but first I would have to learn to drive cars with a standard shift."

—Mi hijo quiere comprar una motocicleta.

"My son wants to buy a motorcycle."

—Yo le **diría** que las motocicletas son muy peligrosas.

"I would tell him that motorcycles are very dangerous."

—Voy a abrir una cuenta en el Banco Nacional.

"I'm going to open an account at the National Bank."

—Yo no **pondría** mi dinero en ese banco.

"I wouldn't put my money in that bank."

Práctica

A. Complete the following dialogues, using the conditional of the verbs in parentheses. Then act them out with a partner.

1. —¿A qué hora _____ (salir) Uds.?
   —No _____ (salir) hasta las ocho.
   —Pero, entonces Uds. no _____ (poder) llegar a la agencia a las ocho y media.
   —Bueno, entonces nosotros _____ (tener) que salir antes.

2. —Teresa va a venir en autobús.
   —Yo no _____ (hacer) eso. Yo _____ (venir) en coche.

3. —¿Tú _____ (saber) arreglar el coche?
   —No, yo _____ (tener) que llevarlo al mecánico. Él lo _____ (poder) revisar.

4. —Quiero comprar una moto. ¿Qué crees tú que me _____ (decir) mamá?
   —Probablemente te _____ (decir) que las motocicletas son muy peligrosas.

5. —¿Tú _____ (poder) vender tu coche por diez mil dólares?
   —No, yo no _____ (poder) cobrar tanto. Mi coche es automático, pero no es nuevo.

6. —¿En qué banco _____ (depositar) tú el dinero?
   —Yo lo _____ (poner) en el Banco de América. Allí tengo yo mi cuenta.

B. With a partner, take turns telling each other what you would do if you won a million dollars in the lottery. Say at least five things each, and then compare your responses with those of other classmates.

3. Some uses of the prepositions a, de, **and** en
Algunos usos de las preposiciones a, de y en

◆ The preposition **a** (*to*, *at*, *in*) is used in the following ways.

1. To introduce the direct object when it is a person,[1] animal, or anything that is given personal characteristics

Esperamos **a** la cajera.	*We're waiting for the cashier.*
Llevé **a** mi perro al veterinario.	*I took my dog to the vet.*

---

[1] When the direct object is not a definite person, the personal **a** is not used: **Busco un buen maestro.**

2. To indicate the time (hour) of day

El coche estará listo **a** las cinco.	*The car will be ready at five.*

3. To express destination or result after verbs of motion when they are followed by an infinitive, a noun, or a pronoun

Siempre venimos **a** alquilar coches aquí.	*We always come to rent cars here.*

4. After the verbs **enseñar, aprender, comenzar,** and **empezar** when they are followed by an infinitive

Voy a **empezar a** arreglar el carro.	*I'm going to start fixing the car.*
Él dijo que me **enseñaría a** manejar.	*He said that he would teach me how to drive.*

5. After the verb **llegar**

Llegaremos a Lima mañana sin falta.	*We will arrive in Lima tomorrow without fail.*

◆ The preposition **de** (*of, from, about*) is used in the following ways.

1. To refer to a specific time of the day or night

Dijeron que vendrían a las ocho **de** la noche.	*They said that they would come at eight in the evening.*

2. To distinguish one from a group when using superlatives

Mi sobrina es la más inteligente **de** la familia.	*My niece is the most intelligent in the family.*

3. To indicate possession or relationship

Carlos es el hijo **del** veterinario.	*Carlos is the vet's son.*
Ésta es la motocicleta **de** mi esposo.	*This is my husband's motorcycle.*

4. To indicate the material something is made of

El reloj es **de** plata.	*The watch is made of silver.*

5. To indicate origin

Ellos son **de** La Habana.	*They are from Havana.*

6. As a synonym of **sobre** or **acerca de** (*about*)

Hablaban **de** los precios de las casas.	*They were speaking about the prices of houses.*

◆ The preposition **en** (*at, in, on, inside, over*) is used in the following ways.

1. to refer to a definite place

Mi coche está **en** la gasolinera.	*My car is at the service station.*

2. To indicate means of transportation

Siempre viajábamos **en** autobús.	*We always travelled by bus.*

3. As a synonym of **sobre** (*on*)

Los libros están **en** la mesa.	*The books are on the table.*

Atención: In Mexico and in most Spanish-speaking countries of Latin America, **por** (*by*) is used with certain means of transportation, whereas **en** is used with other means.

Vamos por avión. (*or* Vamos **en** avión.)
Vamos **por** tren. (*or* Vamos **en** tren.)
but
Vamos **en** autobús.
Vamos **en** automóvil.
Vamos **en** motocicleta.

Práctica

Complete the following dialogues, using **a**, **de**, or **en** as appropriate. Then act them out with a partner.

1. —¿ _____ qué hora llegarán Uds. _____ la agencia _____ viajes?
   —Llegaremos _____ las ocho y media _____ la mañana sin falta.
2. —¿ _____ quién esperan Uds.?
   —Esperamos _____ la cajera.
   —¿Dónde está ella ahora?
   —Está _____ la oficina _____ la agencia.
3. —¿No trajiste _____ tu perro?
   —No, está enfermo. Lo llevé _____ la veterinaria ayer.

4. —¿Para qué fueron Uds. _____ la agencia?
   —Fuimos _____ alquilar un coche _____ cambios
   mecánicos.
   —¿Tú sabes manejar ese tipo de coche?
   —No, pero mi hermano me va _____ enseñar _____
   manejarlo.
5. —¿Quién es esa chica tan hermosa?
   —Es la hermana _____ Raúl. Es la chica más inteligente
   _____ la clase.
   —¿ _____ dónde es ella?
   —Creo que es _____ Perú.
6. —¿ _____ quién es el reloj que está _____ la mesa?
   —Es _____ Aurelio.
   —¿Es _____ plata?
   —No, es _____ oro blanco.
7. —¿ _____ qué estaban hablando Uds.?
   —Estábamos hablando _____ nuestras vacaciones.
   —¿Adónde fueron?
   —Fuimos _____ San Antonio.
   —¿Fueron _____ autobús?
   —No, fuimos _____ automóvil.
8. —¿Dónde está Teresa?
   —Está _____ el banco. Fue _____ cambiar un cheque.
   —¿Para qué necesitaba el dinero?
   —Para pagarle _____ mecánico que arregló el motor
   _____ su coche.

🔊 *En el laboratorio*

The following material is to be used with the tape in the language
laboratory.

I. *Vocabulario*

Repeat each word after the speaker. When repeating words that
are cognates, notice the difference in pronunciation between
English and Spanish.

COGNADOS:	automático el examen
	probablemente el veterinario

NOMBRES:	la agencia de alquiler de automóviles
	el cajero la cuenta la motocicleta
	la moto el motor el perro la plata
	el precio el tren

VERBOS:	alquilar cobrar depositar manejar revisar chequear
ADJETIVOS:	hermoso peligroso
OTRAS PALABRAS Y EXPRESIONES:	cambiar un cheque de cambios mecánicos después hasta sin falta

II. Práctica

A. Rephrase each sentence, using the future tense instead of the expression **ir a** + *infinitive*. Repeat the correct answer after the speaker's confirmation. Listen to the model.

> *Modelo:* Vamos a salir muy tarde.
> **Saldremos muy tarde.**

B. Answer the questions, always using the second choice. Repeat the correct answer after the speaker's confirmation. Listen to the model.

> *Modelo:* —¿Comprarías un coche o una casa?
> **—Compraría una casa.**

C. Answer the following questions in complete sentences, using the cues provided. Repeat the correct answer after the speaker's confirmation. Listen to the model.

> *Modelo:* —¿Cómo van ellos? (coche)
> **—Van en coche.**

1. (la cajera)
2. (las ocho)
3. (autobús)
4. (la mesa)
5. (las vacaciones)
6. (la agencia)
7. (Carlos)
8. (Sí)

III. Para escuchar y entender

1. Listen carefully to the dialogue. It will be read twice.

   (*Diálogo 1*)

   Now the speaker will make statements about the dialogue you just heard. Tell whether each statement is true (**verdadero**) or false (**falso**). The speaker will confirm the correct answer.

2. Listen carefully to the dialogue. It will be read twice.

   (*Diálogo 2*)

   Now the speaker will ask you some questions about the dialogue you just heard. Answer each question, omitting the subject. The speaker will confirm the correct answer. Repeat the correct answer.

LECCIONES 11–15

Lección 11   **A.** Time expressions with **hacer**

How would you say the following in Spanish?

1. "How long have you (*pl.*) been working in San Juan?"
   "We have been working in San Juan for five years."
2. "How long have they been waiting?"
   "They have been waiting for three hours."
3. "How long has she been studying Spanish?"
   "She has been studying Spanish for two years."

B. Irregular preterits

Rewrite the sentences, beginning with the expressions provided. Follow the model.

Modelo: Tenemos que salir. (Ayer)
   Ayer tuvimos que salir.

1. María no está en la clase. (Ayer)
2. No pueden venir. (Anoche)
3. Pongo el dinero en el banco. (El mes pasado)
4. No haces nada. (El domingo pasado)
5. Ella viene con Juan. (Ayer)
6. No queremos venir a clase. (El lunes pasado)
7. Yo no digo nada. (Anoche)
8. Traemos la tostadora. (Ayer)
9. Yo conduzco mi coche. (Anoche)
10. Ellos traducen las lecciones. (Ayer)

C. The imperfect tense

Answer the following questions using the model as a guide.

Modelo: —¿Qué querían ellos? (arroz con pollo)
   —Querían arroz con pollo.

1. ¿Dónde vivían Uds. cuando eran chicos? (en Alaska)
2. ¿Qué idioma hablabas tú cuando eras chico(a)? (inglés)
3. ¿A quién veías siempre cuando eras chico(a)? (a mi abuela)
4. ¿En qué banco ponían Uds. el dinero? (en el Banco de América)
5. ¿A qué hora se acostaban ellos? (a las nueve)

6. ¿Adónde iba Rosa? (a la universidad)
7. ¿Qué compraba Ud.? (arroz)
8. ¿Qué enseñaba Elsa? (español)

D. The affirmative familiar command (**tú** form)

Change the commands from the **Ud.** (*formal*) form to the **tú** (*informal*) form. Follow the model.

Modelo: Salga con los niños.
        Sal con los niños.

1. Venga acá, por favor.
2. Hable con la profesora.
3. Dígame su dirección.
4. Lávese las manos.
5. Póngase el abrigo.
6. Tráiganos el arroz con pollo.
7. Compre los libros.
8. Hágame un favor.
9. Apague la luz.
10. Vaya de compras hoy.
11. Salga temprano.
12. Aféitese aquí.
13. Tenga paciencia.
14. Sea buena.
15. Coma con nosotros.

E. The negative familiar command (**tú** form)

How would you say the following in Spanish?

1. Don't tell (it to) him.
2. Don't go out now.
3. Don't get up.
4. Don't bring the dessert now.
5. Don't drink coffee.
6. Don't talk to them.
7. Don't go to the store.
8. That dress? Don't put it on!
9. Don't do that.

F. Vocabulary

Complete the following sentences, using words learned in **Lección 11.**

1. Ayer fui de _____ porque necesitaba un vestido.
2. Ana, _____ la luz, por favor.

3. Los domingos nosotros siempre comíamos _____ con pollo.
4. No me gusta hacer los _____ de la casa.
5. Ayer hubo una gran _____ en Sears. Todo estaba muy barato.
6. En esa _____ nosotros vivíamos en La Habana.
7. Vamos a tomar un taxi porque ella no quiere _____.
8. Nosotros casi _____ comemos carne.
9. Yo como postre de vez en _____.
10. ¿Vas a salir otra _____?

Lección 12 **A.** The past progressive

Complete the sentences with the past progressive of **hacer, hablar, estudiar, comer, leer, trabajar, escribir,** or **comprar** as appropriate. Use each verb once.

1. Nosotros _____ arroz con pollo cuando llegó Elsa.
2. ¿Qué _____ tú cuando yo llamé?
3. Elena _____ a máquina cuando llegó el Dr. Vargas.
4. Yo _____ por teléfono (*on the phone*) con mi cuñado.
5. ¿Uds. _____ el reloj (*watch*) en la joyería?
6. Ud. _____ el periódico cuando yo vine.
7. Los niños _____ la lección.
8. Roberto _____ en la zapatería cuando yo lo vi.

B. The preterit contrasted with the imperfect

How would you say the following in Spanish?

1. We went to bed at eleven last night.
2. She was typing when I saw her.
3. We used to go to Lima every summer.
4. It was ten-thirty when I called my sister-in-law.
5. She said she wanted to read.

C. Changes in meaning with imperfect and preterit of **conocer, saber,** and **querer**

Complete the sentences with the preterit or the imperfect of the verbs **conocer, saber,** and **querer,** as appropriate.

1. Yo no _____ a los abuelos de María. Los _____ ayer.
2. Nosotros no _____ que ella era casada. Lo _____ anoche.
3. Mamá no fue a la fiesta porque no _____ ir.
4. Yo no _____ ir a la fiesta, pero cuando _____ que Carlos iba a ir, decidí ir también.

D. En and **a** as equivalents of *at*

Write sentences using the words provided with **en** or **a**, as appropriate. Follow the model.

Modelo: Yo / estar / universidad
       Yo estoy en la universidad.

1. Nosotros / llegar / aeropuerto / seis y media
2. Mi cuñada / estar / casa
3. Ellos / estar / joyería
4. La fiesta / ser / las doce
5. ¿Raúl / estar / clase?

E. Vocabulary

Complete the following sentences, using words learned in **Lección 12.**

1. Mi cuñada compró ayer un _____ de baño nuevo.
2. Ellos vieron el sombrero en el _____ de JC Penney.
3. No podemos irnos. Tenemos que _____ aquí _____ el día.
4. Necesito la _____ de escribir.
5. Voy a _____ con Rosa a las cinco.
6. El mes pasado fuimos de _____ a México.
7. No quiero ir sola. ¿Por qué no vamos _____ tú y yo?
8. Tengo que estar en el _____ a las ocho porque el avión sale a las ocho y media.
9. El esposo de mi hermana es mi _____.
10. Nos gusta ir al centro _____ a mirar _____.

A. The preterit of stem-changing verbs (**e:i** and **o:u**)   **Lección 13**

Rewrite the sentences, beginning with the expressions provided. Follow the model.

Modelo: Él no pide dinero. (Ayer)
       Ayer él no **pidió** dinero.

1. Ella elige el anillo de oro. (Ayer)
2. Marta no duerme bien. (Anoche)
3. No le pido nada. (Ayer)
4. Ella te miente. (La semana pasada)
5. Ellos sirven los refrescos. (El sábado pasado)
6. No lo repito. (Ayer)
7. Ella sigue estudiando. (Anoche)
8. Tú no consigues nada. (El lunes pasado)

B. The expression **acabar de**

Answer the following questions in the affirmative, using **acabar de** in your answer. Follow the model.

Modelo: —¿Ya estudió Juan la lección?
　　　　 —Sí, **acaba de estudiarla.**

1. ¿Ya encontraste el collar?
2. ¿Ya vendiste la casa?
3. ¿Ya compraron ellos las corbatas?
4. ¿Ya arreglaron Uds. la escalera mecánica?
5. ¿Ya llegaron los estudiantes?

C. Special construction with **gustar, doler,** and **hacer falta**

Complete the following sentences with the appropriate forms of **gustar, doler,** and **hacer falta.**

1. No _____ esas sortijas. Prefiero aquéllas.
2. ¿Qué _____, señora? ¿Un camisón?
3. A Marta _____ la cabeza. ¿Tienes aspirinas?
4. A nosotros no _____ dinero. No necesitamos comprar nada.
5. ¿ _____ a Ud. esta chaqueta, o prefiere la otra?
6. A Rodolfo _____ un traje. ¿Puedes comprárselo?
7. A mí _____ los pies (feet).
8. A nosotros no _____ caminar. ¿Podemos ir en coche?

D. **¿Qué?** and ¿**cuál**? used with **ser**

How would you say the following in Spanish?

1. What is a raincoat?
2. What is your address?
3. What is a library?
4. What is your telephone number?
5. What are his ideas about this?

E. Vocabulary

Complete the following sentences, using words learned in **Lección 13.**

1. Voy a tomar dos _____ porque me _____ la cabeza.
2. Ayer en el accidente _____ cuatro personas.
3. Ellos _____ de llegar.
4. Ayer no me _____ nada en la fiesta. Estuvo muy aburrida.
5. El anillo es de _____.

6. La escalera _____ no funciona.
7. Me voy a poner la _____ porque tengo frío.
8. Ella _____ un collar muy bonito ayer.
9. Otro nombre para anillo es _____.
10. Nos _____ de ellos en el aeropuerto.

A. Hace meaning *ago*   **Lección 14**

Write two sentences for each set of items. Follow the model.

Modelo: Un año / yo / conocer / él
    Hace un año que yo lo conocí.
    Yo lo conocí hace un año.

1. tres meses / nosotros / llegar / a California
2. dos horas / el chico / tomar / café
3. dos días / ellos / terminar / la lección
4. veinte años / ella / venir / a esta ciudad
5. dos días / tú / llenar / el tanque

B. The past participle

Complete the following chart.

Infinitive	Past Participle
1. trabajar	1. trabajado
2. recibir	2. _____
3. _____	3. vuelto
4. usar	4. _____
5. escribir	5. _____
6. _____	6. ido
7. aprender	7. _____
8. _____	8. abierto
9. cubrir	9. _____
10. comer	10. _____
11. _____	11. visto
12. hacer	12. _____
13. ser	13. _____
14. _____	14. dicho
15. cerrar	15. _____
16. _____	16. muerto
17. _____	17. roto
18. dormir	18. _____
19. estar	19. _____
20. _____	20. puesto

C. Past participles used as adjectives

How would you say the following in Spanish?

1. The book is written in English.
2. The window is broken.
3. The door is open.
4. Are the banks closed?
5. The table is covered.

D. The present perfect tense

Complete the sentences with the present perfect of **hablar, hacer, abrir, venir, decir, estudiar escribir, tener, poner, romper,** or **comer,** as appropriate. Use each verb once.

1. Yo _____ muchas veces a este lugar.
2. ¿_____ Uds. la lección?
3. Nosotros todavía no _____ con el mecánico.
4. Ella me _____ que tengo que venir el sábado y el domingo.
5. ¿No _____ (tú) las cartas todavía?
6. Hoy nosotros no _____ nada, porque no _____ tiempo.
7. ¿Quién _____ las puertas?
8. ¿Dónde _____ Ud. las sillas?
9. Elena y Carlos no _____ todavía.
10. Ellos _____ el parabrisas.

E. The past perfect (pluperfect) tense

How would you say the following in Spanish?

1. I had already brought the battery.
2. They had not called the clerk.
3. They had broken the windows.
4. He had already seen the professor.
5. Had you covered the tables, Miss Peña?

F. Vocabulary

Complete the following sentences, using words learned in **Lección 14.**

1. Voy a la estación de _____ porque necesito comprar _____.
2. Otro nombre para batería es _____.
3. Tengo que llenar el tanque porque está casi _____.
4. Tengo que cambiar la _____ porque está _____.
5. Voy a llamar al club _____ porque necesito una grúa.

6. ¿Qué _____ de aceite usa Ud.? ¿Penzoil?
7. ¿Cuánto tiempo _____ que Ud. llenó el tanque de su coche?
8. El coche no está listo todavía porque necesita varias piezas de _____.

A. The future tense

Complete the following sentences, using the future tense of the verb in parentheses.

1. ¿Cuándo _____ (ir) Uds. a la agencia de alquiler de automóviles?
2. El cajero _____ (venir) mañana a las ocho.
3. Ellos _____ (pagar) la cuenta el viernes.
4. ¿Tú _____ (llevar) al perro al veterinario?
5. El examen _____ (ser) mañana.
6. ¿Dónde _____ (poner) tú la moto?
7. Ellos _____ (manejar) mi coche.
8. El mecánico _____ (revisar) los frenos.
9. ¿Qué _____ (hacer) Uds. el domingo por la tarde?
10. Yo _____ (alquilar) un coche el próximo sábado.

B. The conditional tense

Complete the sentences with the conditional tense of **servir, poner, haber, trabajar, seguir, vender, levantarse, preferir,** or **ir.** Use each verb once.

1. Él dijo que nosotros _____ a Europa el verano próximo.
2. ¿Ellos _____ su casa a ese precio? Yo creo que sí.
3. ¿Dijo Ud. que no _____ clases esta tarde?
4. Yo no _____ el café en la terraza.
5. Tú no _____ en una gasolinera.
6. ¿_____ Ud. su dinero en ese banco?
7. ¿Qué _____ Uds., ir a México o ir a Guatemala?
8. ¿_____ Uds. estudiando español?
9. ¿_____ tú a las tres de la mañana?

C. Some uses of the prepositions **a, de,** and **en**

How would you say the following in Spanish?

1. We won't arrive at the university at six.
2. Did you take your dog to the vet, María?
3. Later we will travel by plane.
4. She's at the car rental agency.
5. What are they talking about?

D. Vocabulary

Complete the following sentences, using words learned in **Lección 15.**

1. Necesito alquilar un coche. Voy a la _____ de alquiler de automóviles.
2. Mi mamá dice que las motocicletas son muy _____.
3. Yo no sé manejar coches de cambios _____; sólo sé manejar coches _____.
4. Voy al banco para _____ cien dólares en mi cuenta.
5. Los aretes de Rosalía no son de oro; son de _____.
6. El mecánico va a _____ el motor del auto.
7. Mañana sin _____ voy a llevar a mi perro al veterinario.
8. El _____ de español fue muy difícil.

Lección

16

1. **The present subjunctive**
2. **The subjunctive with verbs of volition**
3. **The absolute superlative**

Vocabulario

NOMBRES
el asiento seat
el boleto[1] ticket
el descuento discount
la estación de trenes train
  station
el fin de semana weekend
el itinerario, el horario
  schedule
el rápido, el expreso
  express train

VERBOS
  aconsejar to advise
  buscar to look for, to
    pick up, to get
  esperar to hope
  mandar to order
  negar (e:ie) to deny
  recomendar (e:ie) to
    recommend

reservar to reserve
rogar (o:ue) to beg
sugerir (e:ie) to suggest

ADJETIVOS
  bello(a) beautiful
  bueno(a) kind
  difícil difficult
  largo(a) long
  lento(a) slow
  mareado(a) dizzy
  rápido(a) fast

**OTRAS PALABRAS Y
EXPRESIONES**
  cuanto antes as soon as
    possible
  por ciento per cent
  sumamente extremely

1. The present subjunctive
El presente de subjuntivo

Uses of the subjunctive

While the indicative mood is used to express events that are factual and definite, the subjunctive mood is used to refer to events or conditions that the speaker views as uncertain, unreal, or hypothetical. Since the subjunctive mood reflects feelings or attitudes towards events or conditions, certain expressions of volition, doubt, surprise, fear, and so forth are followed by the subjunctive.

Except for its use in main clauses to express commands, the Spanish subjunctive is most often used in subordinate or dependent clauses.

The subjunctive is also used in English, although not as often as in Spanish. For example:

I suggest that he arrive tomorrow.

[1] Used when traveling by train or by bus.

The expression that requires the use of the subjunctive is in the main clause, *I suggest*. The subjunctive appears in the subordinate clause, *that he arrive tomorrow*. The subjunctive mood is used because the action of arriving is not yet realized; it is only what is *suggested* that he do.

There are four major concepts that require the use of the subjunctive in Spanish.

1. *Volition:* demands, wishes, advice, persuasion, and other impositions of will

Ella **quiere** que yo **compre** los boletos.	*She wants me to buy the tickets.*
Te **aconsejo** que **vayas** en el rápido.	*I advise you to go on the express train.*
Deseo que **vengas** con nosotros.	*I want you to come with us.*

2. *Emotion:* pity, joy, fear, surprise, hope, regret, etc.

Espero que Uds. **puedan** venir.	*I hope that you can come.*
Siento mucho que Luisa **esté** mareada.	*I'm very sorry that Luisa is dizzy.*

3. *Doubt, disbelief,* and *denial:* uncertainty, negated facts

Dudo que nos **den** un diez por ciento de descuento.	*I doubt that they'll give us a ten percent discount.*
No es verdad que el horario **cambie** la próxima semana.	*It isn't true that the schedule is changing next week.*
Ella **niega** que Juan **sea** su novio.	*She denies that Juan is her boyfriend.*

4. *Unreality:* expectations, indefiniteness, nonexistence

Busco a **alguien** que **pueda** hacerlo.	*I'm looking for someone who can do it.*
¿Hay **alguien** en la clase que **hable** alemán?	*Is there anyone in the class who speaks German?*
No hay **nadie** aquí que **sepa** su dirección.	*There is nobody here who knows his address.*

Formation of the present subjunctive

The present subjunctive is formed by dropping the **-o** from the stem of the first person singular of the present indicative and adding the following endings.

The Present Subjunctive of Regular Verbs		
-ar *Verbs*	**-er** *Verbs*	**-ir** *Verbs*
trabajar	**comer**	**vivir**
trabaje	coma	viva
trabajes	comas	vivas
trabaje	coma	viva
trabajemos	comamos	vivamos
trabajen	coman	vivan

ATENCIÓN: Notice that the endings for **-er** and **-ir** verbs are the same.

The following table shows you how to form the first person singular of the present subjunctive from the infinitive of the verb.

Verb	First Person Singular (Indicative)	Stem	First Person Singular (Present Subjunctive)
habl**ar**	hablo	**habl-**	hable
aprend**er**	aprendo	**aprend-**	aprenda
escrib**ir**	escribo	**escrib-**	escriba
dec**ir**	digo	**dig-**	diga
hac**er**	hago	**hag-**	haga
tra**er**	traigo	**traig-**	traiga
ven**ir**	vengo	**veng-**	venga
conoc**er**	conozco	**conozc-**	conozca

Práctica

Give the present subjunctive of the following verbs.

1. **yo:** comer, venir, hablar, hacer, salir, ponerse
2. **tú:** decir, ver, traer, trabajar, escribir, conocer
3. **él:** vivir, aprender, salir, estudiar, levantarse, hacer
4. **nosotros:** escribir, caminar, poner, desear, tener, afeitarse
5. **ellos:** salir, hacer, llevar, conocer, ver, bañarse

Subjunctive forms of stem-changing verbs

Stem-changing **-ar** and **-er** verbs maintain the basic pattern of the present indicative. Their stems undergo the same changes in the present subjunctive.

recomendar *(to recommend)*		recordar *(to remember)*	
recomiende	recomendemos	recuerde	recordemos
recomiendes		recuerdes	
recomiende	recomienden	recuerde	recuerden

entender *(to understand)*		mover *(to move)*	
entienda	entendamos	mueva	movamos
entiendas		muevas	
entienda	entiendan	mueva	muevan

Stem-changing **-ir** verbs change the unstressed **e** to **i** and the unstressed **o** to **u** in the first person plural:

mentir *(to lie)*		dormir *(to sleep)*	
mienta	mintamos	duerma	durmamos
mientas		duermas	
mienta	mientan	duerma	duerman

Subjunctive forms of irregular verbs

dar	estar	saber	ser	ir
dé	esté	sepa	sea	vaya
des	estés	sepas	seas	vayas
dé	esté	sepa	sea	vaya
demos	estemos	sepamos	seamos	vayamos
den	estén	sepan	sean	vayan

◆ The subjunctive of **hay** (impersonal form of **haber**) is **haya.**

Práctica

Give the present subjunctive of the following verbs.

1. **yo:** dormir, mover, cerrar, sentir, ser
2. **tú:** mentir, volver, ir, dar, recordar
3. **ella:** estar, saber, perder, dormir, ser
4. **nosotros:** pensar, recordar, dar, morir, cerrar
5. **ellos:** ver, preferir, dar, ir, saber

2. The subjunctive with verbs of volition

El subjuntivo usado con verbos de deseo

All impositions of will, as well as indirect or implied commands, require the subjunctive in subordinate clauses. The subject in the main clause must be different from the subject in the subordinate clause.

◆ Some verbs of volition:

aconsejar	*to advise*	querer	
desear		recomendar	*to recommend*
mandar	*to order*	rogar	*to beg*
necesitar		sugerir	*to suggest*
pedir			

◆ Note the sentence structure for the use of the subjunctive in Spanish.

Yo quiero	que	*Ud.* estudie.
main clause		subordinate clause
I want		*you* to study.

—Quiero ir a Sevilla este fin de semana.
"*I want to go to Seville this weekend.*"

—Entonces **te aconsejo** que **compres** los boletos cuanto antes.
"*Then I advise you to buy the tickets as soon as possible.*"

—Sí, voy a **pedirle** a Ernesto que me **lleve** a la estación de trenes para comprarlos.
"*Yes, I'm going to ask Ernesto to take me to the train station to buy them.*"

—**Te sugiero** que **viajes** por la noche.
"*I suggest you travel at night.*"

—¿Por qué?
"*Why?*"

—Porque el tren de por la noche es más rápido.
"*Because the night train is faster.*"

—¿Qué quieren hacer Uds. hoy?
"*What do you want to do today?*"

—Queremos ir al aeropuerto para reservar los asientos para el vuelo del sábado.
"*We want to go to the airport to reserve the seats for the Saturday flight.*"

—Yo no puedo ir con Uds. porque mi hermano **quiere** que **vaya a** la estación a buscarle un itinerario.

"I can't go with you because my brother wants me to go to the station to get him a schedule."

ATENCIÓN: If there is no change of subject, the infinitive is used.

—¿Adónde quiere **ir** Ud.?
—Quiero **ir** a Sevilla.

Práctica

A. Change the following sentences according to the new beginnings.

> *Modelo:* Yo quiero buscar los libros. Yo quiero que tú...
> Yo quiero que tú **busques**[1] los libros.

1. Nosotros queremos comprar los boletos.
   Nosotros queremos que Uds....
2. Yo necesito reservar un asiento.
   Yo necesito que tú...
3. Ella desea ir a la estación de trenes.
   Ella desea que nosotros...
4. ¿Ud. quiere tomar el rápido?
   ¿Ud. quiere que ellos... ?
5. Mis padres desean conseguir un itinerario.
   Mis padres desean que yo...
6. Oscar necesita estar allí a las diez.
   Oscar necesita que Ud....
7. Carlos quiere ir a buscar a su hermana.
   Carlos quiere que Marta...

B. Use your imagination to complete the following sentences, using the infinitive or the subjunctive, as appropriate.

1. Yo le sugiero a mi amigo(a) que...
2. Ellos necesitan que tú...
3. Nosotros queremos...
4. Mis padres me ruegan que...
5. Yo necesito...
6. El (La) profesor(a) nos manda que...
7. Yo les recomiendo que...
8. Mi hermano(a) desea...
9. Yo te pido que...
10. Mi madre siempre me aconseja que...

---

[1] Verbs ending in -car change **c** to **qu** in the present subjunctive. For other verbs with orthographic changes, see Appendix B, p. 291.

C. With a partner, act out the following dialogues in Spanish.

1. "My friend needs the tickets."
   "I suggest that you give them to him as soon as possible, Anita."
2. "I need to be in Seville this afternoon."
   "I advise you to take the express train, miss."
3. "I'm dizzy."
   "Then I recommend that you lie down, Miss Vega."
4. "I want to go to the airport to reserve a seat."
   "Why don't you ask your friend to do it, Paquito?"
5. "I recommend that you travel during the weekend, sir."
   "Why?"
   "Because you can get a ten percent discount."

3. The absolute superlative
El superlativo absoluto

In Spanish, there are two ways of expressing a high degree of a given quality without comparing one person or thing to another.

♦ By modifying the adjective with an adverb **(muy, sumamente).**

—¿Cómo estuvo el vuelo?	*"How was the flight?"*
—Estuvo **muy** aburrido y fue **sumamente** largo.	*"It was very boring and extremely long."*

♦ By adding the suffix **-ísimo (-a, -os, -as)** to the adjective. This form is known as the absolute superlative. If the word ends in a vowel, the vowel is dropped before adding the suffix. Notice that the **í** of the suffix always has a written accent:

alt**o**	alt-	**ísimo**	alt**í**simo
ocupad**a**	ocupad-	**ísima**	ocupad**í**sima
lent**os**	lent-	**ísimos**	lent**í**simos
buen**as**	buen-	**ísimas**	buen**í**simas
difícil	dificil-	**ísimo**	dificil**í**simo

—¿Fuiste a Madrid el verano pasado?	*"Did you go to Madrid last summer?"*
—Sí, es una ciudad **bellísima,** pero es **dificilísimo** conducir allí.	*"Yes, it is a very beautiful city, but it is extremely difficult to drive there."*
—¿Pueden ir al aeropuerto con nosotros?	*"Can you go to the airport with us?"*
—No, estamos **ocupadísimas.**	*"No, we are extremely busy."*

Práctica

Change the underlined words in the following sentences to the absolute superlative.

1. Mi novia es <u>muy bella.</u>
2. Mi novio es <u>sumamente alto.</u>
3. Ellos están <u>muy ocupados.</u>
4. Es <u>muy fácil</u> llegar a la estación de trenes.
5. Ellas son <u>muy buenas.</u>
6. La cajera está <u>sumamente ocupada.</u>
7. Ellos son <u>muy lentos.</u>
8. Las clases son <u>sumamente difíciles</u> allí.
9. Ella está <u>sumamente mareada.</u>
10. El tren es <u>muy rápido.</u>

En el laboratorio

The following material is to be used with the tape in the language laboratory.

I. Vocabulario

Repeat each word after the speaker.

NOMBRES:	el asiento el boleto el descuento la estación de trenes el fin de semana el itinerario el horario el rápido el expreso
VERBOS:	aconsejar buscar esperar mandar negar recomendar reservar rogar sugerir
ADJETIVOS:	bello bueno difícil largo lento mareado rápido
OTRAS PALABRAS Y EXPRESIONES:	cuanto antes por ciento sumamente

II. Práctica

A. Say what Carmen wants everybody to do, using the present subjunctive and the cues provided. Repeat the correct answer after the speaker's confirmation. Listen to the model.

Modelo: ¿Qué quiere Carmen que yo haga? (reservar el asiento)
Quiere que Ud. reserve el asiento.

1. (comprar los boletos)
2. (ir a la estación de trenes)
3. (buscar el horario)
4. (darle un descuento)
5. (estar aquí a las dos)
6. (pedir un itinerario)
7. (viajar en el rápido)
8. (venir cuanto antes)
9. (cerrar la puerta)
10. (volver mañana)

B. Rephrase each sentence, changing **muy** + *adjective* to the absolute superlative. Repeat the correct answer after the speaker's confirmation. Listen to the model.

Modelo: Mi novio es muy alto.
Mi novio es altísimo.

III. Para escuchar y entender

1. Listen carefully to the narration. It will be read twice.

(*Narración*)

Now the speaker will make statements about the narration you just heard. Tell whether each statement is true (**verdadero**) or false (**falso**). The speaker will confirm the correct answer.

2. Listen carefully to the dialogue. It will be read twice.

(*Diálogo 1*)

Now the speaker will make statements about the dialogue you just heard. Tell whether each statement is true (**verdadero**) or false (**falso**). The speaker will confirm the correct answer.

3. Listen carefully to the dialogue. It will be read twice.

(*Diálogo 2*)

Now the speaker will ask you some questions about the dialogue you just heard. Answer each question, omitting the subject. The speaker will confirm the correct answer. Repeat the correct answer.

Lección

17

1. **The subjunctive to express emotion**
2. **The subjunctive with some impersonal expressions**
3. **Formation of adverbs**

Vocabulario

COGNADOS

la **calculadora** calculator
el **contrato** contract
  especial special
  general general
la **literatura** literature

necesario(a) necessary
posible possible
probable probable
reciente recent

NOMBRES
el (la) **abogado(a)** lawyer
la **beca** scholarship
la **conferencia** lecture
el (la) **consejero(a)** adviser
el **examen final** final exam
el **examen parcial**
  midterm exam
la **física** physics
la **matrícula** tuition
la **nota** grade
la **química** chemistry
el **requisito** requirement

VERBOS
  alegrarse (de) to be glad
  firmar to sign
  matricularse to register
  sentir (e:ie) to regret,
  to be sorry
  temer to fear
  terminar to finish

ADJETIVOS
claro(a) clear
cuidadoso(a) careful
fácil easy

OTRAS PALABRAS Y
EXPRESIONES
  conviene it is advisable
  es difícil it's unlikely
  es lástima it is a pity
  es mejor it is better
  es seguro it is certain
  ojalá if only . . . , I hope
  pronto soon
  puede ser it may be
  sacar una nota to get a
  grade

1. The subjunctive to express emotion

El subjuntivo para expresar emoción

In Spanish, the subjunctive is always used in a subordinate clause when the verb in the main clause expresses any kind of emotion, such as fear, joy, pity, hope, pleasure, surprise, anger, regret, and sorrow.

◆ Some verbs of emotion:

alegrarse (de) *to be glad*   **sentir (e:ie)** *to regret, to be sorry*

esperar *to hope*   **temer** *to fear*

—¿Vas a hablar con tu consejero hoy?
—Sí, y **espero** que me **diga** qué requisitos generales debo tomar.

"Are you going to talk with your adviser today?"
"Yes, and I hope he'll tell me what general requirements I have to take."

—¿Vas a tomar la clase de literatura española?
—Sí, ya me matriculé.
—**Me alegro** de que **podamos** tomarla juntos.

"Are you going to take the Spanish literature class?"
"Yes, I registered already."
"I'm glad that we can take it together."

—Mañana tengo dos exámenes parciales, uno en química y otro en física. **Temo** que mis notas no **sean** buenas.
—Entonces tienes que estudiar. **Siento** que no **puedas** ir con nosotros a la conferencia.

"Tomorrow I have two midterm exams, one in chemistry and the other in physics. I'm afraid that my grades won't be good."
"Then you have to study. I'm sorry that you can't go with us to the lecture."

ATENCIÓN: The subject of the subordinate clause must be different from that of the main clause for the subjunctive to be used. If there is no change of subject, the infinitive is used instead.

—¿Vas a terminar el trabajo para las cinco?
—Temo no **poder** terminarlo tan pronto.

"Are you going to finish the work by five?"
"I'm afraid I won't be able to finish it so soon."

—Tengo el examen final mañana.
—Espero que **saques** una buena nota.

"I have the final exam tomorrow."
"I hope that you get a good grade."

Práctica

A. Complete the dialogues, using the infinitive or the present subjunctive as appropriate. Then act them out with a partner.

1. —Temo no _____ (poder) ir a la conferencia con Uds.
   —Espero que tú _____ (poder) ir la semana que viene.

    2. —Esperamos _____ (sacar) una buena nota en el examen
       final.
      —Temo que Uds. no _____ (poder) estudiar mucho.
    3. —No puedo matricularme en la clase de literatura.
      —Siento que tú no _____ (tomar) la clase conmigo.
      —Yo también siento no _____ (poder) tomarla.
    4. —Jorge se alegra de no _____ (tener) que tomar la clase
       de física.
      —Espero que tampoco (él) _____ (tener) que tomar la de
       química.
    5. —Me alegro de _____ (ver) que has sacado una buena
       nota en literatura.
      —¡Espero _____ (poder) sacar una buena nota en química!

B. Use your imagination to complete the following sentences with
either the subjunctive or the infinitive, as appropriate.

    1. Yo espero que mi profesor(a)...
    2. Nosotros nos alegramos de...
    3. Yo temo...
    4. Siento que Uds...
    5. Ellos sienten no...
    6. Yo me alegro de que mis padres...
    7. Nosotros tememos que...
    8. Mis amigos se alegran de que...

2. The subjunctive with some impersonal expressions
El subjuntivo con algunas expresiones impersonales

In Spanish, some impersonal expressions that convey emotion,
uncertainty, unreality, or an indirect or implied command are followed by a verb in the subjunctive. This occurs only when the verb
of the subordinate clause has an expressed subject. The most common impersonal expressions include the following.

conviene *it is advisable*	**es mejor** *it is better*
es difícil *it is unlikely*	**es necesario** *it is necessary*
es importante *it is important*	**ojalá** *if only . . . ! or I hope . . .*
es (im)posible *it is (im)possible*	**puede ser** *it may be*
es lástima *it is a pity*	

—¿Crees que va a llover
mañana?

"*Do you think it's going to
rain tomorrow?*"

—**Ojalá** que no **llueva**
porque **es posible** que
Enrique me **lleve** al
partido de tenis.

"*I hope it won't rain, because
it's possible that Enrique will
take me to the tennis
match.*"

—¿Viene hoy el abogado?

"*Is the lawyer coming today?*"

—**Es difícil** que **venga** hoy.

"*It is unlikely that he'll come
today.*"

—¿Cuándo quiere Ud. que
yo escriba las cartas?

"*When do you want me to
write the letters?*"

—**Es importante** que las
escriba hoy.

"*It is important that you
write them today.*"

—¿Cuándo quiere Ud. que
los estudiantes tomen el
examen?

"*When do you want the
students to take the exam?*"

—**Es mejor** que lo **tomen**
en seguida.

"*It is better that they take
it right away.*"

—**Es lástima** que Ud. no
pueda conseguir una beca.

"*It is a pity that you can't get
a scholarship.*"

—Sí, porque yo no tengo
dinero para pagar la
matrícula.

"*Yes, because I don't have
money to pay the tuition.*"

—¿Cuándo tengo que
matricularme?

"*When do I have to register?*"

—**Es necesario** que **se
matricule** hoy.

"*It is necessary that you
register today.*"

ATENCIÓN: When the impersonal expression implies certainty, the
indicative is used.

—¿Vienen ellos hoy?

"*Are they coming today?*"

—Sí, **es seguro** que **vienen**
hoy.

"*Yes, it is certain that they'll
come today.*"

When a sentence is completely impersonal (that is, when no
subject is stated), the expressions on page 236 are followed by the
infinitive.

—¿Cuándo vamos a firmar
el contrato?

"*When are we going to sign
the contract?*"

—**Conviene firmarlo** esta
semana.

"*It is advisable to sign it
this week.*"

Práctica

A. Complete the following sentences using the infinitive, the indicative, or the subjunctive.

1. Conviene que Uds. _____ (tomar) los requisitos ahora.
2. Es imposible _____ (matricularse) a esta hora.
3. Es mejor que ellos no _____ (ir) a la conferencia.
4. Ojalá que el consejero _____ (venir) pronto.
5. Es seguro que la profesora nos _____ (dar) un examen parcial hoy.
6. Es difícil que él _____ (conseguir) una beca.
7. Es seguro que la abogada _____ (tener) el contrato.
8. Es importante _____ (ir) a la conferencia de hoy.

B. With a partner, act out the following dialogues in Spanish.

1. "I don't know what classes to take . . ."
   "It's advisable to take the general requirements first."
2. "Will the lawyer be here today?"
   "It's unlikely that he'll come today."
3. "It's a pity that Marta can't pay the tuition."
   "I hope that she gets a scholarship."
4. "Do you think it's necessary to see the adviser?"
   "Yes, it's very important to speak with her."
5. "It may be that they'll sign the contract tomorrow."
   "I hope their lawyer can be there."

3. Formation of adverbs
Formación de adverbios

> **Adverb** a word that modifies a verb, an adjective, or another adverb. It answers the questions "How?", "When?", "Where?": She walked **slowly.** She'll be here **tomorrow.** She is **here.**

Most Spanish adverbs are formed by adding **-mente** (the equivalent of *-ly* in English) to the adjective.

especial *special*	especial**mente** *specially, especially*
reciente *recent*	reciente**mente** *recently*
probable *probable*	probable**mente** *probably*
general *general*	general**mente** *generally*

◆ If the adjective ends in **-o,** the ending changes to **-a** before adding **-mente.**

lent**o** *slow*	lent**amente** *slowly*
rápid**o** *rapid*	rápid**amente** *rapidly*
clar**o** *clear*	clar**amente** *clearly*

◆ If two or more adverbs are used together, both change the **-o** to **-a,** but only the last adverb takes the **-mente** ending.

lent**a** y cuidados**amente**   *slowly and carefully*

◆ If the adjective has a written accent mark, the corresponding adverb retains it.

fácil   fácilmente

—Traje esta calculadora **especialmente** para Ud.
—Gracias.

"I brought this calculator especially for you."
"Thanks."

—El niño escribe la carta **lenta** y **cuidadosamente.**
—¡Pero la escribe muy bien!

"The child is writing the letter slowly and carefully."
"But he is writing it very well!"

Práctica

A. Complete the following sentences, using appropriate adverbs.

1. Ella habló _____ y _____, pero no la entendí.
2. _____ ellos van a tomar el examen hoy.
3. _____ estudio por la noche.
4. Compré una calculadora _____.
5. Ellos caminan _____.
6. Trajo los libros de literatura _____ para mí.
7. Ellos escriben _____.

B. How would you say the following sentences in Spanish?

1. She reads slowly.
2. Do it carefully, Miss Peña.
3. The chair is especially for you, sir.
4. She is going to do it rapidly, but carefully.
5. When did you see it, ma'am? Recently?
6. The lesson? We can translate it easily.

🔲 *En el laboratorio*

The following material is to be used with the tape in the language laboratory.

I. *Vocabulario*

Repeat each word after the speaker. When repeating words that are cognates, notice the difference in pronunciation between English and Spanish.

COGNADOS:	la calculadora el contrato especial general la literatura necesario posible probable reciente
NOMBRES:	el abogado la beca la conferencia el consejero el examen final el examen parcial la física la matrícula la nota la química el requisito
VERBOS:	alegrarse de firmar matricularse sentir temer terminar
ADJETIVOS:	claro cuidadoso fácil
OTRAS PALABRAS Y EXPRESIONES:	conviene es difícil es lástima es mejor es seguro ojalá pronto puede ser sacar una nota

II. *Práctica*

A. Restate each of the following sentences, inserting the cue at the beginning and making any necessary changes. Repeat the correct answer after the speaker's confirmation. Listen to the model.

Modelo: El cliente firma el contrato. (Espero)
> **Espero que el cliente firme el contrato.**

1. (Temo)
2. (Espero)
3. (Siento)
4. (Temo)
5. (Me alegro)
6. (Espero)
7. (Espero)
8. (Me alegro)

B. Restate each of the following sentences, inserting the cue at the beginning and making any necessary changes. Repeat the correct answer after the speaker's confirmation. Listen to the model.

Modelo: Él conduce muy rápido. (Es difícil)
         Es difícil que él conduzca muy rápido.

1. (No conviene)
2. (Es necesario)
3. (Es imposible)
4. (Es mejor)
5. (Puede ser)
6. (Ojalá)
7. (Es lástima)
8. (Es importante)

C. Give the adverb that corresponds to each adjective. Repeat the correct answer after the speaker's confirmation. Listen to the model.

Modelo: especial
         especialmente

III. Para escuchar y entender

1. Listen carefully to the dialogue. It will be read twice.

(Diálogo 1)

Now the speaker will make statements about the dialogue you just heard. Tell whether each statement is true **(verdadero)** or false **(falso).** The speaker will confirm the correct answer.

2. Listen carefully to the dialogue. It will be read twice.

(Diálogo 2)

Now the speaker will make statements about the dialogue you just heard. Tell whether each statement is true **(verdadero)** or false **(falso).** The speaker will confirm the correct answer.

3. Listen carefully to the dialogue. It will be read twice.

(Diálogo 2)

Now the speaker will ask you some questions about the dialogue you just heard. Answer each question, omitting the subject. The speaker will confirm the correct answer. Repeat the correct answer.

1. **The subjunctive to express doubt, disbelief, and denial**
2. **The subjunctive to express indefiniteness and nonexistence**
3. **Diminutive suffixes**

Vocabulario

la ambulancia ambulance	**la emergencia** emergency
el (la) dentista dentist	**el (la) paramédico(a)** paramedic

NOMBRES
el árbol tree
el consultorio doctor's office
el dolor pain
la inyección shot, injection
la muleta crutch
el (la) paciente patient
la pierna leg
la radiografía X-ray
la sala ward room
la sala de emergencia emergency room
la sala de rayos X X-ray room
el tobillo ankle

VERBOS
cuidar to take care
dudar to doubt

enyesar to put a cast on
fracturarse, romperse to break (a bone)

ADJETIVOS
seguro(a) sure

OTRAS PALABRAS Y EXPRESIONES
en este momento at this moment
poner una inyección to give a shot
todos los días everyday

1. The subjunctive to express doubt, disbelief, and denial
El subjuntivo para expresar duda, incredulidad y negación

In Spanish, the subjunctive mood is always used in a subordinate clause when the main clause expresses doubt, uncertainty, or disbelief.

◆ Doubt or uncertainty

—Necesito hablar con el médico.
—**Dudo** que él **esté** en su consultorio hoy, y **no estoy seguro** de que **pueda** verla mañana.

"I need to speak with the doctor."
"I doubt that he is in his office today, and I'm not sure that he can see you tomorrow."

—¿Puedes llevar a Teresa a la
sala de emergencia? **Dudo**
que **sea** necesario llamar
una ambulancia.
—Sí, la llevo en seguida.

*"Can you take Teresa to the
emergency room? I doubt that
it's necessary to call an
ambulance."*
"Yes, I'll take her right away."

ATENCIÓN: In the affirmative, the verb **dudar** *(to doubt)* takes the
subjunctive in the subordinate clause even when there is no
change of subject.

—¿Puedes ir conmigo al
médico?
—**(Yo) dudo** que **(yo) pueda**
ir contigo hoy.

*"Can you go to the doctor
with me?"*
*"I doubt that I can go with
you today."*

When the speaker expresses no doubt and is certain of the real-
ity, the indicative is used.

—¿Llamaron a los
paramédicos?
—Sí, y **no dudo** que
vienen en seguida.

"Did they call the paramedics?"

*"Yes, and I don't doubt that
they will come right away."*

—¿**Está** Ud. **seguro** de que
él **tiene** que usar muletas?
—Sí, se rompió la pierna[1]
ayer.

*"Are you sure that he has to
use crutches?"*
*"Yes, he broke his leg
yesterday."*

◆   Disbelief

The verb **creer** *(to believe, to think)* is followed by the subjunctive when used in negative sentences in which it expresses
disbelief.

—Carlos dice que lo van a
llevar a la sala de rayos X.

—¿Para qué? **No creo** que él
necesite una radiografía.

*"Carlos says that they are going
to take him to the X-ray
room."*
*"What for? I don't think he
needs an X-ray."*

Creer is followed by the indicative in affirmative sentences in
which it expresses belief.

—¿Enrique se fracturó el
tobillo?[1]
—Sí, y **creo** que **tienen** que
enyesárselo.

"Did Enrique break his ankle?"

*"Yes, and I think they have to
put it in a cast."*

---

[1] Note that the definite article, rather than the possessive adjective, is used in Spanish
with parts of the body.

◆ Denial

When the main clause denies what is said in the subordinate clause, the subjunctive is used.

—Dicen que esa dentista
  tiene unos mil pacientes.
—**Es verdad** que **tiene**
  muchos pacientes, pero
  no es verdad que **tenga**
  mil.

"They say that dentist has
about a thousand patients."
"It's true that she has many
patients, but it's not true
that she has a thousand."

ATENCIÓN: When the clause confirms rather than denies what is said in the subordinate clause, the indicative is used. **Es verdad** que **tiene** muchos pacientes.

Práctica

A. Complete the following dialogues, using the present indicative or the present subjunctive of the verbs in parentheses. Then act them out with a partner.

1. —¿Tus padres pueden llevarme al hospital?
   —Estoy seguro de que _____ (poder) llevarte, pero dudo que _____ (ir) ahora.
2. —¿Tú crees que voy a necesitar usar muletas?
   —Creo que _____ (tener) que usarlas, pero no creo que las _____ (necesitar) por más de tres semanas.
3. —¿Adónde llevaron a Marta?
   —Creo que _____ (estar) en la sala de emergencia.
4. —Roberto se rompió una pierna.
   —Sí, y estoy seguro de que el médico _____ (tener) que enyesársela.
5. —Yo creo que Antonio _____ (ser) paramédico y _____ (manejar) una ambulancia.
   —Es verdad que _____ (manejar) una ambulancia, pero no es verdad que _____ (ser) paramédico.

B. Use your imagination to complete the following sentences with either the subjunctive or the indicative, as appropriate.

1. Yo estoy seguro de que mis padres…
2. Dudo que la casa del profesor…
3. Es verdad que yo…
4. No estoy seguro de que mi amigo…
5. No es verdad que mi familia…
6. No creo que mi nota en esta clase…
7. No dudo que mis amigos…
8. Creo que el profesor…

2. The subjunctive to express indefiniteness and nonexistence
El subjuntivo para expresar lo indefinido y lo no existente

The subjunctive is always used when a subordinate clause refers to someone or something that is indefinite, unspecified, or nonexistent.

—Ellos **buscan una** enfermera que **pueda** cuidar al paciente en su casa.	*"They are looking for a nurse who can take care of the patient in his home."*
—No conozco a **ninguna** enfermera que **quiera** hacer eso.	*"I don't know any nurse who wants to do that."*
—¿**Hay alguien** aquí que **pueda** ponerme una inyección ahora mismo? Tengo mucho dolor.	*"Is there anyone here who can give me a shot right now? I have a lot of pain."*
—No, porque todos están ocupados en este momento.	*"No, because everybody is busy at this moment."*

ATENCIÓN: If the subordinate clause refers to existent, definite, or specific persons or things, the indicative is used.

Conozco a una enfermera que **puede** cuidar al paciente en su casa. **Hay alguien** aquí que **puede** ponerme una inyección ahora mismo.

Práctica

A. Complete the following dialogues, using the present subjunctive or the present indicative of the verbs in parentheses. Then act them out with a partner.

1. —¿Hay alguna enfermera que no _____ (estar) ocupada en este momento?
   —Sí, hay una en el consultorio del Dr. Vargas que no _____ (estar) ocupada ahora.
2. —Necesito a alguien que _____ (poder) cuidar a los niños.
   —Yo conozco a una señora que _____ (cuidar) niños en su casa.
3. —Daniel se fracturó el tobillo y necesitamos llevarlo al hospital. ¿Hay alguien aquí que _____ (tener) coche?
   —Sí, aquí hay varias personas que _____ (tener) coche.

4. —¿Hay alguien que _____ (saber) dónde están las ra-
diografías del Sr. Rojas?
—Sí, están en la sala de rayos X.
5. —Yo necesito ponerme una inyección todos los días.
¿Conoces a alguien que _____ (poder) enseñarme a
hacerlo?
—No, no conozco a nadie que _____ (poder) enseñarte.
6. —¿Qué buscan ellos?
—Buscan un médico que no _____ (tener) muchos
pacientes.
7. —¿Conoces a algún dentista que _____ (ser) bueno y que
_____ (trabajar) los sábados?
—Sí, el Dr. Rodríguez _____ (ser) muy bueno y _____
(trabajar) los sábados.

B. Use your imagination to complete the following sentences with
either the subjunctive or the indicative, as appropriate.

1. Yo quiero una casa que...
2. No hay ningún restaurante que...
3. En mi familia no hay nadie que...
4. Yo vivo en una casa que...
5. Conozco a una chica (un chico) que...
6. En mi clase de español hay muchos estudiantes que...
7. En la ciudad donde yo vivo hay muchos restaurantes que...
8. Yo no conozco a nadie que...

3. Diminutive suffixes
Los sufijos diminutivos

To express the idea of small size, and also to denote affection, special suffixes are used in Spanish. The most common suffixes are
-ito(a) and **-cito(a).** There are no set rules for forming the diminutive, but usually if the word ends in **-a** or **-o,** the vowel is dropped
and **-ito(a)** is added.

niño	niñ + **ito** =	**niñito**	(little boy)
niña	niñ + **ita** =	**niñita**	(little girl)
abuelo	abuel + **ito** =	**abuelito**	(grandpa)
Ana	An + **ita** =	**Anita**	(Annie)

◆ If the word ends in a consonant other than **-n** or **-r,** the suffix
-ito(a) is added.

árbol + **ito** =	**arbolito**	(little tree)
Luis + **ito** =	**Luisito**	(Louie)

◆ If the word ends in **-e, -n,** or **-r,** the suffix **-cito(a)** is added.

coche   + **cito** =   **cochecito**   *(little car)*
mujer   + **cita** =   **mujercita**   *(little woman)*
Carmen + **cita** =   **Carmencita**   *(Carmen)*

—Hola, **abuelito.** ¿Me   "*Hello, grandpa. Did you*
  trajiste el **arbolito** de   *bring me the little*
  Navidad?   *Christmas tree?*"
—Sí, **Tomasito.**   "*Yes, Tommy.*"

—Me gusta tu **cochecito.**   "*I like your little car.*"
—Gracias, **Carmencita.**   "*Thanks, Carmen.*"

Práctica

Give the diminutive form of each of the following words.

1. primo   6. hermana
2. escuela   7. dolor
3. árbol   8. Juan
4. Raúl   9. Adela
5. coche   10. mamá

📼 *En el laboratorio*

The following material is to be used with the tape in the language laboratory.

I. Vocabulario

Repeat each word after the speaker. When repeating words that are cognates, notice the difference in pronunciation between English and Spanish.

COGNADOS: la ambulancia   el dentista
                 la emergencia   el paramédico

NOMBRES: el árbol   el consultorio   el dolor
                 la inyección   la muleta   el paciente
                 la pierna   la radiografía   la sala
                 la sala de emergencia
                 la sala de rayos X   el tobillo

VERBOS: cuidar   dudar   enyesar   fracturarse
                 romperse

ADJETIVO: seguro

OTRAS PALABRAS   en este momento   poner una inyección
Y EXPRESIONES: todos los días

II. Práctica

A. Restate each of the following sentences, inserting the cue at the beginning and making any necessary changes. Repeat the correct answer after the speaker's confirmation. Listen to the model.

Modelo: No dudo que el médico viene hoy. (Dudo)
Dudo que el médico venga hoy.

1. (No estoy seguro)	6. (Hay alguien)
2. (No creo)	7. (Creen)
3. (Es verdad)	8. (Estamos seguros)
4. (Tememos)	9. (No hay nadie)
5. (Necesito)	10. (No es verdad)

B. The speaker will say some nouns. Change each one to the dimunitive form.

III. Para escuchar y entender

1. Listen carefully to the narration. It will be read twice.

(Narración 1)

Now the speaker will make statements about the narration you just heard. Tell whether each statement is true **(verdadero)** or false **(falso).** The speaker will confirm the correct answer.

2. Listen carefully to the dialogue. It will be read twice.

(Diálogo)

Now the speaker will make statements about the dialogue you just heard. Tell whether each statement is true **(verdadero)** or false **(falso).** The speaker will confirm the correct answer.

3. Listen carefully to the narration. It will be read twice.

(Narración 2)

Now the speaker will ask you some questions about the narration you just heard. Answer each question, omitting the subject. The speaker will confirm the correct answer. Repeat the correct answer.

Lección

19

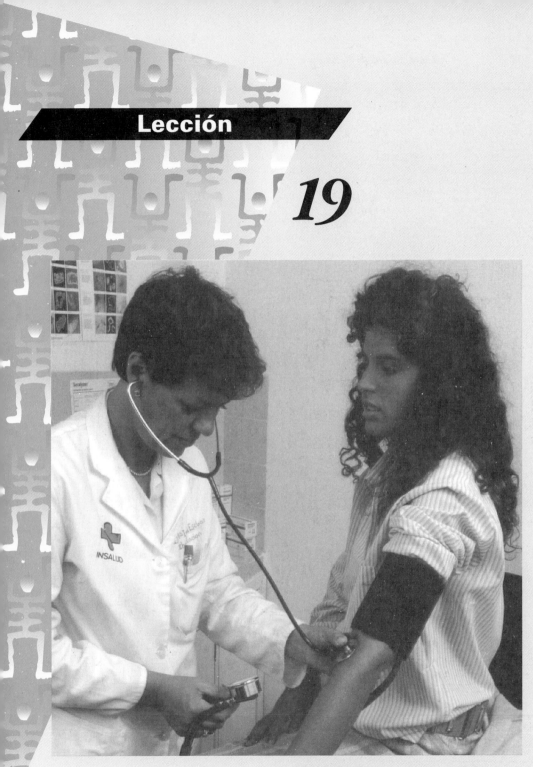

1. The subjunctive after certain conjunctions
2. The present perfect subjunctive
3. Uses of the present perfect subjunctive

Vocabulario

COGNADOS

horrible horrible	**el testamento** testament,
el resultado result	will
el termómetro	
thermometer	

NOMBRES
el análisis test
la autopista freeway
el (la) ayudante assistant
el (la) cirujano(a) surgeon
la fiebre fever, temperature
el jarabe syrup
el (la) oculista eye doctor
la operación, la cirugía
  surgery
el (la) pasajero(a) passenger
la pastilla pill
el peso weight

VERBOS
  bajar to go down, to
  decrease

chocar to collide
sobrevivir to survive

OTRAS PALABRAS Y
EXPRESIONES
  a menos que unless
  antes de que before
  en caso de que in case
  en cuanto, tan pronto
  como as soon as
  hacer ejercicio to exercise
  hasta que until
  para que in order that
  ponerse a dieta to go on
  a diet
  sin que without

1. The subjunctive after certain conjunctions

El subjuntivo después de ciertas conjunciones

The subjunctive is used after conjunctions of time when the main clause refers to the future or is a command.

◆ Some conjunctions of time.

tan pronto como	*as soon as*
en cuanto	*as soon as*
hasta que	*until*
cuando	*when*

—Eva, ¿cuándo va a llamarte
  el doctor?
—Me llamará **tan pronto
  como sepa** el resultado
  de los análisis.

*"Eva, when is the doctor going
  to call you?"*
*"He will call me as soon as he
  finds out the results of the
  tests."*

—Carlos, ¿a qué hora van a
empezar la operación?

"Carlos, at what time are
they going to begin the
surgery?"

—La van a empezar **en**
cuanto llegue el ayudante
de la cirujana.

"They're going to begin it
as soon as the surgeon's
assistant arrives."

—Tomás, ¿cuándo vamos a
salir para el hospital?

"Tomás, when are we going
to leave for the hospital?"

—No podemos salir **hasta**
que el carro **esté**
arreglado.

"We can't leave until the car
is fixed."

—**Cuando llegue** Marta,
dígale que **compre** el
jarabe y un termómetro.

"When Marta arrives, tell
her to buy the syrup and a
thermometer."

—Muy bien. Se lo diré
cuando venga.

"Very well. I'll tell her when
she comes."

ATENCIÓN: If the action already happened or if there is no indica-
tion of a future action, the indicative is used after the conjunction of time.

—¿A qué hora van a empezar
la operación?

"At what time are they going
to begin the surgery?"

—Siempre empiezan **en**
cuanto llegan los
cirujanos.

"They always begin as soon
as the surgeons arrive."

—¿Qué haces con el niño
cuando tú tienes que
trabajar?

"What do you do with the
child when you have to
work?"

—**Cuando** yo **trabajo,** mi
mamá viene a cuidarlo.

"When I work, my mother
comes to take care of him."

◆ There are certain conjunctions that, by their very meaning,
imply uncertainty or conditional fulfillment; they are therefore
always followed by the subjunctive. Here are some of them.

a menos que	*unless*	**en caso de que**	*in case*
antes de que	*before*	**para que**	*in order that*
con tal que	*provided that*	**sin que**	*without*

—¿Va Ud. a firmar el
testamento hoy?

"Are you going to sign the
will today?"

—No puedo firmarlo **sin**
que mi abogado lo **lea.**

"I can't sign it without my
lawyer reading it."

—¿Vas a tomar las pastillas esta noche?	*"Are you going to take the pills tonight?"*
—Sí, voy a tomarlas **a menos que** me **baje** la fiebre.	*"Yes, I'm going to take them unless the fever goes down."*

Práctica

A. Complete the following dialogues, using the present indicative or the present subjunctive of the verbs in parentheses. Then act them out with a partner.

1. —¿Cuándo vas a volver a la oficina?
   —En cuanto me _____ (bajar) la fiebre y me _____ (sentir) mejor.
2. —¿Cuándo te va a llamar Jorge?
   —No me va a llamar hasta que el doctor le _____ (dar) el resultado de los análisis.
3. —¿Qué vas a hacer?
   —Voy a llamar a Tito para que me _____ (traer) el jarabe cuando _____ (venir) esta tarde.
4. —Todos los días, yo llamo a mamá tan pronto como _____ (llegar) a casa.
   —Cuando (tú) la _____ (llamar) hoy, dile que me mande las pastillas.
5. —¿Vas a comprar el termómetro?
   —No puedo comprarlo a menos que tú me _____ (llevar) a la farmacia.
6. —¿Te vas a ir de vacaciones?
   —No puedo irme antes de que el cirujano _____ (decidir) si necesito la operación o no.
   —Yo puedo quedarme contigo en caso de que (tú) me _____ (necesitar).
7. —¿Por qué tomas estas pastillas?
   —Porque son muy buenas. Siempre me siento mejor en cuanto las _____ (tomar).
8. —Tengo que salir de casa sin que los niños me _____ (ver).
   —Sí, porque cuando tú _____ (irse), ellos siempre lloran (*cry*).

B. Use your imagination to complete the following sentences with the present indicative or the present subjunctive, as appropriate.

1. No te bajará la fiebre a menos que...
2. El cirujano va a comenzar la operación en cuanto...
3. Ella siempre me llama tan pronto como...
4. Todas las noches lo espero hasta que...

5. Voy a limpiar la casa en caso de que…
6. Carlos siempre llama a su abogado cuando…
7. No puedo ir al hospital antes de que…
8. No puedo comprarte el jarabe sin que tú…

2. The present perfect subjunctive
El pretérito perfecto de subjuntivo

The present perfect subjunctive is formed with the present subjunctive of the auxiliary verb **haber** and the past participle of the main verb.

The Present Perfect Subjunctive		
Present Subjunctive of haber	**+**	*Past Participle of the Main Verb*
yo	**haya**	**hablado**
tú	**hayas**	**comido**
Ud. él ella	**haya**	**vivido**
nosotros	**hayamos**	**hecho**
Uds. ellos ellas	**hayan**	**puesto**

Práctica

Conjugate the following verbs in the present perfect subjunctive for each subject given.

1. **yo:** hacer, venir, comer, levantarse
2. **tú:** trabajar, poner, decir, acostarse
3. **ella:** escribir, cerrar, abrir, sentarse
4. **nosotros:** romper, hablar, llegar, vestirse
5. **ellos:** morir, vender, alquilar, bañarse

3. Uses of the present perfect subjunctive
Usos del pretérito perfecto de subjuntivo

The present perfect subjunctive is used in the same way as the present perfect tense in English, but only in sentences that require the subjunctive in the subordinate clause. It describes events that have ended prior to the time indicated in the main clause.

—¿Ya han pagado Uds. la cuenta del oculista?

"Have you already paid the eye doctor's bill?"

—No recuerdo... no, **no creo** que la **hayamos pagado** todavía.

"I don't remember . . . No, I don't think we've paid it yet."

—Hubo un accidente en la autopista. Chocaron dos autobuses, y **temo** que **hayan muerto** todos los pasajeros.

"There was an accident on the freeway. Two buses collided and I fear that all the passengers (have) died."

—¡Qué horrible![1] **Ojalá** que algunos **hayan sobrevivido.**

"How horrible! I hope that some (of them) (have) survived."

—Inés se ha puesto a dieta.

"Inés has gone on a diet."

—Sí, pero **no creo** que **haya perdido** mucho peso porque nunca hace ejercicio.

"Yes, but I don't think she has lost a lot of weight because she never exercises."

Práctica

A. Complete the following dialogues, using the present perfect subjunctive. Then act them out with a partner.

1. —¿Crees que el cirujano ha terminado ya la operación?
   —No, no creo que la _____ (terminar).
2. —Dicen que Mario se ha puesto a dieta.
   —Dudo que se _____ (poner) a dieta, porque él no necesita perder peso. Además, él siempre hace ejercicio.
3. —Ha habido *(There has been)* un accidente en la autopista. Chocaron un ómnibus y un coche.
   —Ojalá que no _____ (morir) nadie.
   —Temo que los pasajeros del coche no _____ (sobrevivir).
   —¡Qué horrible!
4. —Gloria ha ido a la oculista.
   —Me alegro de que _____ (decidir) ir, porque no ve muy bien.
5. —¿Hay alguien aquí que _____ (estar) en México este verano?
   —No, aquí no hay nadie que _____ (ir) a México.
6. —¿El Sr. Vega ya ha hecho el testamento?
   —No, no creo que lo _____ (hacer) todavía.

[1] The Spanish equivalent of *how* + adjective is **qué** + adjective.

B. Use your imagination to complete the following sentences, using the present perfect subjunctive.

1. Yo me alegro de que mis padres…
2. Ojalá que tú…
3. Yo no creo que mi médico…
4. Mi familia espera que yo…
5. El (La) profesor(a) espera que nosotros…
6. Yo siento que Uds.…
7. En mi familia no hay nadie que…
8. Yo dudo que mi hermano(a)…

🔲 *En el laboratorio*

The following material is to be used with the tape in the language laboratory.

I. *Vocabulario*

Repeat each word after the speaker. When repeating words that are cognates, notice the different in pronunciation between English and Spanish.

COGNADOS:	horrible el resultado el termómetro el testamento
NOMBRES:	el análisis la autopista el ayudante el cirujano la fiebre el jarabe el oculista la operación la cirugía el pasajero la pastilla el peso
VERBOS:	bajar chocar sobrevivir
OTRAS PALABRAS Y EXPRESIONES:	a menos que antes de que en caso de que en cuanto tan pronto como hacer ejercicio hasta que para que ponerse a dieta sin que

II. *Práctica*

A. Restate each of the following sentences, inserting the cue at the beginning and making any necessary changes. Repeat the correct answer after the speaker's confirmation. Listen to the model.

Modelo: Siempre me llama tan pronto como llega. (Me va a llamar)
   Me va a llamar tan pronto como llegue.

1. (Los voy a llamar)
2. (Voy a comprar)
3. (Ella va a venir)
4. (No voy a poder hacer nada)
5. (Van a traer)
6. (Vamos a estar aquí)

B. Restate each of the following sentences, inserting the cue at the beginning and using the present perfect subjunctive. Make any other necessary changes. Repeat the correct answer after the speaker's confirmation. Listen to the model.

Modelo: El doctor ha llegado. (Espero)
 Espero que el doctor haya llegado.

III. Para escuchar y entender

1. Listen carefully to the dialogue. It will be read twice.

(Diálogo 1)

Now the speaker will make statements about the dialogue you just heard. Tell whether each statement is true **(verdadero)** or false **(falso).** The speaker will confirm the correct answer.

2. Listen carefully to the dialogue. It will be read twice.

(Diálogo 2)

Now the speaker will make statements about the dialogue you just heard. Tell whether each statement is true **(verdadero)** or false **(falso).** The speaker will confirm the correct answer.

3. Listen carefully to the dialogue. It will be read twice.

(Diálogo 3)

Now the speaker will ask you some questions about the dialogue you just heard. Answer each question, omitting the subject. The speaker will confirm the correct answer. Repeat the correct answer.

Lección

20

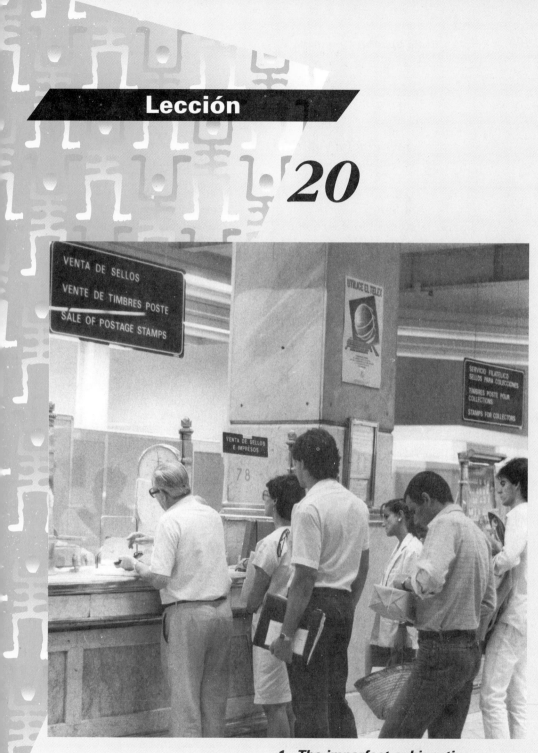

1. **The imperfect subjunctive**
2. **Uses of the imperfect subjunctive**
3. **If clauses**

Vocabulario

americano(a) American
el consulado consulate

el crédito credit
la fotocopia photocopy

NOMBRES
la billetera wallet
la computadora computer
el correo post office
la cortina curtain
la diligencia errand
la entrevista interview
el informe report
el (la) jefe(a) boss, chief
el paquete package
el préstamo loan
la reunión, la junta
    meeting
el talonario de cheques
    checkbook

VERBOS
asistir (a) to attend
devolver (o:ue) to return
    (something), to give back
preocuparse to worry
recoger to pick up

OTRAS PALABRAS Y
EXPRESIONES
echar al correo to mail
hacer diligencias to do
    errands
un montón a lot

1. The imperfect subjunctive
El imperfecto de subjuntivo

The Imperfect Subjunctive

Verb	Preterit, Third Person Plural	Stem	Imperfect Subjunctive	
hablar	hablaron	**habla-**	que yo habla-	**ra**
comer	comieron	**comie-**	que tú comie-	**ras**
vivir	vivieron	**vivie-**	que Ud. vivie-	**ra**
traer	trajeron	**traje-**	que él traje-	**ra**
ir	fueron	**fue-**	que ella fue-	**ra**
saber	supieron	**supie-**	que nosotros supié-	**ramos**
decir	dijeron	**dije-**	que Uds. dije-	**ran**
poner	pusieron	**pusie-**	que ellos pusie-	**ran**
estar	estuvieron	**estuvie-**	que ellas estuvie-	**ran**

The imperfect subjunctive is the simplest past tense of the subjunctive. It is formed in the same way for all verbs, regular and irregular. The **-ron** ending of the third person plural of the preterit is dropped and the following endings are added to the stem: **-ra, -ras, -ra, -ramos, -ran.**[1]

◆ Notice the written accent mark in the first person plural form.

Práctica

Give the imperfect subjunctive of the following verbs.

1. **yo:**	bajar, aprender, abrir, cerrar, estar, acostarse
2. **tú:**	salir, sentir, temer, recordar, venir, ponerse
3. **Ud.:**	llevar, romper, morir, revisar, volar, alegrarse
4. **nosotros:**	esperar, traer, pedir, volver, servir, vestirse
5. **ellos:**	tener, ser, dar, estar, poder, irse

2. Uses of the imperfect subjunctive
Usos del imperfecto de subjuntivo

◆ The imperfect subjunctive is always used in a subordinate clause when the verb of the main clause is in the past and requires the subjunctive mood.

—¿Qué te sugirió él?   *"What did he suggest to you?"*
—Me **sugirió** que **pidiera**   *"He suggested that I ask for a*
un préstamo en el banco.   *loan at the bank."*
—¿Lo pediste?   *"Did you ask for it?"*
—No, porque como no   *"No, because since I don't have*
tengo crédito **temí** que   *credit I was afraid that they*
no me lo **dieran.**   *wouldn't give it to me."*

—Mamá me **pidió** que   *"Mom asked me to buy stamps*
comprara estampillas y   *and to mail these letters."*
que **echara** estas cartas
al correo.
—A mí me **dijo** que **fuera** a   *"She told me to go to the*
la tintorería para recoger   *cleaners to pick up the*
las cortinas.   *curtains."*
—Y a papá le **pidió** que   *"And she asked Dad to do*
hiciera otras diligencias.   *other errands."*

---

[1] See Appendix B: Verbs, for the **-se** endings of the imperfect subjunctive, which are less frequently used.

—El jefe me **dio** el
informe para que **hiciera**
fotocopias y las **llevara** al
consulado americano.

—¿Ya lo hiciste?

—No, porque también me
dijo que **escribiera** a
máquina un montón de
cartas.

*"The boss gave me for the
report so that I could make
photocopies of it and take them
to the American consulate."*

"Did you do it already?"

*"No, because he also told me to
type a lot of letters."*

◆ The imperfect subjunctive is also used when the verb of the
main clause is in the present, but the subordinate clause refers to
the past.

—Es una lástima que no
pudieras asistir a la
reunión ayer.

—No pude ir porque tuve
que ir a una entrevista.

*"It's a pity that you weren't
able to attend the meeting
yesterday."*

*"I couldn't go because I had
to go to an interview."*

◆ The imperfect subjunctive form of **querer (quisiera)** is used as
a polite form of request.

—**Quisiera** pedirle un favor.   *"I would like to ask you a favor."*

Práctica

A. Complete the following dialogues using the imperfect subjunctive. Then act them out with a partner.

1. —Anita, te dije que _____ (hacer) fotocopias de este
informe.
—No pude porque papá me pidió que _____ (ir) a la
oficina de correos.

2. —Mamá quería que yo _____ (recoger) las cortinas en la
tintorería.
—A mí me pidió que _____ (hacer) un montón de
diligencias.

3. —Es una lástima que Julio no _____ (poder) ir a la
entrevista ayer.
—No pudo ir porque su jefe le pidió que _____ (asistir) a
una junta.

4. —Siento que ellos no te _____ (dar) el préstamo.
—Era difícil que me lo _____ (dar) porque no tengo
buen crédito.

5. —Alicia nos pidió que _____ (comprar) estampillas y que
_____ (echar) unas cartas al correo.
—¡Pero mamá quería que (nosotros) _____ (ir) con ella al
consulado americano!

B. Use your imagination to complete the following sentences, using the imperfect subjunctive.

1. Siento que ayer tú no…
2. Yo les pedí a mis amigos que…
3. Mis padres querían que yo…
4. El profesor nos dijo que…
5. Yo quería que mi hermano(a)…
6. Yo me alegré de que Uds.…

3. *If* clauses
Cláusulas que comienzan con si

In Spanish, the imperfect subjunctive is used in a clause introduced by **si** *(if)* when it refers to statements considered contrary to fact, hypothetical, or unlikely to happen. The resultant clause usually has a verb in the conditional.

Si yo fuera Ud.…	*If I were you…*
—**Si** yo **tuviera** dinero, iría de vacaciones con Uds.	*"If I had money, I would go on vacation with you."*
—¿No te lo puede prestar tu padre?	*"Can't your father lend it to you?"*
—No, porque **si** mi padre me lo **prestara,** tendría que devolvérselo antes de septiembre, y yo necesito el dinero para pagar la matrícula.	*"No, because if my father were to lend it to me,[1] I would have to give it back to him before September, and I need the money to pay for registration."*
—**Si tuviéramos** tiempo, podríamos llevar estos paquetes al correo ahora.	*"If we had time, we could take these packages to the post office now."*
—No te preocupes. Podemos llevarlos mañana.	*"Don't worry. We can take them tomorrow."*
—No puedo comprar la computadora porque no tengo mi talonario de cheques.	*"I can't buy the computer because I don't have my checkbook."*
—**Si** yo **fuera** tú, usaría una tarjeta de crédito.	*"If I were you, I would use a credit card."*
—Tienes razón. Si tengo mi *MasterCard* en la billetera voy a usarla.	*"You're right. If I have my MasterCard in my wallet I am going to use it."*

---

[1] Many colloquial English speakers use the simple past tense to express a contrary-to-fact or hypothetical situation, *e.g.,* "… if my father **lent** it to me."

ATENCIÓN: When an *if*-clause is not contrary to fact or hypothetical, or when there is a possibility that the situation it describes will happen, the indicative is used.

—Vamos a comprar los   *"We are going to buy the*
   billetes **si** nos **dan** el   *tickets if they give us the*
   dinero.   *money."*

◆ The present subjunctive is **never** used with an *if*-clause.

Práctica

A. Complete the following dialogues, using the imperfect subjunctive. Then act them out with a partner.

   1. —Si yo _____ (tener) dinero, le compraría una computadora a Pepe.
      —Si yo _____ (ser) tú, no le compraría nada.
   2. —Si Estrella me _____ (devolver) el dinero que le presté yo, podría pagar mis cuentas.
      —Estoy segura de que si ella _____ (poder), te lo devolvería.
   3. —Ernesto se preocupa mucho por sus hijos.
      —Yo también me preocuparía si mis hijos _____ (ser) como los de él.
   4. —Si Carolina _____ (venir) hoy, podríamos ir al consulado juntas.
      —Si nosotras no _____ (trabajar) hoy, iríamos contigo.
   5. —Si tú _____ (tener) un examen y un amigo te _____ (pedir) que _____ (hacer) un montón de diligencias, ¿qué harías?
      —Le diría que no.

B. Use your imagination to complete the following sentences, using either the imperfect subjunctive or the present indicative, as appropriate.

   1. Yo llevaría el paquete al correo si...
   2. Ella te compraría una billetera si...
   3. Nosotros pagaríamos con un cheque si...
   4. Haré las fotocopias hoy si...
   5. Ellos van a asistir a la reunión si...
   6. ¿Qué harías tú si...?
   7. Mi papá pediría un préstamo si...
   8. Te voy a devolver el dinero si...

🔲 *En el laboratorio*

The following material is to be used with the tape in the language laboratory.

I. *Vocabulario*

Repeat each word after the speaker. When repeating words that are cognates, notice the difference in pronunciation between English and Spanish.

COGNADOS:	americano el consulado el crédito la fotocopia
NOMBRES:	la billetera la computadora el correo la cortina la diligencia la entrevista el informe el jefe el paquete el préstamo la reunión la junta el talonario de cheques
VERBOS:	asistir devolver preocuparse recoger
OTRAS PALABRAS Y EXPRESIONES:	echar al correo hacer diligencias un montón

II. *Práctica*

A. Restate each of the following sentences, inserting the cue at the beginning and making any necessary changes. Repeat the correct answer after the speaker's confirmation. Listen to the model.

Modelo: Ella quiere que yo vaya con él. (Ella quería)
   Ella quería que yo fuera con él.

1. (Fue una lástima)
2. (No creí)
3. (Esperaba)
4. (Dudábamos)
5. (No había nadie)
6. (Necesitaba)
7. (No quería)
8. (No creían)

B. Restate each of the following sentences, inserting the cue at the beginning and making any necessary changes. Repeat the correct answer after the speaker's confirmation. Listen to the model.

Modelo: Iré si tengo tiempo. (Iría)
> **Iría si tuviera tiempo.**

1. (Le hablaría)
2. (Compraríamos)
3. (Lo harían)
4. (Se lo diría)
5. (Vendríamos)
6. (Me alegraría)
7. (Lo compraría)
8. (Lo haríamos)

III. Para escuchar y entender

1. Listen carefully to the narration. It will be read twice.

(Narración)

Now the speaker will make statements about the narration you just heard. Tell whether each statement is true (**verdadero**) or false (**falso**). The speaker will confirm the correct answer.

2. Listen carefully to the dialogue. It will be read twice.

(Diálogo 1)

Now the speaker will make statements about the dialogue you just heard. Tell whether each statement is true (**verdadero**) or false (**falso**). The speaker will confirm the correct answer.

3. Listen carefully to the dialogue. It will be read twice.

(Diálogo 2)

Now the speaker will ask you some questions about the dialogue you just heard. Answer each question, omitting the subject. The speaker will confirm the correct answer. Repeat the correct answer.

¿Cuánto sabe usted ahora?

LECCIONES 16–20

A. The present subjunctive

Lección 16

Complete the following sentences, using the Spanish equivalent of the verbs in parentheses in the present subjunctive. Follow the model.

Modelo: ...que yo _____ *(speak)*
  ...que yo **hable**

1. ...que nosotros _____ *(close)*
2. ...que ellos _____ *(go)*
3. ...que tú _____ *(open)*
4. ...que Pablo _____ *(recommend)*
5. ...que Ud. _____ *(leave)*
6. ...que yo _____ *(return)*
7. ...que Uds. _____ *(want)*
8. ...que ella _____ *(understand)*
9. ...que nosotros _____ *(have)*
10. ...que las chicas _____ *(put)*
11. ...que tú _____ *(bring)*
12. ...que los estudiantes _____ *(give)*
13. ...que yo _____ *(be:* **estar)**
14. ...que Teresa _____ *(be:* **ser)**
15. ...que Uds. _____ *(know:* **saber)**

B. The subjunctive with verbs of volition

How would you say the following in Spanish?

1. "Do you want to go to the hospital with me, Anita?"
   "I can't. Alberto wants me to go to the train station with him."
2. "What do you want to do this weekend, Pedro?"
   "I don't know...What do you suggest that I do?"
   "I suggest that you study."
3. "Do you need me to bring you the train schedule, Miss Rojas?"
   "Yes, and I beg you to come this afternoon, Mr. Varela."
   "What time do you want me to be at your house?"
   "At two."
4. "I am going to ask him to buy the tickets."
   "I prefer to buy them this afternoon."

C. The absolute superlative

Change the following to the absolute superlative.

1. sumamente difícil
2. muy lenta
3. sumamente buenas
4. muy alto
5. muy largo
6. sumamente rápido
7. muy inteligentes
8. sumamente fáciles

D. Vocabulario

Complete the following sentences, using words learned in **Lección 16**.

1. ¡Son las cinco! Tienes que salir cuanto _____ .
2. Me dieron un _____ del diez por _____ .
3. Quiero reservar un _____ para el vuelo a Mérida.
4. Todos los trenes son muy lentos, menos *(except for)* el _____ .
5. Vamos a estar en la _____ de trenes a las diez.
6. Alberto dice que ella es muy bonita. ¡Yo no lo _____!

Lección 17   **A.** The subjunctive to express emotion

How would you say the following in Spanish?

1. "I hope to get the scholarship."
   "I'm afraid you can't get it because your grades are not very good."
2. "I'm glad to be here with you, Anita."
   "I hope that you can go to the party with me tonight, Carlos."
3. "I'm afraid we cannot register in the physics class."
   "I'm sorry you don't have the money, girls . . . "
4. "We hope to take a literature class."
   "We're glad that you want to take literature."

B. The subjunctive with some impersonal expressions

Complete the following sentences, using the present subjunctive or the infinitive, as appropriate.

1. Conviene _____ (matricularse) en agosto.
2. Es difícil que mi abogado _____ (poder) verme mañana.
3. Es importante _____ (sacar) buenas notas.
4. Es posible que ellos me _____ (dar) una beca.
5. Es lástima que esa clase _____ (ser) un requisito.
6. Yo creo que es mejor no _____ (firmar) el contrato.
7. Es necesario _____ (tomar) una clase de química.
8. Ojalá que el profesor _____ (tener) tiempo de preparar la conferencia.

C. Formation of adverbs

Complete the following sentences, using the Spanish equivalent of the words in parentheses.

1. Ella vino _____ para verte. *(especially)*
2. Tomé una clase de literatura _____ . *(recently)*
3. Yo hablé _____ y _____, y los estudiantes me entendieron. *(slowly* and *clearly)*
4. Nosotros _____ nos levantamos a las seis. *(generally)*
5. Ellos todos lo hacen muy _____. *(easily)*

D. Vocabulary

Complete the sentences, using words learned in **Lección 17.**

1. Necesito la _____ para mi clase de matemáticas.
2. El examen _____ es en octubre y el examen _____ es en diciembre.
3. No es _____. ¡Es muy difícil!
4. No puedo tomar clases. No tengo dinero para pagar la

   _____ .

5. Puede _____ que la profesora vuelva mañana.
6. Ud. no necesita traer dinero porque no es _____ comprar nada.
7. Estudiamos las ideas de Isaac Newton en nuestra clase de

   _____ .

8. Mi _____ quiere que tome una clase de física.

A. The subjunctive to express doubt, disbelief, and denial   **Lección 18**

How would you say the following in Spanish?

1. "Dr. Soto says she can take care of my patients."
   "I'm sure she can."
2. "I don't think the doctor is in his office."
   "Then I have to call his house."
3. "I doubt that Mr. Soto can take his wife to the emergency room."
   "Can her daughter take her?"
   "I don't think she's home."
4. "I'm sure that she needs crutches!"
   "It's true that her leg hurts, but it isn't true that she needs crutches . . . "

B. The subjunctive to express indefiniteness and nonexistence

Rephrase these sentences according to the new beginnings.

1. Tengo un paciente que es de México.
   No tengo ningún paciente…

2. Hay alguien que puede llevarlo a la sala de rayos X.
   No hay nadie...
3. Hay una enfermera que habla español.
   No hay ninguna enfermera...
4. Hay dos personas aquí que saben poner inyecciones.
   Busco a alguien...
5. Necesito a alguien que cuide a mis hijos.
   Hay una señora...

C. Diminutive suffixes

Give the diminutive form of the following words.

1. Carmen
2. árbol
3. niños
4. café
5. Juan

6. favor
7. piernas
8. brazo
9. hermana
10. noche

D. Vocabulario

Complete the following sentences, using words learned in
Lección 18.

1. Lo llevaron al hospital en una _____ .
2. Se rompió la pierna. Va a necesitar _____ para caminar.
3. Lo llevaron a la _____ de emergencia.
4. El doctor está en su _____ .
5. Lo llevaron a la sala de rayos X para hacerle una _____ .
6. Le van a _____ una inyección.
7. Yo me rompí el brazo; me lo van a _____ .
8. En este _____ llegan los paramédicos.

Lección 19 **A.** The subjunctive after certain conjunctions

Complete the following sentences, using the Spanish equivalent
of the words in parentheses.

1. No va a hacer testamento hasta que _____ . *(her lawyer
   comes)*
2. Yo siempre espero hasta que mi ayudante _____ el resultado. *(brings me)*
3. Yo podré ir a trabajar en cuanto _____ . *(the fever goes
   down)*
4. Cuando ella _____ su peso, se va a poner a dieta. *(knows)*
5. No sobrevivirán a menos que _____ al hospital inmedia-
   tamente. *(they take them)*
6. En cuanto el cirujano _____ al hospital, siempre habla
   con sus ayudantes. *(arrives)*

7. No te sentirás mejor a menos que _____ estas pastillas.
   (you take)
8. Voy a comprar aspirinas en caso de que Adela _____ .
   (has a fever)

B. The present perfect subjunctive

Give the present perfect subjunctive of the verbs given.

1. ...que yo _____ (llegar)
2. ...que Uds. _____ (volver)
3. ...que Teresa _____ (ir)
4. ...que tú _____ (decir)
5. ...que nosotros _____ (hacer)
6. ...que Ud. _____ (preferir)
7. ...que Carlos _____ (abrir)
8. ...que los niños _____ (poner)

C. Uses of the present perfect subjunctive

Rephrase the following sentences according to the new beginnings.

1. Nosotros hemos hecho el trabajo.
   Ellos no creen que nosotros...
2. Yo he estado enfermo.
   Ella duda que yo...
3. Han muerto muchos.
   No es verdad que...
4. Ha ido a México.
   No hay nadie que...
5. Tú le has escrito una carta.
   Ella no cree que tú...
6. Ellos han hablado con la enfermera.
   Espero que...
7. Uds. no han visto a sus pacientes.
   Siento que Uds...
8. Ana y yo hemos ido a su consultorio.
   No es cierto...

D. Vocabulario

Complete the following sentences, using words learned in **Lección 19.**

1. Los _____ ya están en el tren.
2. Necesito el _____ para ver si tiene fiebre.
3. Hubo un accidente en la _____ .
4. Te traje un _____ para la tos *(cough)*.

5. Tengo que salir _____ de que lleguen los chicos.
6. Yo voy a hacer _____ y ella se va a poner a _____.

Lección 20   **A.** The imperfect subjunctive

Give the imperfect subjunctive of the verbs given.

1. ...que ellos _____ (asistir)
2. ...que tú _____ (ser)
3. ...que nosotros _____ (devolver)
4. ...que Estela _____ (ir)
5. ...que yo _____ (recoger)
6. ...que Roberto _____ (poder)
7. ...que Ud. _____ (querer)
8. ...que Uds. _____ (dar)
9. ...que Luis y yo _____ (hacer)
10. ...que las niñas _____ (traer)

B. Uses of the imperfect subjunctive

Rephrase the following sentences according to the new beginnings.

1. Yo tuve que trabajar.
   No era verdad que yo...
2. Nosotros pusimos el dinero en el banco.
   Ella quería que nosotros...
3. Tú fuiste al correo.
   Tu papá te dijo que...
4. Ellos hicieron las diligencias.
   La Sra. Rojas quería que ellos...
5. Ud. llevó el paquete.
   Yo quería que Ud...
6. Uds. hablaron con el jefe.
   Nosotros esperábamos que Uds...
7. María estuvo enferma.
   Yo sentí mucho que María...
8. Esteban perdió la billetera.
   Yo temía que Esteban...

C. *If* clauses

Complete the following sentences, using the Spanish equivalent of the words in parentheses.

1. _____, le diré que tú la necesitas. *(If I see her)*
2. _____, no haría eso. *(If I were you)*
3. _____, iría contigo. *(If she had time)*

4. _____, podré comprar las cortinas. *(If he gives me the money)*
5. _____, llegaríamos mañana. *(If we went by car)*
6. _____, te va a traer el dinero. *(If she can come)*
7. _____, podríamos ir con ellos, Anita. *(If you wanted to)*
8. Iré al banco _____, *(if they go with me)*

D. Vocabulario

Complete the following sentences, using words learned in **Lección 20.**

1. Voy a poner el dinero en la _____.
2. ¿Tu _____ es Apple o I.B.M.?
3. Voy a escribir un _____ para mi clase de historia.
4. No tengo dinero para comprar el coche. Voy a pedir un _____.
5. ¿Tienes tu _____ de cheques?
6. Ellos _____ a la Universidad de Salamanca.
7. Tengo un _____ de cartas para _____ al correo.

Appendix A

Spanish Pronunciation

Vowels

There are five distinct vowels in Spanish: **a, e, i, o,** and **u.** Each vowel has only one basic, constant sound. The pronunciation of each vowel is constant, clear, and brief. The length of the sound is practically the same whether it is produced in a stressed or unstressed syllable.[1]

While producing the sounds of the English stressed vowels that most closely resemble the Spanish ones, the speaker changes the position of the tongue, lips, and lower jaw, so that the vowel actually starts as one sound and then *glides* into another. In Spanish, however, the tongue, lips, and jaw keep a constant position during the production of the sound.

    English: ban*a*na   **Spanish:** ban*a*na

The stress falls on the same vowel and syllable in both Spanish and English, but the English stressed *a* is longer than the Spanish stressed **a.**

    English: ban*a*na   **Spanish:** ban*a*na

Note also that the English stressed *a* has a sound different from the other *a*'s in the word, while the Spanish **a** sound remains constant.

a in Spanish sounds similar to the English *a* in the word *father.*

alta	casa	palma	Ana
cama	Panamá	alma	apagar

e is pronounced like the English *e* in the word *eight.*

mes	entre	este	deje
ese	encender	teme	prender

i has a sound similar to the English *ee* in the word *see.*

fin	ir	sí	sin	dividir	Trini	difícil

o is similar to the English *o* in the word *no,* but without the glide.

toco	como	poco	roto
corto	corro	solo	loco

---

[1] In a stressed syllable, the prominence of the vowel is indicated by its loudness.

u is pronounced like the English *oo* sound in the word *shoot*, or the *ue* sound in the word *Sue*.

su	Lulú	Úrsula	cultura
un	luna	sucursal	Uruguay

Diphthongs and Triphthongs

When unstressed **i** or **u** falls next to another vowel in a syllable, it unites with that vowel to form what is called a *diphthong*. Both vowels are pronounced as one syllable. Their sounds do not change; they are only pronounced more rapidly and with a glide. For example:

tra**i**ga	L**i**dia	tre**i**nta	s**i**ete	**oi**go	ad**ió**s
Aurora	ag**u**a	b**u**eno	antig**u**o	c**i**u**dad	L**u**is

A *triphthong* is the union of three vowels: a stressed vowel between two unstressed ones (**i** or **u**) in the same syllable. For example: Parag**uay,** estud**iéi**s.

NOTE: Stressed **i** and **u** do not form diphthongs with other vowels, except in the combinations **iu** and **ui**. For example, **rí**-o, sa-**bí**-ais.

In syllabication, diphthongs and triphthongs are considered a single vowel; their components cannot be separated.

Consonants

p   Spanish **p** is pronounced in a manner similar to the English *p* sound, but without the puff of air that follows after the English sound is produced.

pesca	pude	puedo	parte	papá
postre	piña	puente	Paco	

k   The Spanish **k** sound, represented by the letters **k**; **c** before **a**, **o**, **u**, or a consonant; and **qu** (before **e** and **i**), is similar to the English *k* sound, but without the puff of air.

casa	comer	cuna	clima	acción	que
quinto	queso	aunque	kiosko	kilómetro	

t   Spanish **t** is produced by touching the back of the upper front teeth with the tip of the tongue. It has no puff of air as in the English *t*.

todo	antes	corto	Guatemala	diente
resto	tonto	roto	tanque	

d The Spanish consonant **d** has two different sounds depending on its position. At the beginning of an utterance and after **n** or **l**, the tip of the tongue presses the back of the upper front teeth.

día	domo	dice	dolor	dar
anda	Aldo	caldo	el deseo	un domicilio

In all other positions the sound of **d** is similar to the *th* sound in the English word *they*, but softer.

medida	todo	nada	nadie	medio
puedo	moda	quedo	nudo	

g The Spanish consonant **g** is similar to the English *g* sound in the word *guy* except before **e** or **i**.

goma	glotón	gallo	gloria	lago	alga
gorrión	garra	guerra	angustia	algo	Dagoberto

j The Spanish sound **j** (or **g** before **e** and **i**) is similar to a strongly exaggerated English *h* sound.

gemir	juez	jarro	gitano	agente
juego	giro	bajo	gente	

b
v There is no difference in sound between Spanish **b** and **v**. Both letters are pronounced alike. At the beginning of an utterance or after **m** or **n**, **b** and **v** have a sound identical to the English *b* sound in the word *boy*.

vivir	beber	vamos	barco	enviar
hambre	batea	bueno	vestido	

When pronounced between vowels, the Spanish **b** and **v** sound is produced by bringing the lips together but not closing them, so that some air may pass through.

sábado	autobús	yo voy	su barco

y
ll In most countries, Spanish **ll** and **y** have a sound similar to the English sound in the word *yes*.

el llavero	trayecto	su yunta	milla
oye	el yeso	mayo	yema
un yelmo	trayectoria	llama	bella

NOTE: When it stands alone or is at the end of a word, Spanish **y** is pronounced like the vowel **i**.

rey	hoy	y	doy	buey
muy	voy	estoy	soy	

r The sound of Spanish **r** is similar to the English *dd* sound in the word *ladder*.

crema	aroma	cara	arena	aro
harina	toro	oro	eres	portero

rr Spanish **rr** and also **r** in an initial position and after **n, l,** or **s** are pronounced with a very strong trill. This trill is produced by bringing the tip of the tongue near the alveolar ridge and letting it vibrate freely while the air passes through the mouth.

rama	carro	Israel	cierra	roto
perro	alrededor	rizo	corre	Enrique

s Spanish **s** is represented in most of the Spanish world by the letters **s, z,** and **c** before **e** or **i**. The sound is very similar to the English sibilant *s* in the word *sink*.

sale	sitio	presidente	signo
salsa	seda	suma	vaso
sobrino	ciudad	cima	canción
zapato	zarza	cerveza	centro

h The letter **h** is silent in Spanish.

hoy	hora	hilo	ahora
humor	huevo	horror	almohada

ch Spanish **ch** is pronounced like the English *ch* in the word *chief*.

hecho	chico	coche	Chile
mucho	muchacho	salchicha	

f Spanish **f** is identical in sound to the English *f*.

difícil	feo	fuego	forma
fácil	fecha	foto	fueron

l Spanish **l** is similar to the English *l* in the word *let*.

dolor	lata	ángel	lago	sueldo
los	pelo	lana	general	fácil

m Spanish **m** is pronounced like the English *m* in the word *mother*.

mano	moda	mucho	muy
mismo	tampoco	multa	cómoda

n In most cases, Spanish **n** has a sound similar to the English *n*.

nada	nunca	ninguno	norte
entra	tiene	sienta	

The sound of Spanish **n** is often affected by the sounds that occur around it. When it appears before **b, v,** or **p,** it is pronounced like an **m.**

tan bueno	toman vino	sin poder
un pobre	comen peras	siguen bebiendo

ñ   Spanish **ñ** is similar to the English *ny* sound in the word *canyon.*

señor	otoño	ñoño	uña
leña	dueño	niños	años

x   Spanish **x** has two pronunciations depending on its position. Between vowels the sound is similar to English *ks.*

examen	exacto	boxeo	éxito
oxidar	oxígeno	existencia	

When it occurs before a consonant, Spanish **x** sounds like *s.*

expresión	explicar	extraer	excusa
expreso	exquisito	extremo	

NOTE: When **x** appears in **México** or in other words of Mexican origin, it is pronounced like the Spanish letter **j.**

Rhythm

Rhythm is the variation of sound intensity that we usually associate with music. Spanish and English each regulate these variations in speech differently, because they have different patterns of syllable length. In Spanish the length of the stressed and unstressed syllables remains almost the same, while in English stressed syllables are considerably longer than unstressed ones. Pronounce the following Spanish words, enunciating each syllable clearly.

es-tu-dian-te	bue-no	Úr-su-la
com-po-si-ción	di-fí-cil	ki-ló-me-tro
po-li-cí-a	Pa-ra-guay	

Because the length of the Spanish syllables remains constant, the greater the number of syllables in a given word or phrase, the longer the phrase will be.

Linking

In spoken Spanish, the different words in a phrase or a sentence are not pronounced as isolated elements but are combined together. This is called *linking*.

Pepe come pan.
Tomás toma leche.
Luis tiene la llave.
la mano de Roberto

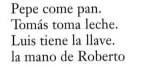

Pe-pe-co-me-pan
To-más-to-ma-le-che
Luis-tie-ne-la-lla-ve
la-ma-no-de-Ro-ber-to

1. The final consonant of a word is pronounced together with the initial vowel of the following word.

   Carlos anda
   un ángel
   el otoño
   unos estudios interesantes

   Car-lo-san-da
   u-nán-gel
   e-lo-to-ño
   u-no-ses-tu-dio-sin-te-re-san-tes

2. A diphthong is formed between the final vowel of a word and the initial vowel of the following word. A triphthong is formed when there is a combination of three vowels (see rules for the formation of diphthongs and triphthongs on page 276).

   su hermana
   tu escopeta
   Roberto y Luis
   negocio importante
   lluvia y nieve
   ardua empresa

   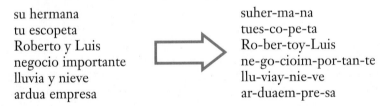

   suher-ma-na
   tues-co-pe-ta
   Ro-ber-toy-Luis
   ne-go-cioim-por-tan-te
   llu-viay-nie-ve
   ar-duaem-pre-sa

3. When the final vowel of a word and the initial vowel of the following word are identical, they are pronounced slightly longer than one vowel.

   A-n*a*l-can-za   Ana alcanza   tie-n*e*-so   tiene eso
   l*o*l-vi-do   lo olvido   Ad*a*-tien-de   Ada atiende

   The same rule applies when two identical vowels appear within a word.

   cr*e*s   cr*e*es
   Te-rán   Te*h*erán
   c*o*r-di-na-ción coordinación

4. When the final consonant of a word and the initial consonant of the following word are the same, they are pronounced as one consonant with slightly longer than normal duration.

e-*l*a-do   el lado   tie-ne-*s*ed   tienes sed
Car-lo-*s*al-ta   Carlos salta

Intonation

Intonation is the rise and fall of pitch in the delivery of a phrase or a sentence. In general, Spanish pitch tends to change less than English, giving the impression that the language is less emphatic.

As a rule, the intonation for normal statements in Spanish starts in a low tone, raises to a higher one on the first stressed syllable, maintains that tone until the last stressed syllable, and then goes back to the initial low tone, with still another drop at the very end.

Tu amigo viene mañana.   José come pan.
Ada está en casa.   Carlos toma café.

Syllable Formation in Spanish

General rules for dividing words into syllables are as follows.

Vowels

1. A vowel or a vowel combination can constitute a syllable.

a-lum-no   a-bue-la   Eu-ro-pa

2. Diphthongs and triphthongs are considered single vowels and cannot be divided.

bai-le   puen-te   Dia-na   es-tu-diáis   an-ti-guo

3. Two strong vowels (**a, e, o**) do not form a diphthong and are separated into two syllables.

em-ple-ar   vol-te-ar   lo-a

4. A written accent on a weak vowel (**i** or **u**) breaks the diphthong, thus the vowels are separated into two syllables.

trí-o   dú-o   Ma-rí-a

Consonants

1. A single consonant forms a syllable with the vowel that follows it.

   po-der   ma-no   mi-nu-to

   NOTE: **ch, ll,** and **rr** are considered single consonants: **co-che, a-ma-ri-llo, pe-rro.**

2. When two consonants appear between two vowels, they are separated into two syllables.

   al-fa-be-to   cam-pe-ón   me-ter-se   mo-les-tia

   EXCEPTION: When a consonant cluster composed of **b, c, d, f, g, p,** or **t** with **l** or **r** appears between two vowels, the cluster joins the following vowel: **so-bre, o-tros, ca-ble, te-lé-gra-fo.**

3. When three consonants appear between two vowels, only the last one goes with the following vowel.

   ins-pec-tor   trans-por-te   trans-for-mar

   EXCEPTION: When there is a cluster of three consonants in the combinations described in rule 2, the first consonant joins the preceding vowel and the cluster joins the following vowel: **es-cri-bir, ex-tran-je-ro, im-plo-rar, es-tre-cho.**

Accentuation

In Spanish, all words are stressed according to specific rules. Words that do not follow the rules must have a written accent to indicate the change of stress. The basic rules for accentuation are as follows.

1. Words ending in a vowel, **n,** or **s** are stressed on the next-to-the-last syllable.

   hi-jo   **ca**-lle   **me**-sa   fa-**mo**-sos
   flo-**re**-cen   **pla**-ya   **ve**-ces

2. Words ending in a consonant, except **n** or **s,** are stressed on the last syllable.

   ma-**yor**   a-**mor**   tro-pi-**cal**
   na-**riz**   re-**loj**   co-rre-**dor**

3. All words that do not follow these rules must have the written accent.

ca-**fé**	**lá**-piz	**mú**-si-ca	sa-**lón**
án-gel	**lí**-qui-do	fran-**cés**	**Víc**-tor
sim-**pá**-ti-co	rin-**cón**	a-**zú**-car	**dár**-se-lo
sa-**lió**	**dé**-bil	e-**xá**-me-nes	**dí**-me-lo

4. Pronouns and adverbs of interrogation and exclamation have a written accent to distinguish them from relative pronouns.

—¿**Qué** comes? *"What are you eating?"*
—La pera que él no comió. *"The pear that he did not eat."*

—¿**Quién** está ahí? *"Who is there?"*
—El hombre a quien tú llamaste. *"The man whom you called."*

—¿**Dónde** está? *"Where is he?"*
—En el lugar donde trabaja. *"At the place where he works."*

5. Words that have the same spelling but different meanings take a written accent to differentiate one from the other.

el	*the*	él	*he, him*	te	*you*	té	*tea*
mi	*my*	mí	*me*	si	*if*	sí	*yes*
tu	*your*	tú	*you*	mas	*but*	más	*more*

Appendix B

Verbs

Regular Verbs
Model **-ar, -er, -ir** *verbs*

INFINITIVE		
amar (*to love*)	**comer** (*to eat*)	**vivir** (*to live*)

GERUND		
amando (*loving*)	**comiendo** (*eating*)	**viviendo** (*living*)

PAST PARTICIPLE		
amado (*loved*)	**comido** (*eaten*)	**vivido** (*lived*)

Simple Tenses

Indicative Mood

PRESENT		
(*I love*)	(*I eat*)	(*I live*)
am**o**	com**o**	viv**o**
am**as**	com**es**	viv**es**
am**a**	com**e**	viv**e**
am**amos**	com**emos**	viv**imos**
am**áis**[1]	com**éis**	viv**ís**
am**an**	com**en**	viv**en**

IMPERFECT		
(*I used to love*)	(*I used to eat*)	(*I used to live*)
am**aba**	com**ía**	viv**ía**
am**abas**	com**ías**	viv**ías**
am**aba**	com**ía**	viv**ía**
am**ábamos**	com**íamos**	viv**íamos**
am**abais**	com**íais**	viv**íais**
am**aban**	com**ían**	viv**ían**

---

[1] **Vosotros amáis:** The **vosotros** form of the verb is used primarily in Spain. This form has not been used in this text.

PRETERIT

(I loved)	*(I ate)*	*(I lived)*
am**é**	com**í**	viv**í**
am**aste**	com**iste**	viv**iste**
am**ó**	com**ió**	viv**ió**
am**amos**	com**imos**	viv**imos**
am**asteis**	com**isteis**	viv**isteis**
am**aron**	com**ieron**	viv**ieron**

FUTURE

(I will love)	*(I will eat)*	*(I will live)*
amar**é**	comer**é**	vivir**é**
amar**ás**	comer**ás**	vivir**ás**
amar**á**	comer**á**	vivir**á**
amar**emos**	comer**emos**	vivir**emos**
amar**éis**	comer**éis**	vivir**éis**
amar**án**	comer**án**	vivir**án**

CONDITIONAL

(I would love)	*(I would eat)*	*(I would live)*
amar**ía**	comer**ía**	vivir**ía**
amar**ías**	comer**ías**	vivir**ías**
amar**ía**	comer**ía**	vivir**ía**
amar**íamos**	comer**íamos**	vivir**íamos**
amar**íais**	comer**íais**	vivir**íais**
amar**ían**	comer**ían**	vivir**ían**

Subjunctive Mood

PRESENT

([that] I [may] love)	*([that] I [may] eat)*	*([that I [may] live)*
am**e**	com**a**	viv**a**
am**es**	com**as**	viv**as**
am**e**	com**a**	viv**a**
am**emos**	com**amos**	viv**amos**
am**éis**	com**áis**	viv**áis**
am**en**	com**an**	viv**an**

IMPERFECT (two forms: **-ra, -se**)

([that] I [might] love)	*([that] I [might] eat)*	*([that] I [might] live)*
am**ara(-ase)**	com**iera(-iese)**	viv**iera(-iese)**
am**aras(-ases)**	com**ieras(-ieses)**	viv**ieras(-ieses)**
am**ara(-ase)**	com**iera(-iese)**	viv**iera(-iese)**
am**áramos**	com**iéramos**	viv**iéramos**
(-ásemos)	**(-iésemos)**	**(-iésemos)**
am**arais(-aseis)**	com**ierais(-ieseis)**	viv**ierais(-ieseis)**
am**aran(-asen)**	com**ieran(-iesen)**	viv**ieran(-iesen)**

Imperative Mood (Command Forms)

(love)	*(eat)*	*(live)*
am**a** (tú)	com**e** (tú)	viv**e** (tú)
am**e** (Ud.)	com**a** (Ud.)	viv**a** (Ud.)
am**emos** (nosotros)	com**amos** (nosotros)	viv**amos** (nosotros)
am**ad** (vosotros)	com**ed** (vosotros)	viv**id** (vosotros)
am**en** (Uds.)	com**an** (Uds.)	viv**an** (Uds.)

Compound Tenses

PERFECT INFINITIVE

haber amado	**haber comido**	**haber vivido**

PERFECT PARTICIPLE

habiendo amado	**habiendo comido**	**habiendo vivido**

Indicative Mood

PRESENT PERFECT

(I have loved)	*(I have eaten)*	*(I have lived)*
he amado	he comido	he vivido
has amado	has comido	has vivido
ha amado	ha comido	ha vivido
hemos amado	hemos comido	hemos vivido
habéis amado	habéis comido	habéis vivido
han amado	han comido	han vivido

PLUPERFECT

(I had loved)	*(I had eaten)*	*(I had lived)*
había amado	había comido	había vivido
habías amado	habías comido	habías vivido
había amado	había comido	había vivido
habíamos amado	habíamos comido	habíamos vivido
habíais amado	habíais comido	habíais vivido
habían amado	habían comido	habían vivido

FUTURE PERFECT

(I will have loved)	*(I will have eaten)*	*(I will have lived)*
habré amado	habré comido	habré vivido
habrás amado	habrás comido	habrás vivido
habrá amado	habrá comido	habrá vivido
habremos amado	habremos comido	habremos vivido
habréis amado	habréis comido	habréis vivido
habrán amado	habrán comido	habrán vivido

CONDITIONAL PERFECT

(I would have loved)	*(I would have eaten)*	*(I would have lived)*
habría amado	habría comido	habría vivido
habrías amado	habrías comido	habrías vivido
habría amado	habría comido	habría vivido
habríamos amado	habríamos comido	habríamos vivido
habríais amado	habríais comido	habríais vivido
habrían amado	habrían comido	habrían vivido

Subjunctive Mood

PRESENT PERFECT

([that] I [may] have loved)	*([that] I [may] have eaten)*	*([that] I [may] have lived)*
haya amado	haya comido	haya vivido
hayas amado	hayas comido	hayas vivido
haya amado	haya comido	haya vivido
hayamos amado	hayamos comido	hayamos vivido
hayáis amado	hayáis comido	hayáis vivido
hayan amado	hayan comido	hayan vivido

PLUPERFECT

(two forms: **-ra, -se**)

([that] I [might] have loved)	*([that] I [might] have eaten)*	*([that] I [might] have lived)*
hubiera(-iese) amado	hubiera(-iese) comido	hubiera(-iese) vivido
hubieras(-ieses) amado	hubieras(-ieses) comido	hubieras(-ieses) vivido
hubiera(-iese) amado	hubiera(-iese) comido	hubiera(-iese) vivido
hubiéramos(-iésemos) amado	hubiéramos(-iésemos) comido	hubiéramos(-iésemos) vivido
hubierais(-ieseis) amado	hubierais(-ieseis) comido	hubierais(-ieseis) vivido
hubieran(-iesen) amado	hubieran(-iesen) comido	hubieran(-iesen) vivido

Stem-Changing Verbs

The -ar *and* -er *stem-changing verbs*

Stem-changing verbs are those that have a change in the root of the verb. Verbs that end in **-ar** and **-er** change the stressed vowel **e** to **ie,** and the stressed **o** to **ue.** These changes occur in all persons, except the first- and second-persons plural of the present indicative, present subjunctive, and command.

INFINITIVE	PRESENT INDICATIVE	IMPERATIVE	PRESENT SUBJUNCTIVE
cerrar	cierro	—	cierre
(to close)	cierras	cierra	cierres
	cierra	cierre	cierre
	cerramos	cerremos	cerremos
	cerráis	cerrad	cerréis
	cierran	cierren	cierren
perder	pierdo	—	pierda
(to lose)	pierdes	pierde	pierdas
	pierde	pierda	pierda
	perdemos	perdamos	perdamos
	perdéis	perded	perdáis
	pierden	pierdan	pierdan
contar	cuento	—	cuente
(to count,	cuentas	cuenta	cuentes
to tell)	cuenta	cuente	cuente
	contamos	contemos	contemos
	contáis	contad	contéis
	cuentan	cuenten	cuenten
volver	vuelvo	—	vuelva
(to return)	vuelves	vuelve	vuelvas
	vuelve	vuelva	vuelva
	volvemos	volvamos	volvamos
	volvéis	volved	volváis
	vuelven	vuelvan	vuelvan

Verbs that follow the same pattern include the following.

acertar   to guess right
acordarse   to remember
acostar(se)   to go to bed
almorzar   to have lunch
atravesar   to go through
cegar   to blind
cocer   to cook
colgar   to hang
comenzar   to begin
confesar   to confess
costar   to cost
demostrar   to demonstrate,
   to show
despertar(se)   to wake up
empezar   to begin
encender   to light, to turn on
encontrar   to find

entender   to understand
llover   to rain
mostrar   to show
mover   to move
negar   to deny
nevar   to snow
pensar   to think, to plan
probar   to prove, to taste
recordar   to remember
resolver   to decide on
rogar   to beg
sentar(se)   to sit down
soler   to be in the habit of
soñar   to dream
tender   to stretch, to unfold
torcer   to twist

The -ir stem-changing verbs

There are two types of stem-changing verbs that end in **-ir:** one type changes stressed **e** to **ie** in some tenses and to **i** in others, and stressed **o** to **ue** or **u;** the second type always changes stressed **e** to **i** in the irregular forms of the verb.

Type I   **e:ie**   or   **i**
         -ir:
               o:ue   or   **u**

These changes occur as follows.

Present Indicative: all persons except the first and second plural change **e** to **ie** and **o** to **ue.** *Preterit:* third person, singular and plural, changes **e** to **i** and **o** to **u.** *Present Subjunctive:* all persons change **e** to **ie** and **o** to **ue,** except the first- and second-persons plural, which change **e** to **i** and **o** to **u.** *Imperfect Subjunctive:* all persons change **e** to **i** and **o** to **u.** *Imperative:* all persons except the second-person plural change **e** to **ie** and **o** to **ue;** first-person plural changes **e** to **i** and **o** to **u.** *Present Participle:* changes **e** to **i** and **o** to **u.**

INFINITIVE	PRESENT	PRETERIT	Imperative	Subjunctive PRESENT	IMPERFECT
		Indicative	*Imperative*	*Subjunctive*	
	PRESENT	PRETERIT		PRESENT	IMPERFECT
sentir	siento	sentí	—	sienta	sintiera(-iese)
(to feel)	sientes	sentiste	siente	sientas	sintieras
	siente	sintió	sienta	sienta	sintiera
PRESENT	sentimos	sentimos	sintamos	sintamos	sintiéramos
PARTICIPLE	sentís	sentisteis	sentid	sintáis	sintierais
sintiendo	sienten	sintieron	sientan	sientan	sintieran
dormir	duermo	dormí	—	duerma	durmiera(-iese)
(to sleep)	duermes	dormiste	duerme	duermas	durmieras
	duerme	durmió	duerma	duerma	durmiera
PRESENT	dormimos	dormimos	durmamos	durmamos	durmiéramos
PARTICIPLE	dormís	dormisteis	dormid	durmáis	durmierais
durmiendo	duermen	durmieron	duerman	duerman	durmieran

Other verbs that follow the same pattern include the following.

advertir to warn		**herir** to wound, to hurt	
arrepentir(se) to repent		**mentir** to lie	
consentir to consent, to pamper		**morir** to die	
convertir(se) to turn into		**preferir** to prefer	
discernir to discern		**referir** to refer	
divertir(se) to amuse oneself		**sugerir** to suggest	

Type II   **-ir: e:i**

The verbs in this second category are irregular in the same tenses as those of the first type. The only difference is that they only have one change: **e:i** in all irregular persons.

INFINITIVE	PRESENT	PRETERIT	Imperative	Subjunctive PRESENT	IMPERFECT
		Indicative	*Imperative*	*Subjunctive*	
	PRESENT	PRETERIT		PRESENT	IMPERFECT
pedir	pido	pedí	—	pida	pidiera(-iese)
(to ask for,	pides	pediste	pide	pidas	pidieras
request)	pide	pidió	pida	pida	pidiera
PRESENT	pedimos	pedimos	pidamos	pidamos	pidiéramos
PARTICIPLE	pedís	pedisteis	pedid	pidáis	pidierais
pidiendo	piden	pidieron	pidan	pidan	pidieran

Verbs that follow this pattern include the following.

competir	to complete	**reír(se)**	to laugh
concebir	to conceive	**reñir**	to fight
despedir(se)	to say good-bye	**repetir**	to repeat
elegir	to choose	**seguir**	to follow
impedir	to prevent	**servir**	to serve
perseguir	to pursue	**vestir(se)**	to dress

Orthographic-Changing Verbs

Some verbs undergo a change in the spelling of the stem in certain tenses, in order to maintain the original sound of the final consonant. The most common verbs of this type are those with the consonants **g** and **c.** Remember that **g** and **c** have a soft sound in front of **e** or **i,** and have a hard sound in front of **a, o,** or **u.** In order to maintain the soft sound in front of **a, o,** and **u, g** and **c** change to **j** and **z,** respectively. And in order to maintain the hard sound of **g** and **c** in front of **e** and **i, u** is added to the **g** (**gu**) and **c** changes to **qu.**

The following important verbs undergo spelling changes in the tenses listed below.

1. Verbs ending in **-gar** change **g** to **gu** before **e** in the first person of the preterit and in all persons of the present subjunctive.

   pagar (*to pay*)
   Preterit: pa**gu**é, pagaste, pagó, etc.
   Pres. Subj.: pa**gu**e, pa**gu**es, pa**gu**e, pa**gu**emos, pa**gu**éis, pa**gu**en

   Verbs that follow the same pattern: **colgar, jugar, llegar, navegar, negar, regar, rogar.**

2. Verbs ending in **-ger** and **-gir** change **g** to **j** before **o** and **a** in the first person of the present indicative and in all persons of the present subjunctive.

   proteger (*to protect*)
   Pres. Ind.: prote**j**o, proteges, protege, etc.
   Pres. Subj.: prote**j**a, prote**j**as, prote**j**a, prote**j**amos, prote**j**áis, prote**j**an

   Verbs that follow the same pattern: **coger, corregir, dirigir, elegir, escoger, exigir, recoger.**

3. Verbs ending in **-guar** change **gu** to **gü** before **e** in the first person of the preterit and in all persons of the present subjunctive.

averiguar (*to find out*)
Preterit: averigüé, averiguaste, averiguó, etc.
Pres. Subj.: averigüe, averigües, averigüe, averigüemos,
                averigüéis, averigüen

The verb **apaciguar** follows the same pattern.

4. Verbs ending in **-guir** change **gu** to **g** before **o** and **a** in the first person of the present indicative and in all persons of the present subjunctive.

conseguir (*to get*)
Pres. Ind.: consigo, consigues, consigue, etc.
Pres. Subj.: consiga, consigas, consiga, consigamos, consigáis,
                consigan

Verbs that follow the same pattern: **distinguir, perseguir, proseguir, seguir.**

5. Verbs ending in **-car** change **c** to **qu** before **e** in the first person of the preterit and in all persons of the present subjunctive.

tocar (*to touch, to play* [*a musical instrument*])
Preterit: toqué, tocaste, tocó, etc.
Pres. Subj.: toque, toques, toque, toquemos, toquéis, toquen

Verbs that follow the same pattern: **atacar, buscar, comunicar, explicar, indicar, pescar, sacar.**

6. Verbs ending in **-cer** and **-cir** preceded by a consonant change **c** to **z** before **o** and **a** in the first person of the present indicative and in all persons of the present subjunctive.

torcer (*to twist*)
Pres. Ind.: tuerzo, tuerces, tuerce, etc.
Pres. Subj.: tuerza, tuerzas, tuerza, torzamos, torzáis, tuerzan

Verbs that follow the same pattern: **convencer, esparcir, vencer.**

7. Verbs ending in **-cer** and **-cir** preceded by a vowel change **c** to **zc** before **o** and **a** in the first person of the present indicative and in all persons of the present subjunctive.

conocer (*to know, to be acquainted with*)
Pres. Ind.: conozco, conoces, conoce, etc.
Pres. Subj.: conozca, conozcas, conozca, conozcamos,
                conozcáis, conozcan.

Verbs that follow the same pattern: **agradecer, aparecer, carecer, entristecer, establecer, lucir, nacer, obedecer, ofrecer, padecer, parecer, pertenecer, reconocer, relucir.**

8. Verbs ending in **-zar** change **z** to **c** before **e** in the first person of the preterit and in all persons of the present subjunctive.

rezar (*to pray*)
Preterit: recé, rezaste, rezó, etc.
Pres. Subj.: rece, reces, rece, recemos, recéis, recen

Verbs that follow the same pattern: **abrazar, alcanzar, almorzar, comenzar, cruzar, empezar, forzar, gozar.**

9. Verbs ending in **-eer** change the unstressed **i** to **y** between vowels in the third-person singular and plural of the preterit, in all persons of the imperfect subjunctive, and in the present participle.

creer (*to believe*)
Preterit: creí, creíste, creyó, creímos, creísteis, creyeron
Imp. Subj.: creyera, creyeras, creyera, creyéramos, creyerais, creyeran
Pres. Part.: creyendo

Leer and **poseer** follow the same pattern.

10. Verbs ending in **-uir** change the unstressed **i** to **y** between vowels (except **-quir,** which has the silent **u**) in the following tenses and persons.

huir (*to escape, to flee*)
Pres. Part.: huyendo
Pres. Ind.: huyo, huyes, huye, huimos, huís, huyen
Preterit: huí, huiste, huyó, huimos, huisteis, huyeron
Imperative: huye, huya, huyamos, huid, huyan
Pres. Subj.: huya, huyas, huya, huyamos, huyáis, huyan
Imp. Subj.: huyera(ese), huyeras, huyera, huyéramos, huyerais, huyeran

Verbs that follow the same pattern: **atribuir, concluir, constituir, construir, contribuir, destituir, destruir, disminuir, distribuir, excluir, incluir, influir, instruir, restituir, sustituir.**

11. Verbs ending in **-eír** lose one **e** in the third-person singular and plural of the preterit, in all persons of the imperfect subjunctive, and in the present participle.

reír(se) (*to laugh*)
Preterit: reí, reíste, rió, reímos, reísteis, rieron
Imp. Subj.: riera(ese), rieras, riera, rierais, rieran
Pres. Part.: riendo

Freír and **sonreír** follow the same pattern.

12. Verbs ending in **-iar** add a written accent to the **i**, except in the first- and second-persons plural of the present indicative and subjunctive.

fiar(se) (*to trust*)
Pres. Ind.:   fío, fías, fía, fiamos, fiais, fían
Pres. Subj.:   fíe, fíes, fíe, fiemos, fiéis, fíen

Verbs that follow the same pattern: **ampliar, criar, desviar, enfriar, enviar, esquiar, guiar, telegrafiar, vaciar, variar.**

13. Verbs ending in **-uar** (except **-guar**) add a written accent to the **u**, except in the first- and second-persons plural of the present indicative and subjunctive.

actuar (*to act*)
Pres. Ind.:   actúo, actúas, actúa, actuamos, actuáis, actúan
Pres. Subj.:   actúe, actúes, actúe, actuemos, actuéis, actúen

Verbs that follow the same pattern: **acentuar, continuar, efectuar, exceptuar, graduar, habituar, insinuar, situar.**

14. Verbs ending in **-ñir** remove the **i** of the diphthongs **ie** and **ió** in the third-person singular and plural of the preterit and in all persons of the imperfect subjunctive. They also change the **e** of the stem to **i** in the same persons.

teñir (*to dye*)
Preterit: teñí, teñiste, **tiñó,** teñimos, teñisteis, **tiñeron**
Imp. Subj.:   **tiñ**era(ese), **tiñ**eras, **tiñ**era, **tiñ**éramos, **tiñ**erais,
                tiñeran

Verbs that follow the same pattern: **ceñir, constreñir, desteñir, estreñir, reñir.**

Some Common Irregular Verbs

Only those tenses with irregular forms are given below.

adquirir (*to acquire*)
Pres. Ind.:   adquiero, adquieres, adquiere, adquirimos, adquirís,
                adquieren
Pres. Subj.:   adquiera, adquieras, adquiera, adquiramos, adquiráis,
                adquieran
Imperative: adquiere, adquiera, adquiramos, adquirid, adquieran

andar (*to walk*)
Preterit: anduve, anduviste, anduvo, anduvimos, anduvisteis,
              anduvieron
Imp. Subj.:   anduviera (anduviese), anduvieras, anduviera,
                anduviéramos, anduvierais, anduvieran

avergonzarse (*to be ashamed, to be embarrassed*)
Pres. Ind.:   me avergüenzo, te avergüenzas, se avergüenza, nos
               avergonzamos, os avergonzáis, se avergüenzan
Pres. Subj.: me avergüence, te avergüences, se avergüence, nos
               avergoncemos, os avergoncéis, se avergüencen
Imperative: avergüénzate, avergüéncense, avergoncémonos,
               avergonzaos, avergüézense

caber (*to fit, to have enough room*)
Pres. Ind.:   quepo, cabes, cabe, cabemos, cabéis, caben
Preterit: cupe, cupiste, cupo, cupimos, cupisteis, cupieron
Future: cabré, cabrás, cabrá, cabremos, cabréis, cabrán
Conditional: cabría, cabrías, cabría, cabríamos, cabríais, cabrían
Imperative: cabe, quepa, quepamos, cabed, quepan
Pres. Subj.: quepa, quepas, quepa, quepamos, quepáis, quepan
Imp. Subj.:   cupiera (cupiese), cupieras, cupiera, cupiéramos,
               cupierais, cupieran

caer (*to fall*)
Pres. Ind.:   caigo, caes, cae, caemos, caéis, caen
Preterit: caí, caíste, cayó, caímos, caísteis, cayeron
Imperative: cae, caiga, caigamos, caed, caigan
Pres. Subj.: caiga, caigas, caiga, caigamos, caigáis, caigan
Imp. Subj.:   cayera (cayese), cayeras, cayera, cayéramos, cayerais,
               cayeran
Past Part.:   caído

conducir (*to guide, to drive*)
Pres. Ind.:   conduzco, conduces, conduce, conducimos, conducís,
               conducen
Preterit: conduje, condujiste, condujo, condujimos, condujisteis,
               condujeron
Imperative: conduce, conduzca, conduzcamos, conducid,
               conduzcan
Pres. Subj.: conduzca, conduzcas, conduzca, conduzcamos,
               conduzcáis, conduzcan
Imp. Subj.:   condujera (condujese), condujeras, condujera,
               condujéramos, condujerais, condujeran

               (All verbs ending in **-ducir** follow this pattern.)

convenir (*to agree*) See **venir.**

dar (*to give*)
Pres. Ind.:   doy, das, da, damos, dais, dan
Preterit: di, diste, dio, dimos, disteis, dieron
Imperative: da, dé, demos, dad, den
Pres. Subj.: dé, des, dé, demos, deis, den
Imp. Subj.:   diera (diese), dieras, diera, diéramos, dierais, dieran

decir (*to say, to tell*)
Pres. Ind.: digo, dices, dice, decimos, decís, dicen
Preterit: dije, dijiste, dijo, dijimos, dijisteis, dijeron
Future: diré, dirás, dirá, diremos, diréis, dirán
Conditional: diría, dirías, diría, diríamos, diríais, dirían
Imperative: di, diga, digamos, decid, digan
Pres. Subj.: diga, digas, diga, digamos, digáis, digan
Imp. Subj.: dijera (dijese), dijeras, dijera, dijéramos, dijerais, dijeran
Pres. Part.: diciendo
Past Part.: dicho

detener (*to stop, to hold, to arrest*) See **tener**.

entretener (*to entertain, to amuse*) See **tener**.

errar (*to err, to miss*)
Pres. Ind.: yerro, yerras, yerra, erramos, erráis, yerran
Imperative: yerra, yerre, erremos, errad, yerren
Pres. Subj.: yerre, yerres, yerre, erremos, erréis, yerren

estar (*to be*)
Pres. Ind.: estoy, estás, está, estamos, estáis, están
Preterit: estuve, estuviste, estuvo, estuvimos, estuvisteis, estuvieron
Imperative: está, esté, estemos, estad, estén
Pres. Subj.: esté, estés, esté, estemos, estéis, estén
Imp. Subj.: estuviera (estuviese), estuvieras, estuviera, estuviéramos, estuvieras, estuvieran

haber (*to have*)
Pres. Ind.: he, has, ha, hemos, habéis, han
Preterit: hube, hubiste, hubo, hubimos, hubisteis, hubieron
Future: habré, habrás, habrá, habremos, habréis, habrán
Conditional: habría, habrías, habría, habríamos, habríais, habrían
Imperative: he, haya, hayamos, habed, hayan
Pres. Subj.: haya, hayas, haya, hayamos, hayáis, hayan
Imp. Subj.: hubiera (hubiese), hubieras, hubiera, hubiéramos, hubieras, hubieran

hacer (*to do, to make*)
Pres. Ind.: hago, haces, hace, hacemos, hacéis, hacen
Preterit: hice, hiciste, hizo, hicimos, hicisteis, hicieron
Future: haré, harás, hará, haremos, haréis, harán
Conditional: haría, harías, haría, haríamos, haríais, harían
Imperative: haz, haga, hagamos, haced, hagan
Pres. Subj.: haga, hagas, haga, hagamos, hagáis, hagan
Imp. Subj.: hiciera (hiciese), hicieras, hiciera, hiciéramos, hicierais, hicieran
Past Part.: hecho

imponer (*to impose, to deposit*) See **poner.**

introducir (*to introduce, to insert, to gain access*) See **conducir.**

ir (*to go*)
Pres. Ind.:   voy, vas, va, vamos, vais, van
Imp. Ind.:   iba, ibas, iba, íbamos, ibais, iban
Preterit: fui, fuiste, fue, fuimos, fuisteis, fueron
Imperative: ve, vaya, vayamos, id, vayan
Pres. Subj.:   vaya, vayas, vaya, vayamos, vayáis, vayan
Imp. Subj.:   fuera (fuese), fueras, fuera, fuéramos, fuerais, fueran

jugar (*to play*)
Pres. Ind.:   juego, juegas, juega, jugamos, jugáis, juegan
Imperative: juega, juegue, juguemos, jugad, jueguen
Pres. Subj.:   juegue, juegues, juegue, juguemos, juguéis, jueguen

obtener (*to obtain*) See **tener.**

oír (*to hear*)
Pres. Ind.:   oigo, oyes, oye, oímos, óis, oyen
Preterit: oí, oíste, oyó, oímos, oísteis, oyeron
Imperative: oye, oiga, oigamos, oid, oigan
Pres. Subj.:   oiga, oigas, oiga, oigamos, oigáis, oigan
Imp. Subj.:   oyera (oyese), oyeras, oyera, oyéramos, oyerais, oyeran
Pres. Part.:   oyendo
Past Part.:   oído

oler (*to smell*)
Pres. Ind.:   huelo, hueles, huele, olemos, oléis, huelen
Imperative: huele, huela, olamos, oled, huelan
Pres. Subj.:   huela, huelas, huela, olamos, oláis, huelan

poder (*to be able*)
Pres. Ind.:   puedo, puedes, puede, podemos, podéis, pueden
Preterit: pude, pudiste, pudo, pudimos, pudisteis, pudieron
Future: podré, podrás, podrá, podremos, podréis, podrán
Conditional: podría, podrías, podría, podríamos, podríais, podrían
Imperative: puede, pueda, podamos, poded, puedan
Pres. Subj.:   pueda, puedas, pueda, podamos, podáis, puedan
Imp. Subj.:   pudiera (pudiese), pudieras, pudiera, pudiéramos,
                 pudierais, pudieran
Pres. Part.:   pudiendo

poner (*to place, to put*)
Pres. Ind.:   pongo, pones, pone, ponemos, ponéis, ponen
Preterit: puse, pusiste, puso, pusimos, pusisteis, pusieron
Future: pondré, pondrás, pondrá, pondremos, pondréis,
             pondrán
Conditional: pondría, pondrías, pondría, pondríamos, pondríais,
             pondrían

Imperative: pon, ponga, pongamos, poned, pongan
Pres. Subj.: ponga, pongas, ponga, pongamos, pongáis, pongan
Imp. Subj.: pusiera (pusiese), pusieras, pusiera, pusiéramos, pusierais, pusieran
Past Part.: puesto

querer (*to want, to wish, to like*)
Pres. Ind.: quiero, quieres, quiere, queremos, queréis, quieren
Preterit: quise, quisiste, quiso, quisimos, quisisteis, quisieron
Future: querré, querrás, querrá, querremos, querréis, querrán
Conditional: querría, querrías, querría, querríamos, querríais, querrían
Imperative: quiere, quiera, queramos, quered, quieran
Pres. Subj.: quiera, quieras, quiera, queramos, queráis, quieran
Imp. Subj.: quisiera (quisiese), quisieras, quisiera, quisiéramos, quisierais, quisieran

resolver (*to decide on*)
Past Part.: resuelto

saber (*to know*)
Pres. Ind.: sé, sabes, sabe, sabemos, sabéis, saben
Preterit: supe, supiste, supo, supimos, supisteis, supieron
Future: sabré, sabrás, sabrá, sabremos, sabréis, sabrán
Conditional: sabría, sabrías, sabría, sabríamos, sabríais, sabrían
Imperative: sabe, sepa, sepamos, sabed, sepan
Pres. Subj.: sepa, sepas, sepa, sepamos, sepáis, sepan
Imp. Subj.: supiera (supiese), supieras, supiera, supiéramos, supierais, supieran

salir (*to leave, to go out*)
Pres. Ind.: salgo, sales, sale, salimos, salís, salen
Future: saldré, saldrás, saldrá, saldremos, saldréis, saldrán
Conditional: saldría, saldrías, saldría, saldríamos, saldríais, saldrían
Imperative: sal, salga, salgamos, salid, salgan
Pres. Subj.: salga, salgas, salga, salgamos, salgáis, salgan

ser (*to be*)
Pres. Ind.: soy, eres, es, somos, sois, son
Imp. Ind.: era, eras, era, éramos, erais, eran
Preterit: fui, fuiste, fue, fuimos, fuisteis, fueron
Imperative: sé, sea, seamos, sed, sean
Pres. Subj.: sea, seas, sea, seamos, seáis, sean
Imp. Subj.: fuera (fuese), fueras, fuera, fuéramos, fuerais, fueran

suponer (*to assume*) See **poner.**

tener (*to have*)
Pres. Ind.: tengo, tienes, tiene, tenemos, tenéis, tienen
Preterit: tuve, tuviste, tuvo, tuvimos, tuvisteis, tuvieron

Future:	tendré, tendrás, tendrá, tendremos, tendréis, tendrán
Conditional:	tendría, tendrías, tendría, tendríamos, tendríais, tendrían
Imperative:	ten, tenga, tengamos, tened, tengan
Pres. Subj.:	tenga, tengas, tenga, tengamos, tengáis, tengan
Imp. Subj.:	tuviera (tuviese), tuvieras, tuviera, tuviéramos, tuvierais, tuvieran

traducir (*to translate*) See **conducir.**

traer (*to bring*)

Pres. Ind.:	traigo, traes, trae, traemos, traéis, traen
Preterit:	traje, trajiste, trajo, trajimos, trajisteis, trajeron
Imperative:	trae, traiga, traigamos, traed, traigan
Pres. Subj.:	traiga, traigas, traiga, traigamos, traigáis, traigan
Imp. Subj.:	trajera (trajese), trajeras, trajera, trajéramos, trajerais, trajeran
Pres. Part.:	trayendo
Past Part.:	traído

valer (*to be worth*)

Pres. Ind.:	valgo, vales, vale, valemos, valéis, valen
Future:	valdré, valdrás, valdrá, valdremos, valdréis, valdrán
Conditional:	valdría, valdrías, valdría, valdríamos, valdríais, valdrían
Imperative:	vale, valga, valgamos, valed, valgan
Pres. Subj.:	valga, valgas, valga, valgamos, valgáis, valgan

venir (*to come*)

Pres. Ind.:	vengo, vienes, viene, venimos, venís, vienen
Preterit:	vine, viniste, vino, vinimos, vinisteis, vinieron
Future:	vendré, vendrás, vendrá, vendremos, vendréis, vendrán
Conditional:	vendría, vendrías, vendría, vendríamos, vendríais, vendrían
Imperative:	ven, venga, vengamos, venid, vengan
Pres. Subj.:	venga, vengas, venga, vengamos, vengáis, vengan
Imp. Subj.:	viniera (viniese), vinieras, viniera, viniéramos, vinierais, vinieran
Pres. Part.:	viniendo

ver (*to see*)

Pres. Ind.:	veo, ves, ve, vemos, veis, ven
Imp. Ind.:	veía, veías, veía, veíamos, veíais, veían
Preterit:	vi, viste, vio, vimos, visteis, vieron
Imperative:	ve, vea, veamos, ved, vean
Pres. Subj.:	vea, veas, vea, veamos, veáis, vean
Imp. Subj.:	viera (viese), vieras, viera, viéramos, vierais, vieran
Past. Part.:	visto

volver (*to return*)

Past Part.:	vuelto

Appendix C

Careers and Occupations

accountant **contador(a)**
actor **actor**
actress **actriz**
administrator
 administrador(a)
agent **agente**
architect **arquitecto(a)**
artisan **artesano(a)**
artist **artista**
baker **panadero(a)**
bank officer **empleado(a)**
 bancario(a)
bank teller **cajero(a)**
banker **banquero(a)**
barber **barbero(a)**
bartender **barman,**
 cantinero(a)
bill collector **cobrador(a)**
bookkeeper **tenedor(a)**
 de libros
brickmason (bricklayer)
 albañil
butcher **carnicero(a)**
buyer **comprador(a)**
camera operator
 camarógrafo(a)
carpenter **carpintero(a)**
cashier **cajero(a)**
chiropractor **quiropráctico(a)**
clerk **dependiente(a)** *(store)*,
 oficinista *(office)*
computer operator
 computista
construction worker
 obrero(a) de la
 construcción
constructor **constructor(a)**
contractor **contratista**
cook **cocinero(a)**
copilot **copiloto(a)**
counselor **consejero(a)**
dancer **bailarín(ina)**

decorator **decorador(a)**
dental hygienist **higienista**
 dental
dentist **dentista**
designer **diseñador(a)**
detective **detective**
dietician **especialista**
 en dietética
diplomat **diplomático(a)**
director **director(a)**
dockworker **obrero(a)**
 portuario(a)
doctor **doctor(a), médico(a)**
draftsman **dibujante**
dressmaker **modista**
driver **conductor(a)**
economist **economista**
editor **editor(a)**
electrician **electricista**
engineer **ingeniero(a)**
engineering technician
 ingeniero(a) técnico(a)
eye doctor **oculista**
farmer **agricultor(a)**
fashion designer **diseñador(a)**
 de alta costura
fire fighter **bombero(a)**
fisherman **pescador(a)**
flight attendant **auxiliar**
 de vuelo
foreman **capataz,**
 encargado(a)
funeral director
 empresario(a) de
 pompas fúnebres
garbage collector **basurero(a)**
gardener **jardinero(a)**
guard **guardia**
guide **guía**
hairdresser **peluquero(a)**
home economist
 economista doméstico(a)

housekeeper **mayordomo, ama de llaves**
inspector **inspector(a)**
instructor **instructor(a)**
insurance agent **agente de seguros**
interior designer **diseñador(a) de interiores**
interpreter **intérprete**
investigator **investigador(a)**
janitor **conserje**
jeweler **joyero(a)**
journalist **periodista**
judge **juez(a)**
lawyer **abogado(a)**
librarian **bibliotecario(a)**
machinist **maquinista**
maid **criada**
mail carrier **cartero(a)**
manager **gerente**
mechanic **mecánico(a)**
midwife **comadrón(ona), partero(a)**
miner **minero(a)**
model **modelo**
musician **músico(a)**
nurse **enfermero(a)**
optician **óptico(a)**
optometrist **optometrista**
painter **pintor(a)**
paramedic **paramédico(a)**
pharmacist **farmacéutico(a)**
photographer **fotógrafo(a)**
physical therapist **terapista físico(a)**
physician **médico(a)**
pilot **piloto** *(masc., fem.)*, **aviador(a)**
plumber **plomero(a)**
police officer **policía**
printer **impresor(a)**
psychologist **psicólogo(a)**
public relations agent **agente de relaciones públicas**
real estate agent **agente de bienes raíces**
receptionist **recepcionista**

reporter **reportero(a), periodista**
sailor **marinero(a)**
sales representative **vendedor(a)**
scientist **científico(a)**
secretary **secretario(a)**
security guard **guardia**
social worker **trabajador(a) social**
sociologist **sociólogo(a)**
soldier **soldado militar**
stenographer **estenógrafo(a)**
stockbroker **bolsista**
student **estudiante**
supervisor **supervisor(a)**
surgeon **cirujano(a)**
systems analyst **analista de sistemas**
tailor **sastre**
taxi driver **chofer de taxi, taxista**
teacher **maestro(a)** *(elem. school)*, **profesor(a)** *(high school and college)*
technician **técnico(a)**
telephone operator **telefonista**
television and radio announcer **locutor(a)**
television and radio technician **técnico(a) de radio y televisión**
teller **cajero(a)**
therapist **terapista**
travel agent **agente de viajes**
truck driver **camionero(a)**
typist **mecanógrafo(a), dactilógrafo(a)**
undertaker **director(a) de pompas fúnebres**
veterinarian **veterinario(a)**
waiter **mozo, camarero**
waitress **camarera**
watchmaker **relojero(a)**
worker **obrero(a)**
writer **escritor(a)**

Appendix D

Lección 1

A. 1. nosotros (nosotras)   2. ellos   3. ellas   4. Uds.
5. ellos   6. nosotros (nosotras)

B. 1. desean   2. necesitamos   3. estudias   4. tomo
5. trabaja

C. 1. —¿(Ella) necesita las cucharas? / —No, (ella) no
necesita las cucharas; necesita los tenedores.   2. —¿Hablan
(Uds.) italiano? / —No, (nosotros) no hablamos italiano;
hablamos español.   3. —¿El Sr. Vega trabaja en Lima? /
—No, (él) no trabaja en Lima; trabaja en Santiago.

D. 1. trescientos cuarenta y uno   2. setecientos ochenta y
tres   3. mil   4. quinientos setenta y cinco   5. cuatrocientos
sesenta y siete   6. ochocientos noventa y seis

E. 1. a las siete y media de la mañana   2. por la tarde
3. a la una   4. a las siete y cuarto de la tarde (noche)
5. las nueve menos veinticinco

F. 1. mantel   2. inglés / italiano / francés   3. tenedor
4. restaurante   5. tomo / desea   6. pagan

Lección 2

A. 1. (Nosotros) necesitamos las sillas blancas y la mesa
negra.   2. (Yo) necesito dos lápices rojos.   3. (Yo) estudio
con dos chicas (muchachas) muy inteligentes.   4. ¿Necesita
(Ud.) hablar con la chica alemana, señor?

B. 1. bebo / beben   2. leemos / escribimos   3. comes
4. reciben   5. vivo / vive

C. 1. es   2. eres   3. somos / es   4. son   5. soy / es

D. 1. bebes   2. comemos   3. vivo   4. escribe
5. temprano   6. leche   7. Cuántos   8. dónde   9. abrimos
10. bueno

Lección 3

A. 1. Carlos es el hijo de María Iriarte. 2. El primo (La prima) de Ana es de Colombia. 3. El apellido de la chica (muchacha) es Torres. 4. (Ella) necesita el número de teléfono de la Sra. Madera. 5. La casa de David es verde.

B. 1. ¿Ud. necesita (Tú necesitas) la dirección de él o la dirección de ella? 2. La Srta. Vega es nuestra amiga. 3. (Yo) necesito mi coche. 4. ¿(Ud.) necesita hablar con sus hijos, Sr. Varela? 5. ¿Tú llamas a tus padres, Paquito?

C. 1. (Yo) deseo visitar a la Srta. Arévalo. 2. ¿Ud. llama (Tú llamas) a María? 3. Los estudiantes visitan el museo.

D. 1. da / damos 2. vas / van 3. estoy / están 4. vamos 5. estás

E. 1. es / está 2. somos 3. es / es 4. es 5. estoy 6. son 7. es 8. estás 9. es 10. está

F. 1. argentino(a) 2. abuelo 3. Estados 4. profesión 5. tomar 6. llevar 7. Quién 8. quién 9. Cómo 10. dan

Lección 4

A. 1. tiene / tienes 2. vengo 3. tenemos 4. tienen / venimos 5. vienes 6. tienen

B. 1. (Yo) necesito el número de teléfono del Sr. Soto. 2. (Ella) va a la universidad los viernes. 3. (Yo) llamo al gerente los martes. 4. (Ella) es la hija del Sr. Miranda. 5. (Nosotros) vamos al gimnasio los sábados.

C. 1. (Ella) es tan alta como mi hijo. 2. El Hotel Azteca es el más caro de la ciudad. ¡Es el mejor! 3. ¿(Ella) es menor o mayor que David? 4. Colombia es más pequeña que los Estados Unidos. 5. (Yo) tengo poco dinero, pero (él) tiene menos dinero que yo. 6. (Nosotros) estamos tan cansados como tú/Ud., Anita. 7. (Yo) no tengo tantos libros como tú/Ud., Ana. 8. Mi esposa necesita tantas maletas como yo.

D. 1. barato 2. pensión 3. pequeño(a) 4. menor 5. mejor 6. piscina 7. llave 8. peor 9. poco 10. biblioteca

Lección 5

A. 1. (Yo) no tengo hambre, pero tengo mucha sed. 2. Darío tiene diecinueve años. ¿Cuántos años tienes (tú), Paco? 3. ¿Tiene (Ud.) prisa, Srta. Perales? 4. ¿(Tú) tienes frío, papá? ¡(Yo) tengo calor!   5. (Nosotros) tenemos mucho sueño.   6. ¡(Ud.) tiene razón, Sra. Vega! Paquito tiene mucho miedo.

B. 1. quieres / prefiero   2. cierran / empieza
3. entienden / entendemos

C. (*Possibilities; answers may vary.*): 1. Tú vas a leer el libro.
2. Nosotros vamos a comer los sándwiches.   3. Ellos van a estudiar la lección dos.   4. Yo voy a tomar (beber) café.
5. Ella va a estudiar francés.

D. 1. Hoy es miércoles.   2. No me gusta el té.   3. La educación es importante.   4. Vamos a la escuela la próxima semana (la semana próxima).   5. (Yo) no tengo clases los viernes.

E. 1. tercer   2. primero   3. quinta / sexta   4. octavo
5. séptima

F. 1. desayunamos   2. revista   3. empieza (comienza)
4. toalla   5. prefieres   6. entiendes   7. vacaciones   8. piso
9. pierden   10. mes

Lección 6

A. (*Possibilities; answers may vary.*): 1. (Yo) vuelvo a mi casa a las cinco y media.   2. Cuando (nosotros) vamos a México, volamos.   3. Sí, (nosotros) recordamos los verbos irregulares.
4. (Yo) duermo ocho horas.   5. No, (nosotros) no podemos ir a la fiesta.

B. 1. Ellos recuerdan algo.   2. Hay alguien en el cuarto.
3. Yo quiero volar también.   4. Recibimos algunos regalos.
5. Siempre tiene fiestas en su casa.

C. 1. ¿(Ud.) puede (Tú puedes) venir conmigo?   2. ¿(Ud.) va (Tú vas) a trabajar con ellos?   3. El dinero es para ti, Anita.   4. El regalo no es para mí. Es para ella.   5. No, Paco, (yo) no puedo ir contigo.

D. (*Possibilities; answers may vary.*): 1. En los Estados Unidos se habla inglés.   2. Se dice colchón.   3. La oficina de correos se cierra a las tres.   4. Mi nombre se escribe. . .
5. Las bibliotecas se abren a las diez.

E. 1. está estudiando   2. está comiendo   3. estamos leyendo
4. estás diciendo   5. estoy bebiendo

F. 1. vista / mar   2. almuerzan   3. colchón   4. cuesta
5. lugares   6. alcohólicas   7. duerme   8. oficina / correos

Lección 7

A. (*Possibilities; answers may vary.*): 1. (Nosotros) servimos sopa. 2. (Yo) pido Coca-Cola para beber. 3. No, (yo) no digo mi edad. 4. Sí, (yo) sigo en la universidad. 5. Sí, (nosotros) siempre pedimos postre.

B. 1. conduzco 2. salgo 3. pongo 4. traduzco 5. conozco 6. traigo 7. hago 8. veo 9. sé

C. 1. (Yo) conozco a su hijo. 2. (Él) no sabe francés. 3. ¿Sabe (Ud.) nadar, Srta. Vera? 4. ¿Conoce (Ud.) al agente de viajes? 5. ¿Conocen los estudiantes las novelas de Cervantes?

D. 1. Yo las conozco. 2. Uds. van a comprarlo. 3. Nosotros no queremos verte. 4. Ella la sirve. 5. ¿Ud. no me conoce? 6. Él los escribe. 7. Carlos va a visitarnos. 8. Nosotros no lo vemos.

E. 1. agencia 2. nadar 3. memoria 4. reservación 5. pasaportes 6. ocupado(a) 7. poema

Lección 8

A. 1. (Yo) necesito estas pelotas y aquéllas. 2. ¿Quiere (Ud.) este caballo o ése? 3. (Yo) prefiero estos patines, no aquéllos. 4. Papá, ¿quieres (tú) comprar esta raqueta o ésa? 5. (Yo) no quiero comer en este restaurante. (Yo) prefiero aquél. 6. (Yo) no entiendo eso.

B. 1. Me va a comprar unos patines. 2. Le doy la bicicleta. 3. Nos habla en español. 4. Les voy a decir la verdad. 5. Les pregunto la dirección de la oficina. 6. Le estamos escribiendo a nuestro padre. 7. Le escribo los lunes. 8. Le doy la información al entrenador. 9. Te hablo en inglés. 10. No me compran nada.

C. 1. (Yo) voy a preguntarle dónde vive. 2. (Yo) siempre le pido dinero a mi tía. 3. (Ella) siempre pregunta cómo está Ud., Sra. Nieto. 4. (Ellos) me van a pedir la tienda de campaña. 5. (Yo) quiero preguntarle cuántos años tiene (él).

D. 1. ¿El dinero? (Yo) se lo doy mañana, Sr. Peña. 2. (Yo) sé que necesitas el diccionario, Anita, pero (yo) no puedo prestártelo. 3. (Yo) necesito mi mochila. ¿Puede (Ud.) traérmela, Srta. López? 4. ¿Las plumas? (Ella) nos las trae. 5. Cuando (yo) necesito patines, mi mamá me los compra.

E. 1. deportiva 2. quién 3. pelota / raqueta 4. bolsas 5. entradas 6. tío 7. campaña 8. parque

Lección 9

A. 1. No, no son mías.   2. No, no son de ella.   3. No, no es mío.   4. No, no es nuestra.   5. No, no es de ellos.
6. No, no son míos.   7. No, no es nuestra.   8. No, no es de Uds.

B. 1. (Yo) me levanto a las siete, me baño, me visto y salgo a las siete y media.   2. ¿A qué hora se despiertan los niños?
3. (Ella) no quiere sentarse.   4. (Él) se afeita todos los días.
5. ¿(Tú) te acuerdas de tus maestros, Carlitos?
6. (Ellos/Ellas) siempre se están quejando.   7. Primero (ella) acuesta a los niños, y entonces (ella) se acuesta.   8. ¿Quiere (Ud.) probarse estos pantalones, señorita?   9. ¿Dónde van a poner (Uds.) el dinero, señoras?   10. Los estudiantes siempre se duermen en esta clase.

C. 1. Abra   2. Hablen   3. Traiga   4. Vengan   5. cierre
6. Doblen   7. Siga   8. Den   9. Estén   10. sean
11. vaya   12. Vuelva   13. Sirva   14. Pongan
15. Escriban

D. 1. Dígales la verdad, Sr. Mena.   2. ¿El vestido? No me lo traiga ahora, Srta. Ruiz.   3. No se lo diga a mi peluquero(a), por favor.   4. Traigan las bebidas, señores. Tráiganlas a la terraza.   5. No se levante, Sra. Miño.   6. ¿El té? Tráigaselo a las cuatro de la tarde, Sr. Vargas.

E. 1. afeitar   2. peluquería / cabeza / pelo   3. tintorería
4. tarjeta de crédito   5. izquierda   6. mismo   7. acostar
8. derecho

Lección 10

A. 1. Ayer ella entró en la cafetería y comió tallarines.
2. Ayer María le escribió a su suegra.   3. El viernes pasado ella me prestó su abrigo.   4. El año pasado ellos fueron los mejores estudiantes.   5. El sábado pasado ellos te esperaron cerca del supermercado.   6. El verano pasado mi hijo fue a Buenos Aires.   7. Ayer por la mañana le di el impermeable.
8. El lunes pasado nosotros decidimos comprar la aspiradora.
9. Anoche le pregunté la hora.   10. Anoche tú no pagaste por la ropa.   11. El jueves pasado fuimos los primeros.   12. Ayer me dieron muchos problemas.   13. Anoche mi suegro no bebió café.   14. Ayer yo no fui a esquiar.   15. La semana pasada te dimos el suéter.

B. 1. La criada entró por la puerta de atrás.   2. (Ella) pasó por mi casa.   3. (Ella) no vino por la lluvia.   4. Hay vuelos para México los sábados.   5. (Nosotros) vamos por avión.

6. El límite de velocidad es cincuenta y cinco millas por hora.
7. (Yo) necesito la lavadora para mañana.   8. ¿Para quién es
el paraguas?   9. (Yo) necesito el dinero para pagar el
impermeable.   10. (Ella) pagó doscientos dólares por esa
aspiradora.

C. 1. Hace mucho viento hoy.   2. Hace mucho frío, y también nieva / está nevando.   3. Hace mucho calor en Cuba.
4. ¿Qué tiempo hace hoy?   5. ¿Hace sol o está nublado?
6. No hay vuelos por la niebla.

D. 1. abrigo (suéter)   2. límite   3. impermeable   4. lata
5. lavadora   6. prepara (cocina)   7. criada   8. tiempo

Lección 11

A. 1. —¿Cuánto tiempo hace que (Uds.) trabajan en San Juan? /
—Hace cinco años que (nosotros) trabajamos en San Juan.
2. —¿Cuánto tiempo hace que (ellos) esperan? / —Hace tres
horas que (ellos) esperan.   3. —¿Cuánto tiempo hace que (ella)
estudia español? / —Hace dos años que (ella) estudia español.

B. 1. Ayer María no estuvo en la clase.   2. Anoche no
pudieron venir.   3. El mes pasado puse el dinero en el banco.
4. El domingo pasado no hiciste nada.   5. Ayer ella vino con
Juan.   6. El lunes pasado no quisimos venir a clase.
7. Anoche yo no dije nada.   8. Ayer trajimos la tostadora.
9. Anoche yo conduje mi coche.   10. Ayer ellos tradujeron
las lecciones.

C. 1. Vivíamos en Alaska.   2. Hablaba inglés.   3. Veía a mi
abuela.   4. Poníamos el dinero en el Banco de América.
5. Se acostaban a las nueve.   6. Iba a la universidad.
7. Compraba arroz.   8. Enseñaba español.

D. 1. Ven acá, por favor.   2. Habla con la profesora.
3. Dime tu dirección.   4. Lávate las manos.   5. Ponte el
abrigo.   6. Tráenos el arroz con pollo.   7. Compra los
libros.   8. Hazme un favor.   9. Apaga la luz.   10. Ve de
compras hoy.   11. Sal temprano.   12. Aféitate aquí.
13. Ten paciencia.   14. Sé buena.   15. Come con nosotros.

E. 1. No se lo digas (a él).   2. No salgas ahora.   3. No te
levantes.   4. No traigas el postre ahora.   5. No bebas
(tomes) el café.   6. No les hables.   7. No vayas a la tienda.
8. ¿Ese vestido? ¡No te lo pongas!   9. No hagas eso.

F. 1. compras   2. apaga   3. arroz   4. trabajos
5. liquidación (venta)   6. época   7. caminar   8. nunca
9. cuando   10. vez

Lección 12

A. 1. estábamos comiendo   2. estabas haciendo   3. estaba escribiendo   4. estaba hablando   5. estaban comprando   6. estaba leyendo   7. estaban estudiando   8. estaba trabajando

B. 1. (Nosotros) nos acostamos a las once anoche.   2. (Ella) estaba escribiendo a máquina cuando la vi.   3. (Nosotros) íbamos a Lima todos los veranos.   4. Eran las diez y media cuando (yo) llamé a mi cuñada.   5. (Ella) dijo que quería leer.

C. 1. conocía / conocí   2. sabíamos / supimos   3. quiso   4. quería / supe

D. 1. Nosotros llegamos al aeropuerto a las seis y media.   2. Mi cuñada está en casa.   3. Ellos están en la joyería.   4. La fiesta es a las doce.   5. ¿Raul está en la clase?

E. 1. traje   2. catálogo   3. quedarnos / todo   4. máquina   5. encontrarme   6. vacaciones   7. juntos (juntas)   8. aeropuerto   9. cuñado   10. comercial / vidrieras (escaparates)

Lección 13

A. 1. Ayer ella eligió el anillo de oro.   2. Anoche Marta no durmió bien.   3. Ayer no le pedí nada.   4. La semana pasada ella te mintió.   5. El sábado pasado ellos sirvieron los refrescos.   6. Ayer no lo repetí.   7. Anoche ella siguió estudiando.   8. El lunes pasado tú no conseguiste nada.

B. 1. Sí, acabo de encontrarlo.   2. Sí, acabo de venderla.   3. Sí, acaban de comprarlas.   4. Sí, acabamos de arreglarla.   5. Sí, acaban de llegar.

C. 1. me gustan   2. le hace falta   3. le duele   4. nos hace falta   5. Le gusta   6. le hace falta   7. me duelen   8. nos gusta

D. 1. ¿Qué es un impermeable?   2. ¿Cuál es su (tu) dirección?   3. ¿Qué es una biblioteca?   4. ¿Cuál es su (tu) número de teléfono?   5. ¿Cuáles son sus ideas sobre esto?

E. 1. aspirinas / duele   2. murieron   3. acaban   4. divertí   5. oro   6. mecánica   7. chaqueta   8. eligió (vendió)   9. sortija   10. despedimos

Lección 14

A. 1. (a) Hace tres meses que nosotros llegamos a California.   (b) Nosotros llegamos a California hace tres meses.

2. (a) Hace dos horas que el chico tomó café.   (b) El chico tomó café hace dos horas.   3. (a) Hace dos días que ellos terminaron la lección.   (b) Ellos terminaron la lección hace dos días.   4. (a) Hace veinte años que ella vino a esta ciudad. (b) Ella vino a esta ciudad hace veinte años.   5. (a) Hace dos días que tú llenaste el tanque.   (b) Tú llenaste el tanque hace dos días.

B. 2. recibido   3. volver   4. usado   5. escrito   6. ir
7. aprendido   8. abrir   9. cubierto   10. comido   11. ver
12. hecho   13. sido   14. decir   15. cerrado   16. morir
17. romper   18. dormido   19. estado   20. poner

C. 1. El libro está escrito en inglés.   2. La ventana está rota.
3. La puerta está abierta.   4. ¿Están cerrados los bancos?
5. La mesa está cubierta.

D. 1. he venido   2. Han terminado   3. hemos hablado
4. ha dicho   5. has escrito   6. hemos hecho / hemos tenido
7. ha abierto   8. ha puesto   9. han comido   10. han roto

E. 1. (Yo) ya había traído la batería (el acumulador).
2. (Ellos, Ellas) no habían llamado al empleado (a la emplea-
da).   3. (Ellos, Ellas) habían roto las ventanas.   4. (Él) ya
había visto al profesor (a la profesora).   5. ¿Había cubierto
(Ud.) las mesas, Srta. Peña?

F. 1. servicio / gasolina   2. acumulador   3. vacío   4. goma
(llanta) / pinchada   5. automovilístico   6. marca   7. hace
8. repuesto

Lección 15

A. 1. irán   2. vendrá   3. pagarán   4. llevarás   5. será
6. pondrás   7. manejarán   8. revisará   9. harán
10. alquilaré

B. 1. iríamos   2. venderían   3. habría   4. serviría
5. trabajarías   6. Pondría   7. preferirían   8. Seguirían
9. Te levantarías

C. 1. (Nosotros) no llegaremos a la universidad a las seis.
2. ¿Llevaste (tú) a tu perro al veterinario, María?   3. Después
(nosotros) viajaremos en avión.   4. (Ella) está en la agencia de
alquiler de automóviles.   5. ¿De qué están hablando (ellos,
ellas)?

D. 1. agencia   2. peligrosas   3. mecánicos / automáticos
4. depositar   5. plata   6. revisar (chequear)   7. falta
8. examen

Lección 16

A. 1. cerremos   2. vayan   3. abras   4. recomiende
5. salga (se vaya)   6. vuelva (regrese)   7. quieran
8. entienda   9. tengamos   10. pongan   11. traigas
12. den   13. esté   14. sea   15. sepan

B. 1. —¿Quieres ir al hospital conmigo, Anita? / —No
puedo. Alberto quiere que vaya a la estación de trenes
con él.

2. —¿Qué quieres hacer este fin de semana, Pedro? / —No sé...
¿Qué me sugieres que haga? / —Te sugiero que estudies.

3. —¿Necesita Ud. que yo le traiga el horario de trenes, Srta.
Rojas? /—Sí, y le ruego que venga esta tarde, Sr. Varela. / —¿A
qué hora quiere que esté en su casa? / —A las dos.

4. —Voy a pedirle que compre los boletos. / —Yo prefiero
comprarlos esta tarde.

C. 1. dificilísimo(a)   2. lentísima   3. buenísimas   4. altísimo
5. larguísimo   6. rapidísimo   7. inteligentísimos(as)
8. facilísimos(as)

D. 1. antes   2. descuento / ciento   3. asiento   4. rápido
(expreso)   5. estación   6. niego

Lección 17

A. 1. —Espero conseguir la beca. / —Temo que no pueda(s)
conseguirla porque tus (sus) notas no son muy buenas.

2. —Me alegro de estar aquí contigo, Anita. / —Espero que
puedas ir a la fiesta conmigo esta noche, Carlos.

3. —Temo que no podamos matricularnos en la clase de física. /
—Siento que no tengan el dinero, chicas. . .

4. —Esperamos tomar una clase de literatura. / —Nos
alegramos de que quieran tomar literatura.

B. 1. matricularse   2. pueda   3. sacar   4. den   5. sea
6. firmar   7. tomar   8. tenga

C. 1. especialmente   2. recientemente   3. lenta y
claramente   4. generalmente   5. fácilmente

D. 1. calculadora   2. parcial / final   3. fácil   4. matrícula
5. ser   6. necesario   7. física   8. consejero(a)

Lección 18

A. 1. —La Dra. Soto dice que (ella) puede cuidar a mis pacientes. / —Estoy seguro(a) de que puede.

2. —No creo que el doctor (médico) esté en su consultorio. / —Entonces tengo que llamar a su casa.

3. —Dudo que el Sr. Soto pueda llevar a su esposa a la sala de emergencia. / —¿Puede llevarla su hija? / —No creo que esté en casa.

4. —¡(Yo) estoy seguro(a) de que ella necesita muletas! / —Es verdad que le duele la pierna, pero no es verdad que necesite muletas. . .

B. 1. que sea de México.   2. que pueda llevarlo a la sala de rayos X.   3. que hable español.   4. que sepa poner inyecciones.   5. que cuide a mis hijos.

C. 1. Carmencita   2. arbolito   3. niñitos   4. cafecito
5. Juancito   6. favorcito   7. piernitas   8. bracito
9. hermanita   10. nochecita

D. 1. ambulancia   2. muletas   3. sala   4. consultorio
5. radiografía   6. poner   7. enyesar   8. momento

Lección 19

A. 1. venga su abogado(a)   2. me trae   3. la fiebre baje
4. sepa   5. los (las) lleven   6. llega   7. tomes   8. tenga fiebre

B. 1. haya llegado   2. hayan vuelto   3. haya ido   4. hayas dicho   5. hayamos hecho   6. haya preferido   7. haya abierto   8. hayan puesto

C. 1. hayamos hecho el trabajo.   2. haya estado enfermo.
3. hayan muerto muchos.   4. haya ido a México.   5. le hayas escrito una carta.   6. ellos hayan hablado con la enfermera.   7. no hayan visto a sus pacientes.   8. que Ana y yo hayamos ido a su consultorio.

D. 1. pasajeros   2. termómetro   3. autopista   4. jarabe
5. antes   6. ejercicio / dieta

Lección 20

A. 1. asistieran   2. fueras   3. devolviéramos   4. fuera
5. recogiera   6. pudiera   7. quisiera   8. dieran
9. hiciéramos   10. trajeran

B. 1. tuviera que trabajar.   2. pusiéramos el dinero en el banco.   3. fueras al correo.   4. hicieran las diligencias. 5. llevara el paquete.   6. hablaran con el jefe.   7. estuviera enferma.   8. perdiera la billetera.

C. 1. Si la veo   2. Si yo fuera Ud. (tú)   3. Si ella tuviera tiempo   4. Si él me da el dinero   5. Si fuéramos en coche 6. Si ella puede venir   7. Si tú quisieras   8. si ellos van conmigo

D. 1. billetera   2. computadora   3. informe   4. préstamo 5. talonario   6. asisten   7. montón / echar

Vocabularies

The number following each vocabulary item indicates the lesson in which it first appears.

The following abbreviations are used.

adj.	adjective	*Méx.*	México
f.	feminine noun	*pl.*	plural
fam.	familiar	*pron.*	pronoun
form.	formal	*sing.*	singular
m.	masculine noun		

Spanish-English

A

a to, 3; at, 1; in, 15
a la derecha to the right, 9
a la izquierda to the left, 9
a menos que unless, 19
a menudo often, 3
¿a qué hora... ? at what time?, 1
¿a quién? to whom?, 3
abogado(a) (*m., f.*) lawyer, 17
abrigo (*m.*) coat, 10
abril April, PI
abrir to open, 2
abuela (*f.*) grandmother, 3
abuelo (*m.*) grandfather, 3
aburrido(a) boring, bored, 13
acabar de (+ *inf.*) to have just (done something), 13
accidente (*m.*) accident, 13
aceite (*m.*) oil, 14
aconsejar to advise, 16
acordarse (o:ue) (de) to remember, 9
acostar (o:ue) to put to bed, 9
acostarse to go to bed, to lie down, 9
acumulador (*m.*) battery, 14
adiós good-bye, PI

¿adónde? where to?, 3
aeropuerto (*m.*) airport, 12
afeitarse to shave (oneself), 9
agencia agency
— **de alquiler de automóviles** (*f.*) car rental agency, 15
— **de viajes** (*f.*) travel agency, 7
agente de viajes (*m., f.*) travel agent, 7
agosto August, PI
ahora now, 3
— **mismo** right now, 9
alberca (*f.*) swimming pool (*Méx.*), 4
alcohólico(a) alcoholic, 6
alegrarse (de) to be glad, 17
alemán (alemana) German, 2
algo something, anything, 6
alguien someone, anyone, 6
algún any, some, 6
alguna vez ever, 6
algunas veces sometimes, 6
alguno(a) any, some, 6
algunos(as) (*pl.*) any, some, 6
almorzar (o:ue) to have lunch, 6

almuerzo (*m.*)   lunch, 5
alquilar   to rent, 15
alto(a)   tall, 2
allá   over there, 8
allí   there, 6
amarillo(a)   yellow, PI
ambulancia (*f.*)   ambulance, 18
americano(a)   American, 20
amigo(a) (*m., f.*)   friend, 3
amistad (*f.*)   friendship, PII
análisis (*m.*)   test, analysis, 19
anaranjado(a)   orange, PI
anillo (*m.*)   ring, 13
anoche   last night, 10
anteayer   the day before
    yesterday, 12
antes de   before, 9
antes de que   before, 19
año(s)   year(s), PI
apagar   to turn off, 11
apellido (*m.*)   surname, PI
    — de soltera (*m.*)
       maiden name, PI
aprender   to learn, 2
aquel(los), aquella(s) (*adj.*)
    that, those (distant), 8
aquél(los), aquélla(s) (*pron.*)
    that (one), those (distant), 8
aquello (*neuter pron.*)   that, 8
aquí   here, 3
árbol (*m.*)   tree, 18
aretes (*m. pl.*)   earrings, 13
argentino(a)   Argentinian, 3
arreglar   to fix, 13
arroz (*m.*)   rice, 11
    — con pollo (*m.*)
       chicken with rice, 11
asado(a)   roasted, baked, 2
asiento (*m.*)   seat, 16
asistir   to attend, 20
aspiradora (*f.*)   vacuum
    cleaner, 10
aspirina (*f.*)   aspirin, 13
atender (e:ie)   to wait on, to
    attend to, 9
auto (*m.*)   car, automobile, 3
autobús (*m.*)   bus, 3

automático(a)   automatic, 15
automóvil (*m.*)   car,
    automobile, 3
autopista (*f.*)   freeway, 19
avenida (*f.*)   avenue, 7
avión (*m.*)   airplane, 7
ayer   yesterday, 10
ayudante (*m., f.*)   assistant, 19
ayudar   to help, 10
azul   blue, PI

B

bajar   to go down, to
    decrease, 19
banco (*m.*)   bank, 6
bañar(se)   to bathe (oneself), 9
baño (*m.*)   bathroom, 9
barato(a)   inexpensive, 4
barrer   to sweep, 10
básquetbol (*m.*)   basketball, 8
basura (*f.*)   trash, 11
batería (*f.*)   battery, 14
beber   to drink, 2
bebida (*f.*)   drink, 3
beca (*f.*)   scholarship, 17
bello(a)   beautiful, 16
biblioteca (*f.*)   library, 4
bicicleta (*f.*)   bicycle, 8
bien   well, fine, PI
    muy —, ¿y usted?   very
       well, and you?, PI
    no muy —   not very well,
       PI
billete (*m.*)   ticket, 7
billetera (*f.*)   wallet, 20
blanco(a)   white, PI
boleto (*m.*)   ticket, 16
bolsa de dormir (*f.*)
    sleeping bag, 8
bonito(a)   pretty, 3
bote (*m.*)   can (*Méx.*), 10
botiquín (*m.*)   medicine
    cabinet, 9
buenas noches   good
    evening (good night), PI

buenas tardes good afternoon, PI
bueno(a) good, 2; kind, 16
buscar to look for, to pick up, to get, 16

C

caballo (*m.*) horse, 8
cabeza (*f.*) head, 13
café brown, PI; (*m.*) coffee, 2
cafetería (*f.*) cafeteria, 1
cajero(a) (*m., f.*) cashier, 15
calculadora (*f.*) calculator, 17
caliente hot, 2
calle (*f.*) street, PI
cama (*f.*) bed, 6
camarero(a) (*m., f.*) waiter, waitress, 2
cambiar to change, 14
— **un cheque** to cash a check, 15
caminar to walk, 11
camisón (*m.*) nightgown, 13
cansado(a) tired, 3
cárcel (*f.*) jail, 5
carne (*f.*) meat, 7
caro(a) expensive, 4
carro (*m.*) car, automobile, 3
carta (*f.*) letter, 7
cartera (*f.*) purse, 12
casa (*f.*) house, PII
casado(a) married, PI
casi almost, 14
— **nunca** hardly ever, 11
catálogo (*m.*) catalogue, 12
catorce fourteen, PI
cena (*f.*) dinner, 5
centro comercial (*m.*) mall, 12
cepillo (*m.*) brush, 9
cerca de near to, 6
cero zero, PI
cerrar (e:ie) to close, 5
cerveza (*f.*) beer, 1
cien, ciento one hundred, PII
cinco five, PI

cincuenta fifty, PII
cine (*m.*) movie theater, movies, 5
cirugía (*f.*) surgery, 19
cirujano(a) (*m., f.*) surgeon, 19
ciudad (*f.*) city, PI
claro(a) clear, 17
clase (*f.*) class, 4
clima (*m.*) climate, PII
club (*m.*) club, 8
— **automovilístico** (*m.*) auto club, 14
cobija (*f.*) blanket, 6
cobrar to charge, 15
cocina (*f.*) kitchen, 10
cocinar to cook, 10
cocinero(a) (*m., f.*) cook, 11
coche (*m.*) car, automobile, 3
colchón (*m.*) mattress, 6
collar (*m.*) necklace, 13
comenzar (e:ie) to begin, to start, 5
comer to eat, 2
comida (*f.*) meal, food, 2
¿cómo? how?, 3
¿— **es?** what is he (she, it) like?, 3
¿— **está usted?** how are you?, PI
¿— **se dice... ?** how do you say. . . ?, 6
comprar to buy, 5
computadora (*f.*) computer, 20
con with, 3
¿— **quién?** with whom?, 3
— **tal que** provided that, 19
— **vista al mar** with an ocean view, 6
concierto (*m.*) concert, 5
conducir to drive, 7
conferencia (*f.*) lecture, 17
confirmar to confirm, 7
conocer to know, to be familiar with, 7; to meet for the first time, 12

dieciséis sixteen, PI
diecisiete seventeen, PI
diez ten, PI
difícil difficult, 16
diligencia (*f.*) errand, 20
dinero (*m.*) money, PII
dirección (*f.*) address, PI
divertirse (e:ie) to have a
   good time, 13
divorciado(a) divorced, PI
doblar to turn, 9
doce twelve, PI
doctor(a) (*m., f.*) M.D.,
   doctor, PII
dólar (*m.*) dollar, 3
doler (o:ue) to hurt, to
   ache, 13
domicilio (*m.*) address, PI
domingo (*m.*) Sunday, PI
¿dónde? where?, 2
dormir (o:ue) to sleep, 6
dormirse (o:ue) to fall
   asleep, 9
dormitorio (*m.*) bedroom, 9
dos two, PI
doscientos two hundred, PII
dudar to doubt, 18
dueño(a) (*m., f.*) owner, 5

E

echar al correo to mail, 20
edad (*f.*) age, PI
educación (*f.*) education, 5
el the (*m.*), it (*m.*), PII
él he, 1; him, 6
elegir (e:i) to choose, to
   select, 13
ella she, 1; her, 6
ellas they (*f.*), 1; them (*f.*), 6
ellos they (*m.*), 1; them
   (*m.*), 6
embajada (*f.*) embassy, 7
emergencia (*f.*)
   emergency, 18
empezar (e:ie) to begin, to
   start, 5

empleado(a) (*m., f.*) clerk,
   attendant, 14
en in, at, 1; inside, over, 15
   — **casa** at home, 12
   — **caso de que** in case, 19
   — **cuanto** as soon as, 19
   — **esa época** in those
     days, 11
   — **este momento** at this
     moment, 18
   — **seguida** right away, 14
encontrarse (o:ue) (con) to
   meet, 12
enero January, PI
enfermero(a) (*m., f.*) nurse,
   PI
enfermo(a) sick, 3
ensalada (*f.*) salad, 7
enseñar to teach, 11
entender (e:ie) to
   understand, 5
entonces then, in that case, 7
entrada (*f.*) ticket (for an
   event), 8
entrar to enter, to come in, 10
entrenador(a) (*m., f.*)
   trainer, coach, 8
entrevista (*f.*) interview, 20
enyesar to put a cast on, 18
es difícil it's unlikely, 17
es importante it is
   important, 17
es imposible it is
   impossible, 17
es lástima it is a pity, 17
es mejor it is better, 17
es necesario it is
   necessary, 17
es seguro it is certain, 17
escalera (*f.*) stairs, 13
   — **mecánica** (*f.*)
     escalator, 13
escaparate (*m.*) store
   window, 12
escoba (*f.*) broom, 10
escribir to write, 2
   — **a máquina** to type, 12

escuela (*f.*)   school, 5
ese(os), esa(as) (*adj.*)   that, those (nearby), 8
ése(os), ésa(as) (*pron.*)   that (one), those (nearby), 8
eso (*neuter pron.*)   that, 8
espaguetis (*m. pl.*) spaghetti, 10
español (*m.*)   Spanish (language), PII
español(a)   Spanish, 2
especial   special, 17
espejo (*m.*)   mirror, 9
esperar   to wait (for), 4; to hope, 16
esposa (*f.*)   wife, 4
esposo (*m.*)   husband, 4
esquiar   to ski, 8
esquíes (*m. pl.*)   skis, 8
esta noche   tonight, 5
está nublado   it's cloudy, 10
estación de servicio (*f.*) gas station, 14
estación de trenes (*f.*)   train station, 16
estado civil (*m.*)   marital status, PI
Estados Unidos (*m. pl.*) United States, 3
estampilla (*f.*)   stamp, 6
estar   to be, 3
este(a)   this, 6
este(os), esta(s) (*adj.*)   this, these, 8
éste(os), ésta(as) (*pron.*)   this (one), these, 8
esto (*neuter pron.*)   this, 8
estudiante (*m., f.*)   student, 4
estudiar   to study, 1
examen (*m.*)   exam, 15
— **final** (*m.*)   final exam, 17
— **parcial** (*m.*)   midterm exam, 17
excursión (*f.*)   excursion, 6

F

fácil   easy, 17
farmacia (*f.*)   pharmacy, 6
favor (*m.*)   favor, 11
febrero   February, PI
fecha (*f.*)   date, PI
— **de nacimiento** (*f.*) date of birth, PI
feliz   happy, 2
femenino(a)   feminine, PI
fiebre (*f.*)   fever, temperature, 19
fiesta (*f.*)   party, 3
fin de semana (*m.*) weekend, 16
firmar   to sign, 17
física (*f.*)   physics, 17
folleto turístico (*m.*)   tourist brochure, 7
fotocopia (*f.*)   photocopy, 20
fracturarse   to break (a bone), 18
francés (*f.*)   French (language), 1
francés (francesa)   French, 2
frazada (*f.*)   blanket, 6
fregadero (*m.*)   sink, 11
freno (*m.*)   brake, 14
frito(a)   fried, 2
funcionar   to work, to function, 13

G

gasolina (*f.*)   gasoline, 14
gasolinera (*f.*)   gas station, 14
general   general, 17
generalmente   generally, 9
gerente (*m., f.*)   manager, 4
gimnasio (*m.*)   gym, 4
goma (*f.*)   tire, 14
— **pinchada** (*f.*)   flat tire, 14
grande   big, large, 2
gris   gray, PI

grúa (*f.*)   tow truck, 14
guapo(a)   handsome, 2
guía (*m., f.*)   guide, 6
gustar   to like, to be
  pleasing, 13
gusto   pleasure, PI
  el — es mío   the pleasure
  is mine, PI

H

habitación   (*f.*) room, 4
hablar   to speak, to talk, 1
hacer   to do; to make, 7
  — buen (mal) tiempo   to
  be good (bad) weather, 10
  — (mucho) calor   to be
  (very) hot, 10
  — diligencias   to do
  errands, 20
  — ejercicio   to exercise, 19
  — falta   to need, to lack, 13
  — (mucho) frío   to be
  (very) cold, 10
  — sol   to be sunny, 10
  — (mucho) viento   to be
  (very) windy, 10
hasta   until, 15
  — luego   I'll see you later,
  PI
  — mañana   I'll see you
  tomorrow, PI
  — que   until, 19
hay   there is, there are, PII
hay que (+ *inf.*)   one must, 6
helado(a)   frozen, iced, 7
hermana (*f.*)   sister, 3
hermano (*m.*)   brother, 3
hermoso(a)   beautiful, 15
hija (*f.*)   daughter, 3
hijo (*m.*)   son, 3
hijos (*m. pl.*)   children (son[s]
  and daughter[s]), 4
hombre (*m.*)   man, PII
horario (*m.*)   schedule, 16
horrible   horrible, 19
hospital (*m.*)   hospital, 3

hotel (*m.*)   hotel, 4
hoy   today, PI
huevo (*m.*)   egg, 2

I

idea (*f.*)   idea, PII
idioma (*m.*)   language, PII
iglesia (*f.*)   church, 5
impaciente   impatient, 9
impermeable (*m.*)
  raincoat, 10
importante   important, 5
imposible   impossible, 14
información (*f.*)
  information, 7
informe (*m.*)   report, 20
inglés (*m.*)   English
  (language), 1
inglés (inglesa)   English, 2
inteligente   intelligent, 2
invierno (*m.*)   winter, PI
inyección (*f.*)   shot,
  injection, 18
ir   to go, 3
  — a esquiar   to go skiing, 8
  — de compras   to go
  shopping, 11
  — de vacaciones   to go
  on vacation, 12
irse   to leave, to go away, 9
italiano (*m.*)   Italian
  (language), 1
itinerario (*m.*)   schedule, 16

J

jabón (*m.*)   soap, 5
jamás   never, 6
jarabe (*m.*)   syrup, 19
jefe(a) (*m., f.*)   boss, chief, 20
joyería (*f.*)   jewelry store, 12
jueves (*m.*)   Thursday, PI
jugar (u:ue)   to play (a game
  or sport), 8
julio   July, PI
junio   June, PI

junta (*f.*)   meeting, 20
juntos(as)   together, 12

L

la   the (*f.*), PII; her, it (*f.*),
  you (*form. f.*), 7
lámpara (*f.*)   lamp, PII
lápiz (*m.*)   pencil, PII
largo(a)   long, 16
las (*f. pl.*)   the, PII; them, you
  (*f.*), 7
lata (*f.*)   can, 10
lavadora (*f.*)   washing
  machine, 10
lavar   to wash, 9
lavarse la cabeza   to wash
  one's hair, 9
le   (to) her, (to) him, (to) you
  (*form.*), 8
lección (*f.*)   lesson, PII
leche (*f.*)   milk, 2
leer   to read, 2
lengua (*f.*)   language, PII
lento(a)   slow, 16
levantar   to lift, to raise, 9
levantarse   to get up, 9
librería (*f.*)   bookstore, 6
libro (*m.*)   book, PII
límite (*m.*)   limit, 10
  — de velocidad (*m.*)
    speed limit, 10
limpiar   to clean, 10
limpiaparabrisas (*m.*)
  windshield wiper, 14
liquidación (*f.*)   sale, 11
listo(a)   ready, 14
literatura (*f.*)   literature, 17
lo   him, it (*m.*), you
  (*form. m.*), 7
  — siento   I'm sorry, PI
los   the (*m. pl.*), PII; them
  (*m.*), you (*m. pl.*), 7
los (las) dos   both, 10
lugar (*m.*)   place, 13
  — de interés (*m.*)   place
    of interest, 6

  — de nacimiento (*m.*)
    place of birth, PI
  — donde trabaja (*m.*)
    place of work, PI
lunes (*m.*)   Monday, PI
luz (*f.*)   light, PII

LL

llamar   to call, 3
llamarse   to be named, 9
llanta (*f.*)   tire, 14
llave (*f.*)   key, 4
llegar   to arrive, 4
llenar   to fill, 14
llevar   to take (something or
  someone to someplace), 3
llover (o:ue)   to rain, 10
lluvia (*f.*)   rain, 10

M

madera (*f.*)   wood, 3
madre (*f.*)   mom, mother, 3
mal   badly, 4
maleta (*f.*)   suitcase, 4
mamá (*f.*)   mom, mother, 3
mandar   to send, 8; to
  order, 16
manejar   to drive, 15
mano (*f.*)   hand, PII
manta (*f.*)   blanket, 6
mantel (*m.*)   tablecloth, 1
mañana (*f.*)   morning, 1
mañana   tomorrow, 6
máquina de afeitar (*f.*)
  razor, 9
máquina de escribir (*f.*)
  typewriter, 12
mar (*m.*)   ocean, 6
marca (*f.*)   brand, 14
mareado(a)   dizzy, 16
marrón   brown, PI
martes (*m.*)   Tuesday, PI
marzo   March, PI
más   more, 4

masculino(a) masculine, PI
matrícula (*f.*) tuition, 17
matricularse to register, 17
mayo (*m.*) May, PI
mayor older; bigger, 4
me me, 7; (to) me, 8; (to) myself, 9
  — **gusta...** I like . . . , PI
mecánico(a) (*m., f.*) mechanic, 14
media hora half an hour, 11
medianoche (*f.*) midnight, 9
médico(a) (*m., f.*) M.D., doctor, PII
mejor better, 4
menor younger; smaller, 4
menos to, until (with time), 1; less, fewer, 4
mentir (e:ie) to lie, 13
menú (*m.*) menu, 2
mercado (*m.*) market, 4
mes (*m.*) month, 5
mesa (*f.*) table, PII
mesero(a) (*m., f.*) waiter, waitress (*Méx.*), 2
metal (*m.*) metal, 3
mexicano(a) Mexican, 2
mi (*adj.*) my, 3
mí (*pron.*) me, 6
miércoles (*m.*) Wednesday, PI
mil thousand, 1
mirar to look at, 12
  — **vidrieras** to window shop, 12
mío(a) (*adj.*) my, of mine, 9
mío(a) (*pron.*) mine, 9
mochila (*f.*) backpack, 8
moda (*f.*) fashion, 13
momento (*m.*) moment, 9
morado(a) purple, PI
morir (o:ue) to die, 13
moto (*f.*) motorcycle, 15
motocicleta (*f.*) motorcycle, 15
motor (*m.*) engine, 15

mozo (*m.*) waiter, 2
muchacha (*f.*) girl, young woman, 2
muchacho (*m.*) boy, young man, 2
mucho a lot, very much, 2
  — **gusto** it's a pleasure to meet you, PI
mujer (*f.*) woman, PII
muleta (*f.*) crutch, 18
museo (*m.*) museum, 3
muy very, 3

N

nacionalidad (*f.*) nationality, PI
nada nothing, 6
nadar to swim, 7
nadie nobody, no one, 6
necesario(a) necessary, 17
necesitar to need, 1
negar (e:ie) to deny, 16
negro(a) black, PI
neumático (*m.*) tire, 14
nevar (e:ie) to snow, 10
ni... ni neither . . . nor, 6
niebla (*f.*) fog, 10
ningún none, not any, 6
ninguno(a) none, not any, 6
niño(a) (*m., f.*) child, kid, 8
noche (*f.*) evening, 1
nombre (*m.*) name, PI
norteamericano(a) North American (from the U.S.), PI
nos us, 7; (to) us, 8; (to) ourselves, 9
nosotros(as) we, 1; us, 6
nota (*f.*) grade, 17
novela (*f.*) novel, 7
noveno(a) ninth, 5
noventa ninety, PII
novia (*f.*) girlfriend, 3
noviembre November, PI

novio (*m.*) boyfriend, 3
nublado(a) cloudy, 10
nuestro(a) (*adj.*) our, 3
nuestro(s), nuestra(s) (*pron.*) ours, 9
nueve nine, PI
nuevo(a) new, 12
número (*m.*) number, PI
   — **de la licencia para conducir (manejar)** (*m.*) driver's license number, PI
   — **de seguro social** (*m.*) social security number, PI
   — **de teléfono** (*m.*) phone number, PI
nunca never, 6

O

o or, 2
o... o either . . . or, 6
ochenta eighty, PII
ocho eight, PI
octavo(a) eighth, 5
octubre October, PI
oculista (*m., f.*) eye doctor, 19
ocupación (*f.*) occupation, PI
ocupado(a) busy, 7
oficina (*f.*) office, 5
   — **de correos** (*f.*) post office, 6
   — **de turismo** (*f.*) tourist office, 7
ojalá if only . . . , I hope, 17
ómnibus (*m.*) bus, 3
once eleven, PI
operación (*f.*) surgery, 19
oro (*m.*) gold, 13
otoño (*m.*) fall, PI
otra vez again, 11

P

paciencia (*f.*) patience, 11
paciente (*m., f.*) patient, 18

padre (*m.*) dad, father, 3
padres (*m. pl.*) parents, 3
pagar to pay (for), 1
página deportiva (*f.*) sports page, 8
pantalón (*m.*) pants, 9
pantalones (*m. pl.*) pants, 9
papa (*f.*) potato, 2
papá (*m.*) dad, father, 3
paquete (*m.*) package, 20
para to, in order to, 5; for, by, 10
   — **que** in order that, 19
   ¿— **quién?** for whom?, 8
parabrisas (*m.*) windshield, 14
paraguas (*m. sing.*) umbrella, 10
paramédico(a) (*m., f.*) paramedic, 18
parque (*m.*) park, 8
partido (*m.*) game, match, 8
pasado(a) last, 6; past, 10
pasaje (*m.*) ticket, 7
pasajero(a) (*m., f.*) passenger, 19
pasaporte (*m.*) passport, 7
pasar (por) to go by, 10
pase come in, PI
pastel (*m.*) pie, 2
pastilla (*f.*) pill, 19
patata (*f.*) potato (*Spain*), 2
patines (*m. pl.*) skates, 8
pedir (e:i) to request, to ask for, to order, 6
peine (*m.*) comb, 9
peligroso(a) dangerous, 15
pelo (*m.*) hair, 9
pelota (*f.*) ball, 8
peluquería (*f.*) beauty salon, beauty parlor, 9
pensión (*f.*) boarding house, 4
peor worse, 4
pequeño(a) small, little (size), 4
perder (e:ie) to lose, 5
perfume (*m.*) perfume, 9

periódico (*m.*) newspaper, 6
pero but, 1
persona (*f.*) person, 13
perro (*m.*) dog, 15
pescado (*m.*) fish, 2
peso (*m.*) weight, 19
pierna (*f.*) leg, 18
pieza de repuesto (*f.*) spare
    part, 14
piscina (*f.*) swimming pool, 4
piso (*m.*) floor, story, 5
plata (*f.*) silver, 15
playa (*f.*) beach, 6
pluma (*f.*) pen, PII
poco(a) little (quantity), 4
poder (o:ue) to be able, 6
poema (*m.*) poem, 7
pollo (*m.*) chicken, 2
poner to put, to place, 7
    — una inyección to give
        a shot, 18
ponerse to put on, 9
    — a dieta to go on a diet,
        19
por around, along, by, for,
    through, 10
    — ciento per cent, 16
    — favor please, PI
    — hora per hour, 10
    — noche per night, 6
    ¿— qué? why?, 3
    — suerte luckily, 13
porque because, 3
posible possible, 17
postre (*m.*) dessert, 7
precio (*m.*) price, 15
preferir (e:ie) to prefer, 5
preguntar to ask a question, 8
preocuparse to worry, 20
preparar to prepare, 10
presidente(a) (*m., f.*)
    president, 8
préstamo (*m.*) loan, 20
prestar to lend, 8
primavera (*f.*) spring, PI
primero(a) first, 5

primo(a) (*m., f.*) cousin, 3
probable probable, 17
probablemente probably, 15
probar (o:ue) to try, to
    taste, 9
probarse (o:ue) to try on, 9
problema (*m.*) problem, PII
profesión (*f.*) profession, 3
profesor(a) (*m., f.*)
    professor, teacher, PI
programa (*m.*) program, PII
progreso (*m.*) progress, PII
pronto soon, 17
próximo(a) next, 5
pueblo (*m.*) town, 6
puerta (*f.*) door, PII
    — de atrás (*f.*) back
        door, 10

Q

que than, 4 ; that, which, 8
que viene next, 6
¿qué? what?, 2
    ¿— tiempo hace hoy?
        what's the weather like
        today?, 10
    ¿— hora es? what time
        is it?, 1
quedar to be located, 7
quedarse to stay, to
    remain, 12
querer (e:ie) to want, 5
querido(a) dear, 9
¿quién(es)? who?, whom?, 3
química (*f.*) chemistry, 17
quince fifteen, PI
quinto(a) fifth, 5
quitar to take away, to
    remove, 9
quitarse to take off (e.g.,
    one's clothing), 9

R

radiografía (*f.*) X-ray, 18
rápido (*m.*) express train, 16

¡**rápido!**   quick!, 11
rápido(a)   fast, 16
raqueta de tenis (*f.*)   tennis racket, 8
recibir   to receive, 2
reciente   recent, 17
recoger   to pick up, 20
recomendar (e:ie)   to recommend, 16
recordar (o:ue)   to remember, 6
refresco (*m.*)   soft drink, soda, 1
regalar   to give (a present), 8
regalo (*m.*)   present, gift, 6
remolcador (*m.*)   tow truck, 14
repetir (e:i)   to repeat, 7
requisito (*m.*)   requirement, 17
reservación (*f.*)   reservation, 7
reservar   to reserve, 16
restaurante (*m.*)   restaurant, 1
resultado (*m.*)   result, 19
reunión (*f.*)   meeting, 20
revisar   to check, 15
revista (*f.*)   magazine, 5
rogar (o:ue)   to beg, 16
rojo(a)   red, P1
romper   to break, 14
romperse   to break (i.e., a bone), 18
ropa (*f.*)   clothes, clothing, 10
rosado(a)   pink, PI

S

sábado (*m.*)   Saturday, PI
saber   to know how, to know a fact, 7
sacar una nota   to get a grade, 17
sala (*f.*)   ward, room, 18
— **de emergencia** (*f.*) emergency room, 18
— **de rayos x** (*f.*)   X-ray room, 18
salir   to go out, to leave, 7

salsa (*f.*)   sauce, 10
se   (to) himself, (to) herself, (to) yourself (*form.*,), (to) yourselves, (to) themselves, 9
se dice   one says, 6
secadora (*f.*)   dryer, 11
secretario(a) (*m., f.*) secretary, PII
seguir (e:i)   to continue, to follow, 7
— **derecho**   to continue straight ahead, 9
según   according to, 13
segundo(a)   second, 5
seguro(a)   sure, 18
seis   six, PI
sello (*m.*)   stamp, 6
semana (*f.*)   week, 5
sentar (e:ie)   to sit, 9
sentarse (e:ie)   to sit down, 9
sentir (e:ie)   to regret, to be sorry, 17
sentirse (e:ie)   to feel, 12
señor   Mr., sir, gentleman, PI
señora   Mrs., madam, lady, PI
señorita   Miss, young lady, PI
separado(a)   separated, PI
septiembre   September, PI
séptimo(a)   seventh, 5
ser   to be, 2
servilleta (*f.*)   napkin, 1
servir (e:i)   to serve, 6
sesenta   sixty, PII
setenta   seventy, PII
sexo (*m.*)   sex, PI
sexto(a)   sixth, 5
si   if, 8
sí   yes, 1
siempre   always, 3
siete   seven, PI
silla (*f.*)   chair, PII
sin falta   without fail, 15
sin que   without, 19
sistema (*m.*)   system, PII
sobre   about, 13

sobrevivir   to survive, 19
solamente   only, 2
solo(a)   alone, 4
soltero(a)   single, PI
sombrero (*m.*)   hat, 12
sopa (*f.*)   soup, 7
sortija (*f.*)   ring, 13
su (*adj.*)   his, her, its, your
   (*form.*), their, 3
suegra (*f.*)   mother-in-law, 10
suegro (*m.*)   father-in-law, 10
suéter (*m.*)   sweater, 10
sugerir (e:ie)   to suggest, 16
sumamente   extremely,
   highly, 16
supermercado (*m.*)
   supermarket, 10
supervisor(a) (*m., f.*)
   supervisor, 4
suyo(s), suya(s) (*pron.*)
   yours (*form.*), his, hers,
   theirs, 9

T

tallarines (*m. pl.*)   spaghetti, 10
talonario de cheques (*m.*)
   checkbook, 20
también   also, too, 4
tampoco   neither, 6
tan   as, 4
   — pronto como   as soon
      as, 19
tanque (*m.*)   tank, 14
tarde (*f.*)   afternoon, 1
tarde   late, 2
tarjeta (*f.*)   card, 9
   — de crédito (*f.*)   credit
      card, 9
taxi (*m.*)   taxi, 3
te   you (*fam.*), 7; (to) you, 8;
   (to) yourself, 9
   ¿— gusta?   do you like . . .
      ?, PI
té (*m.*)   tea, 2
teatro (*m.*)   theater, 6

teléfono (*m.*)   telephone, PII
telegrama (*m.*)   telegram, PII
televisión (*f.*)   television, PII
temer   to fear, 17
temprano   early, 2
ten paciencia   be patient, 11
tenedor (*m.*)   fork, 1
tener   to have, 4
   — ... años (de edad)   to
      be . . . years old, 5
   — calor   to be hot, 5
   — cuidado   to be careful, 5
   — frío   to be cold, 5
   — hambre   to be hungry, 5
   — miedo   to be afraid, 5
   — prisa   to be in a hurry, 5
   — que (+ *inf.*)   to have to, 4
   — razón   to be right, 5
   — sed   to be thirsty, 5
   — sueño   to be sleepy, 5
tenis (*m.*)   tennis, 8
tercero(a)   third, 5
terminar   to finish, 17
termómetro (*m.*)
   thermometer, 19
terraza (*m.*)   terrace, 9
testamento (*m.*)   will, 19
ti (*fam. sing.*)   you, 6
tía (*f.*)   aunt, 8
tienda (*f.*)   store, 4
   — de campaña (*f.*)   tent, 8
timbre (*m.*)   stamp (Méx.), 6
tintorería (*f.*)   dry cleaners, 9
tío (*m.*)   uncle, 8
tipo (*m.*)   type, 13
toalla (*f.*)   towel, 5
tobillo (*m.*)   ankle, 18
todavía   yet, 9
todo(a)   all, 11
   — el día   all day long, 12
todos(as)   every, 1
   — los días   every day, 18
tomar   to drink, 1; to take
   (i.e., the bus), 3
tomate (*m.*)   tomato, 10
tome asiento   sit down (take
   a seat), PI

tostadora (*f.*)   toaster, 11
trabajar   to work, 1
trabajos de la casa (*m. pl.*)
   household chores, 11
traducir   to translate, 7
traer   to bring, 6
traje (*m.*)   suit, outfit, 13
   — de baño (*m.*)   bathing
      suit, 12
trece   thirteen, PI
treinta   thirty, PI
tren (*m.*)   train, 15
tres   three, PI
tu (*adj.*)   your (*fam.*), 3
tú   you (*fam.*), 1
tuyo(s), tuya(s) (*pron.*)
   yours (*fam. sing.*), 9

U

un(a)   one, PI;   a, an, PII
un montón   a lot, 20
universidad (*f.*)   university, PII
uno   one, PI
unos(as)   some, PII
usar   to use, 14
usted   you (*form. sing.*), 1
ustedes   you (*pl.*) 1

V

vacaciones (*f. pl.*)   vacation, 5
vacío(a)   empty, 14
varios(as)   several, various, 13
veinte   twenty, PI
veinticinco   twenty-five, PI
veinticuatro   twenty-four, PI
veintidós   twenty-two, PI
veintinueve   twenty-nine, PI
veintiocho   twenty-eight, PI
veintiséis   twenty-six, PI

veintisiete   twenty-seven, PI
veintitrés   twenty-three, PI
veintiuno   twenty-one, PI
velocidad (*f.*)   velocity,
   speed, 10
vender   to sell, 13
venir   to come, 4
venta (*f.*)   sale, 11
ventana (*f.*)   window, 9
ver   to see, 7
verano (*m.*)   summer, PI
verdad (*f.*)   truth, 7
verde   green, PI
vestido (*m.*)   dress, 9
vestirse (e:i)   to get dressed, 9
veterinario(a) (*m., f.*)
   veterinarian, 15
viajar   to travel, 5
vidriera (*f.*)   store window, 12
viernes (*m.*)   Friday, PI
vino (*m.*)   wine, 1
   — tinto   red wine, 2
visitar   to visit, 3
viudo(a) (*m., f.*)   widowed, PI
vivir   to live, 2
volar (o:ue)   to fly, 6
volver (o:ue)   to return, to
   come (go) back, 6
vuelo (*m.*)   flight, 10

Y

y   and, 1
ya   already, 13
   — lo creo   I'll say, 5
yo   I, 1

Z

zapatería (*f.*)   shoe store, 12

English-Spanish

A

a un(a), PI
a lot mucho, un montón, 2
about sobre, 13; de, 6
accident accidente *(m.)*, 13
according to según, 13
account cuenta *(f.)*, 15
ache doler (o:ue), 13
address dirección *(f.)*,
　domicilio *(m.)*, PI
advise aconsejar, 16
adviser consejero(a)
　(m., f.), 17
afternoon tarde *(f.)*, 1
afterwards después, 15
again otra vez, 11
age edad *(f.)*, PI
airplane avión *(m.)*, 7
airport aeropuerto *(m.)*, 12
alcoholic alcohólico(a), 6
all todo(a), 11
　—day long todo el día, 12
almost casi, 14
alone solo(a), 4
along por, 10
already ya, 13
also también, 4
always siempre, 3
ambulance ambulancia
　(f.), 18
American americano(a), 20
an un(a), PI
analysis análisis *(m.)*, 19
ankle tobillo *(m.)*, 18
any algún, alguno(a),
　algunos(as), 6
anyone alguien, 6
anything algo, 6
April abril, PI
Argentinian argentino(a)
　(m., f.), 3

around por, 10
arrive llegar, 4
as tan, 4
　—soon as en cuanto, tan
　pronto como, 19
　—soon as possible
　cuanto antes, 4
ask preguntar, 8
　—for pedir (e:i), 6
aspirin aspirina *(f.)*, 13
assistant ayudante *(m., f.)*, 19
at a, 1
　—home en casa, 12
　—this moment en este
　momento, 18
　—what time? ¿a qué
　hora...?, 1
attend asistir, 20
　—to atender (e:ie), 9
August agosto, PI
aunt tía *(f.)*, 8
auto club club
　automovilístico *(m.)*, 14
automatic automático(a), 15
automobile auto *(m.)*, carro
　(m.), coche *(m.)*, 3
avenue avenida *(f.)*, 7

B

back door puerta de atrás
　(f.), 10
backpack mochila *(f.)*, 8
badly mal, 4
baked asado(a), 2
ball pelota *(f.)*, 8
bank banco *(m.)*, 6
basketball básquetbol *(m.)*, 8
bathe *(oneself)* bañar(se), 9
bathing suit traje de baño
　(m.), 12
bathroom baño *(m.)*, 9

battery acumulador *(m.)*, batería *(f.)*, 14
be ser, 2; estar, 2
— **. . . years old** tener... años (de edad), 5
—**able** poder (o:ue), 6
—**afraid** tener miedo, 5
—**careful** tener cuidado, 5
—**cold** tener frío, 5; hacer frío, 10
—**familiar with** conocer, 7
—**glad** alegrarse (de), 17
—**good (bad) weather** hacer buen (mal) tiempo, 10
—**hot** tener calor, 5; hacer calor, 10
—**hungry** tener hambre, 5
—**in a hurry** tener prisa, 5
—**located** quedar, 7
—**named** llamarse, 9
—**patient** tener paciencia, 11
—**pleasing** gustar, 13
—**right** tener razón, 5
—**sleepy** tener sueño, 5
—**sorry** sentir (e:ie), 17
—**thirsty** tener sed, 5
—**(very) windy** hacer (mucho) viento, 10
beach playa *(f.)*, 6
beautiful hermoso(a), 15; bello(a), 16
beauty salon peluquería *(f.)*, 9
because porque, 3
bed cama *(f.)*, 6
bedroom dormitorio *(m.)*, 9
beer cerveza *(f.)*, 1
before antes de, 9; antes de que, 19
beg rogar (o:ue), 16
begin comenzar (e:ie), empezar (e:ie), 5
believe creer, 4
better mejor, 4
bicycle bicicleta *(f.)*, 8

big grande, 2
bill cuenta *(f.)*, 1
black negro, PI
blanket cobija *(f.)*, frazada *(f.)*, manta *(f.)*, 6
blue azul, PI
boarding house pensión *(f.)*, 4
book libro *(m.)*, PII
bookstore librería *(f.)*, 6
bored aburrido(a), 13
boring aburrido(a), 13
boss jefe(a) *(m., f.)*, 20
both los (las) dos, 10
boy chico *(m.)*, muchacho *(m.)*, 2
boyfriend novio *(m.)*, 3
brake freno *(m.)*, 14
brand marca *(f.)*, 14
break romper, 14
—**a bone** fracturarse, romperse, 18
breakfast desayuno *(m.)*, 5
bring traer, 6
broom escoba *(f.)*, 10
brother hermano *(m.)*, 3
brother-in-law cuñado *(m.)*, 12
brown café, marrón, PI
brush cepillo *(m.)*, 9
bus autobús *(m.)* ómnibus *(m)*, 3
busy ocupado(a), 7
but pero, 1
buy comprar, 5
by para, por, 10
—**heart** de memoria, 7

C

cafeteria cafetería *(f.)*, 1
calculator calculadora *(f.)*, 17
call llamar, 3
can bote *(m.)* (Méx.), lata *(f.)*, 10
car auto *(m.)*, automóvil *(m.)* carro *(m.)*, coche *(m.)*, 3

—**rental agency** agencia de alquiler de automóviles *(f.)*, 15
card tarjeta *(f.)*, 9
careful cuidadoso(a), 17
cash a check cambiar un cheque, 15
cashier cajero(a) *(m., f.)*, 15
catalogue catálogo *(m.)*, 12
chair silla *(f.)*, PII
champagne champán *(m.)*, 2
change cambiar, 14
charge cobrar, 15
check cheque *(m.)*, 2; chequear, revisar, 15
checkbook talonario de cheques *(m.)*, 20
chemistry química *(f.)*, 17
chicken pollo *(m.)*, 2
—**with rice** arroz con pollo, 11
chief jefe(a) *(m., f.)*, 20
children (son[s] and daughter[s]) hijos *(m. pl.)*, 4
chocolate chocolate *(m.)*, 2
choose elegir (e:i), 13
church iglesia *(f.)*, 5
city ciudad *(f.)*, PI
class clase *(f.)*, 4
clean limpiar, 10
clear claro(a), 17
clerk empleado(a) *(m., f.)*, 14
climate clima *(m.)*, PII
close cerrar (e:ie), 5
clothes ropa *(f.)*, 10
clothing ropa *(f.)*, 10
cloudy nublado(a), 10
club club *(m.)*, 8
coach entrenador(a) *(m., f.)*, 8
coat abrigo *(m.)*, 10
coffee café *(m.)*, 2
collide chocar, 19
comb peine *(m.)*, 9
come venir, 4
—**back** volver (o:ue), 6
—**in** pase, PI; entrar 10

computer computadora *(f.)*, 20
concert concierto *(m.)*, 5
confirm confirmar, 7
consulate consulado *(m.)*, 20
continue seguir (e:i), 7
—**straight ahead** seguir derecho, 9
contract contrato *(m.)*, 17
conversation conversación *(f.)*, PII
cook cocinar, 10; cocinero(a) *(m.,f.)*, 11
cost costar (o:ue), 6
cousin primo(a) *(m., f.)*, 3
cover cubrir, 14
credit crédito *(m.)*, 20
—**card** tarjeta de crédito *(f.)*, 9
crutch muleta *(f.)*, 18
curtain cortina *(f.)*, 20
cut cortar, 9

D

dad papá, 3
dangerous peligroso(a), 15
date fecha *(f.)*, PI
—**of birth** fecha de nacimiento *(f.)*, PI
daughter hija *(f.)*, 3
day día *(m.)*, PII
dear querido(a), 9
December diciembre, PI
decide decidir, 2
decision decisión *(f.)*, PII
decrease bajar, 19
dentist dentista *(m., f.)*, 18
deny negar (e:ie), 16
deposit depositar, 15
desire desear, 1
dessert postre *(m.)*, 7
die morir (o:ue), 13
difficult difícil, 16
dinner cena *(f.)*, 5
discount descuento *(m.)*, 16

divorced divorciado(a), PI
dizzy mareado(a), 16
do hacer, 7
   —errands hacer
   diligencias, 20
do you like . . . ?
   ¿te gusta?, PI
doctor's office consultorio
   (m.), 18
doctor doctor(a) *(m., f.)*,
   médico(a) *(m., f.)*, PII
dog perro *(m.)*, 15
dollar dólar *(m.)*, 3
door puerta *(f.)*, PII
doubt dudar, 18
dress vestido *(m.)*, 9
drink tomar, 1; bebida *(f.)*,
   beber, 2
drive conducir, 7; manejar, 15
driver's license number
   número de la licencia para
   conducir (manejar), PI
dry cleaners tintorería *(f.)*, 9
dryer secadora *(f.)*, 11

E

early temprano, 2
earrings aretes *(m. pl.)*, 13
easy fácil, 17
eat comer, 2
education educación *(f.)*, 5
egg huevo *(m.)*, 2
eight ocho, PI
eighteen dieciocho, PI
eighth octavo(a), 5
eighty ochenta, PII
either . . . or o... o, 6
eleven once, PI
embassy embajada *(f.)*, 7
emergency room sala de
   emergencia *(f.)*, 18
emergency emergencia
   (f.), 18
empty vacío(a), 14
engine motor *(m.)*, 15
English *(language)* inglés
   (m.), 1

English inglés(a), 2
enter entrar, 10
errand diligencia *(f.)*, 20
escalator escalera
   mecánica, 13
evening noche *(f.)*, 1
ever alguna vez, 6
every todos(as), 1
   —day todos los días, 18
exam examen *(m.)*, 15
excursion excursión *(f.)*, 6
exercise hacer ejercicio, 19
expensive caro(a), 4
express train rápido *(m.)*, 16
extremely sumamente, 16
eye doctor oculista
   (m., f.), 19

F

fall otoño *(f.)*, PI
fall asleep dormirse (o:ue), 9
fashion moda *(f.)*, 13
fast rápido(a), 16
father padre, papá, 3
father-in-law suegro *(m.)*, 10
favor favor *(m.)*, 11
fear temer, 17
February febrero, PI
feel sentirse (e:ie), 12
feminine femenino(a), PI
fever fiebre *(f.)*, 19
fewer menos, 4
fifteen quince, PI
fifth quinto(a), 5
fifty cincuenta, PII
fill llenar, 14
final exam examen final
   (m.), 17
fine bien, PI
finish terminar, 17
first primero(a), 5
fish pescado *(m.)*, 2
five cinco, PI
fix arreglar, 13
flat tire goma pinchada *(f.)*, 14
flight vuelo *(m.)*, 10
floor *(story)* piso *(m.)*, 5

fly volar (o:ue), 6
fog niebla (f.), 10
follow seguir (e:i), 7
food comida (f.), 2
for para, por, 10
   —whom ¿para quién?, 8
fork tenedor (m.), 1
forty cuarenta, PII
four cuatro, PI
fourteen catorce, PI
fourth cuarto(a), 5
freeway autopista (f.), 19
French (*language*) francés
   (f.), 1
French francés (francesa), 2
Friday viernes, PI
fried frito(a), 2
friend amigo(a) (m., f.), 3
friendship amistad (f.), PII
from de, 3
frozen helado(a), 7
function funcionar, 13

G

game (*match*) partido (m.), 8
gas station estación de
   servicio (f.), gasolinera
   (f.), 14
gasoline gasolina (f.), 14
general general, 17
generally generalmente, 9
gentleman señor, PI
German alemán (alemana), 2
get buscar, 16
   —a grade sacar una
     nota, 17
   —dressed vestirse (e:i), 9
   —up levantarse, 9
gift regalo, 6
girl chica (f.), muchacha
   (f.), 2
girlfriend novia (f.), 3
give dar, 3
   —a present regalar, 8
   —a shot poner una
     inyección, 18
   —back devolver (o:ue), 20

go ir, 3
   —away irse, 9
   —by pasar (por), 10
   —down bajar, 19
   —on a diet ponerse a
     dieta, 19
   —on vacation ir de
     vacaciones, 12
   —out salir, 7
   —shopping ir de
     compras, 11
   —skiing ir a esquiar, 8
   —to bed acostarse (o:ue), 9
gold oro (m.), 13
good bueno(a), 2
good afternoon buenas
   tardes, PI
good evening (*good night*)
   buenas noches, PI
goodbye adiós, PI
grade nota (f.), 17
grandfather abuelo (m.), 3
grandmother abuela (f.), 3
gray gris, PI
green verde, PI
guide guía (m.), 6
gym gimnasio (m.), 4

H

hair pelo (m.), 9
half an hour media hora,
   11
hand mano (f.), PII
handsome guapo(a), 2
happy feliz, 2
hardly ever casi nunca, 11
hat sombrero (m.), 12
have tener, 4
   —a good time divertirse
     (e:ie), 13
   —breakfast desayunar, 5
   —just (*done something*)
     acabar de (+ *inf.*), 13
   —lunch almorzar (o:ue), 6
   —to tener que (+ *inf.*), 4
he él, 1
head cabeza (f.), 13

help ayudar, 10
her su, 3; ella, 6; la, 7; le, 8
here aquí, 3
hers suyo(s), suya(s), 9
herself se, 9
highly sumamente, 16
him él, 6; lo, 7; le; 8
himself se, 9
his su, 3; suyo(s),
  suya(s), 9
hope esperar, 16
horrible horrible, 19
horse caballo (*m.*), 8
hospital hospital (*m.*), 3
hot caliente, 2
hotel hotel (*m.*), 4
house casa (*f.*), PII
household chores trabajos
  de la casa (*m. pl.*), 11
how? ¿cómo?, 3
  —are you? ¿cómo está
    usted?, PI
  —do you say . . . ? ¿cómo
    se dice... ?, 6
  —long ago . . . ? ¿cuánto
    tiempo hace que... ?, 14
  —long ¿cuánto tiempo?, 11
  —many? ¿cuántos(as)?, 2
  —much ¿cuánto(a)?, 5
hurt doler (o:ue), 13
husband esposo (*m.*), 4

I

I yo, 1
I hope ojalá, 17
I like . . . me gusta..., PI
I'll say ya lo creo, 5
I'll see you later hasta
  luego, PI
I'll see you tomorrow hasta
  mañana, PI
I'm sorry lo siento, PI
idea idea (*f.*), PII
if si, 8
if only ojalá, 17
impatient impaciente, 9

important importante, 5
impossible imposible, 14
in a, 15; en, 1
  —case en caso de que, 19
  —order that para que, 19
  —order to para, 5
  —that case entonces, 7
  —those days en esa
    época, 11
inexpensive barato(a), 4
information información
  (*f.*), 7
injection inyección (*f.*), 18
intelligent inteligente, 2
interview entrevista (*f.*), 20
it (*f.*) la, lo, 7
Italian (*language*) italiano
  (*m.*), 1
its su (adj.), 3

J

jacket chaqueta (*f.*), 13
jail cárcel (*f.*), 5
January enero, PI
jewelry store joyería (*f.*), 12
July julio, PI
June junio, PI

K

key llave (*f.*), 4
kind bueno(a), 16
kitchen cocina (*f.*), 10
know conocer, saber, 7

L

lady señora, PI
lamp lámpara (*f.*), PII
language idioma (*m.*),
  lengua (*f.*), PII
last pasado(a), 6
  —night anoche, 10
late tarde, 2
later después, 15
lawyer abogado(a) (*m., f.*), 17
learn aprender, 2

leave   salir, 7
lecture   conferencia *(f.)*, 17
leg   pierna *(f.)*, 18
lend   prestar, 8
less   menos, 4
lesson   lección *(f.)*, PII
letter   carta *(f.)*, 7
library   biblioteca, 4
lie   mentir (e:ie), 13
lie down   acostarse (o:ue), 9
lift   levantar, 9
light   luz *(f.)*, PII
like   gustar, 13
limit   límite *(m.)*, 10
literature   literatura *(f.)*, 17
little   poco(a) *(quantity)*,
   pequeño(a) *(size)*, 4
live   vivir, 2
loan   préstamo *(m.)*, 20
long   largo(a), 16
look at   mirar, 12
look for   buscar, 16
lose   perder (e:ie), 5
luckily   por suerte, 13
lunch   almuerzo *(m.)*, 5

M

madam   señora, PI
magazine   revista *(f.)*, 5
maiden name   apellido de
   soltera *(m.)*, PI
mail   echar al correo, 20
make   hacer, 7
mall   centro comercial
   (m.), 12
man   hombre *(m.)*, PII
manager   gerente *(m., f.)*, 4
March   marzo, PI
marital status   estado civil
   (m.), PI
market   mercado *(m.)*, 4
married   casado(a), PI
masculine   masculino, PI
mattress   colchón *(m.)*, 6
May   mayo, PI

me   mí, 6; me, 7
meal   comida *(f.)*, 2
meat   carne *(f.)*, 7
mechanic   mecánico(a)
   (m., f.), 14
medicine cabinet   botiquín
   (m.), 9
meet for the first time
   conocer, 12
meet   encontrarse (o:ue), 12
meeting   junta *(f.)*, reunión
   (f.), 20
menu   menú *(m.)*, 2
metal   metal *(m.)*, 3
Mexican   mexicano(a), 2
midnight   medianoche *(f.)*, 9
midterm exam   examen
   parcial *(m.)*, 17
milk   leche *(f.)*, 2
mine   mío(a), 9
mirror   espejo *(m.)*, 9
mom   mamá, 3
moment   momento *(m.)*, 9
Monday   lunes, PI
money   dinero *(m.)*, PII
month   mes *(m.)*, 5
more   más, 4
morning   mañana *(f.)*, 1
mother   madre *(f.)*, 3
mother-in-law   suegra *(f.)*, 10
motorcycle   moto *(f.)*, 15;
   motocicleta *(f.)*, 15
movie theater   cine *(m.)*, 5
movies   cine *(m.)*, 5
Mr.   señor, PI
Mrs.   señora, PI
much   mucho, 2
museum   museo *(m.)*, 3
must, to have to, should
   deber (+ *inf.*), 3
my   mi, 3 mío(a), 9
myself   me, 9

N

name   nombre *(m.)*, PI
napkin   servilleta *(f.)*, 1

nationality nacionalidad *(f.)*, PI
near to cerca de, 6
necessary necesario(a), 17
necklace collar *(m.)*, 13
need necesitar, 1
neither tampoco, 6
neither . . . nor ni... ni, 6
never jamás, 6; nunca, 6
new nuevo(a), 12
newspaper diario *(m.)*, periódico *(m.)*, 6
next próximo(a), 5; que viene, 6
nightgown camisón *(m.)*, 13
nine nueve, PI
nineteen diecinueve, PI
ninety noventa, PII
ninth noveno(a), 5
niño(a) *(m., f.)* child, 8
no one nadie, 6
nobody nadie, 6
none ninguno(a), ningún, 6
North American *(from the U.S.)* norteamericano(a), PI
not any ningún, ninguno(a), 6
not very well no muy bien, PI
nothing nada, 6
novel novela *(f.)*, 7
November noviembre, PI
now ahora, 3
number número *(m.)*, PI
nurse enfermero(a) *(m., f.)*, PI

O

obtain conseguir (e:i), 7
occupation ocupación *(f.)*, PI
ocean mar *(m.)*, 6
October octubre, PI
of de, 3
of mine mío(a) *(adj.)*, 9
office oficina *(f.)*, 5

often a menudo, 3
oil aceite *(m.)*, 14
older mayor, 4
once in a while de vez en cuando, 11
one uno, un(a), PI
one hundred cien, ciento, PII
one must hay que (+ *inf.*), 6
one says se dice, 6
only solamente, 2
open abrir, 2
or o, 2
orange anaranjado, PI
order mandar, 16; pedir (e:i), 6
our nuestro(a) *(adj.)*, 3
ours nuestro(s), nuestra(s), 9
ourselves nos, 9
over there allá, 8
owner dueño(a) *(m., f.)*, 5

P

package paquete *(m.)*, 20
pants pantalón *(m.)*; pantalones *(m. pl.)*, 9
paramedic paramédico(a) *(m., f.)*, 18
parents padres *(m.)*, 3
park parque *(m.)*, 8
party fiesta *(f.)*, 3
passenger pasajero(a) *(m., f.)*, 19
passport pasaporte *(m.)*, 7
past y *(with time expressions)*, 1; pasado(a), 10
patience paciencia *(f.)*, 11
patient paciente *(m., f.)*, 18
pay *(for)* pagar, 1
pen pluma *(f.)*, PII
pencil lápiz *(m.)*, PII
per hour por hora, 10
per night por noche, 6
percent por ciento, 16
perfume perfume *(m.)*, 9
person persona *(f.)*, 13

pharmacy farmacia *(f.)*, 6
phone number número de teléfono, PI
photocopy fotocopia *(f.)*, 20
physics física *(f.)*, 17
pick up buscar, 16; recoger, 20
pie pastel *(m.)*, 2
pill pastilla *(f.)*, 19
pink rosado, PI
place poner, 7; lugar *(m.)*, 13
 —**of birth** lugar de nacimiento, PI
 —**of interest** lugar de interés, 6
 —**of work** lugar donde trabaja, PI
play *(a game or sport)* jugar, 8
please por favor, PI
poem poema *(m.)*, 7
possible posible, 17
post office oficina de correos *(f.)*, 6; correo *(m.)*, 20
potato papa *(f.)*, patata *(f.)*, 2
prefer preferir (e:ie), 5
prepare preparar, 10
present regalo *(m.)*, 6
president presidente(a) *(m., f.)*, 8
pretty bonito(a), 3
price precio *(m.)*, 15
probable probable, 17
probably probablemente, 15
problem problema *(m.)*, PII
profession profesión *(f.)*, 3
program programa *(m.)*, PII
progress progreso *(m.)*, PII
provided that con tal que, 19
purple morado, PI
purse cartera *(f.)*, 12
put poner, 7
 —**a cast on** enyesar, 18
 —**to bed** acostar (o:ue), 9
put on ponerse, 9

R

rain llover (o:ue); lluvia *(f.)*, 10
raincoat impermeable *(m.)*, 10
raise levantar, 9
razor máquina de afeitar *(f.)*, 9
read leer, 2
ready listo(a), 14
receive recibir, 2
recent reciente, 17
recommend recomendar (e:ie), 16
red rojo, PI
red wine vino tinto, 2
register matricularse, 17
regret sentir (e:ie), 17
remain quedarse, 12
remember recordar (o:ue), 6; acordarse (o:ue) (de), 9
remove quitar, 9
rent alquilar, 15
repeat repetir (e:i), 17
report informe *(m.)*, 20
request pedir (e:i), 6
requirement requisito *(m.)*, 17
reservation reservación *(f.)*, 7
reserve reservar, 16
restaurant restaurante *(m.)*, 1
result resultado *(m.)*, 19
return volver (o:ue), 6; *(something)* devolver (o:ue), 20
rice arroz *(m.)*, 11
right away en seguida, 14
right now ahora mismo, 9
ring anillo *(m.)*, sortija *(f.)*, 13
roasted asado(a), 2
room cuarto *(m.)*, habitación *(f.)*, 4

S

salad   ensalada *(f.)*, 7
sale   liquidación *(f.)*, venta *(f.)*, 11
Saturday   sábado, PI
sauce   salsa *(f.)*, 10
say   decir (e:i), 6
  —goodbye   despedirse (e:i), 13
schedule   horario *(m.)*, itinerario *(m.)*, 16
scholarship   beca *(f.)*, 17
school   escuela *(f.)*, 5
seat   asiento *(m.)*, 16
second   segundo(a), 5
secretary   secretario(a) *(m., f.)*, PII
see   ver, 7
select   elegir (e:i), 13
sell   vender, 13
send   mandar, 8
separated   separado(a), PI
September   septiembre, PI
servant   criado(a) *(m., f.)*, 10
serve   servir (e:i), 6
seven   siete, PI
seventeen   diecisiete, PI
seventh   séptimo(a), 5
seventy   setenta, PII
several   varios(as), 13
sex   sexo, PI
shampoo   champú *(m.)*, 9
shave *(oneself)*   afeitarse, 9
she   ella, 1
shoe store   zapatería *(f.)*, 12
short   corto(a), 9
shot   inyección *(f.)*, 18
sick   enfermo(a), 3
sign   firmar, 17
silver   plata *(f.)*, 15
single   soltero(a), PI
sink   fregadero *(m.)*, 11
sir   señor, PI
sister   hermana *(f.)*, 3
sister-in-law   cuñada *(f.)*, 12

sit   sentar (e:ie), 9
  —down   sentarse (e:ie), 9
  —down *(take a seat)* tome asiento, PI
six   seis, PI
sixteen   dieciséis, PI
sixth   sexto(a), 5
sixty   sesenta, PII
skates   patines *(m. pl.)*, 8
ski   esquiar, 8
skis   esquíes *(m. pl.)*, 8
sleep   dormir (o:ue), 6
sleeping bag   bolsa de dormir *(f.)*, 8
slow   lento(a), 16
small   pequeño(a), 4
smaller   menor, 4
snow   nevar (e:ie), 10
soap   jabón *(m.)*, 5
social security number   número de seguro social, PI
soda   refresco *(m.)*, 1
soft drink   refresco *(m.)*, 1
some   unos(as), PII; algunos(as) *(pl.)*, algún, alguno(a), 6
someone   alguien, 6
something   algo, 6
sometimes   algunas veces, 6
son   hijo *(m.)*, 3
soon   pronto, 17
soup   sopa *(f.)*, 7
spaghetti   espaguetis *(m. pl.)*, tallarines *(m. pl.)*, 10
Spanish *(language)*   español *(m.)*, PII
Spanish   español(a), 2
spare part   pieza de repuesto *(f.)*, 14
speak   hablar, 1
special   especial, 17
speed limit   límite de velocidad *(m.)*, 10
speed   velocidad *(f.)*, 10
spoon   cuchara *(f.)*, 1

sports page página deportiva *(f.)*, 8
spring primavera *(f.)*, PI
stairs escalera *(f.)*, 13
stamp timbre *(m.) (Méx.)*, estampilla *(f.)*, sello *(m.)*, 6
start comenzar (e:ie), 5, empezar (e:ie), 5
stay quedarse, 12
store window escaparate *(m.)*, vidriera *(f.)*, 12
store tienda *(f.)*, 4
street calle *(f.)*, PI
student estudiante *(m., f.)*, 4
study estudiar, 1
suggest sugerir (e:ie), 16
suit, outfit traje *(m.)*, 13
suitcase maleta *(f.)*, 4
summer verano *(m.)*, PI
Sunday domingo, PI
supermarket supermercado *(m.)*, 10
supervisor supervisor(a) *(m., f.)*, 4
sure seguro(a), 18
surgeon cirujano(a) *(m., f.)*, 19
surgery cirugía *(f.)*, operación *(f.)*, 19
surname apellido *(m.)*, PI
survive sobrevivir, 19
sweater suéter *(m.)*, 10
sweep barrer, 10
swim nadar, 7
swimming pool alberca *(f.) (Méx.)*, piscina *(f.)*, 4
syrup jarabe *(m.)*, 19
system sistema *(m.)*, PII

T

table mesa *(f.)*, PII
tablecloth mantel *(m.)*, 1
take tomar, 3; *(something or someone to someplace)* llevar, 3
—**away** quitar, 9
—**care** cuidar, 18

take off *(i.e., one's clothing)* quitarse, 9
talk hablar, 1
tall alto(a), 2
tank tanque *(m.)*, 14
taste probar (o:ue), 9
taxi taxi *(m.)*, 3
tea té, 2
teach enseñar, 11
teacher profesor(a) *(m., f.)*, PI
telegram telegrama *(m.)*, PII
telephone teléfono *(m.)*, PII
television televisión *(f.)*, PII
tell decir (e:i), 6
ten diez, PI
tennis tenis *(m.)*, 8
—**racquet** raqueta de tenis *(f.)*, 8
tent tienda de campaña *(f.)*, 8
tenth décimo(a), 5
terrace terraza *(m.)*, 9
test análisis *(m.)*, 19
than que, 4
that aquel(los), aquella(s) *(adj.)*, 8; aquello *(neuter pron.)*, 8; ese(os), esa(as) *(adj.)*, 8; eso *(neuter pron.)*, 8; que, 8
that (one) aquél, aquélla *(pron.)*, 8; ése, ésa *(pron.)*, 8
the el, la, las, los, PII
the day before yesterday anteayer, 12
the pleasure is mine el gusto es mío, PI
theater teatro *(m.)*, 6
their su *(adj.)*, 3
theirs suyo(s), suya(s) *(pron.)*, 9
them ellas, ellos, 6; las, los, 7; les, 8
themselves se, 9
then entonces, 7
there allí, 6
—**are** hay, PII
—**is** hay, PII

thermometer termómetro
  (m.), 19
these estos, estas *(adj.)*, 8
these (ones) éstos, éstas
  (pron.), 8
they ellas, ellos, 1
think creer, 4
third tercero(a), 5
thirteen trece, PI
thirty treinta, PI
this este(a), 6; *(adj.)*, 8
this esto *(neuter pron.)*, 8
this (one) éste, ésta
  (pron.), 8
those *(distant)* aquellos,
  aquellas *(adj.)*, 8
those *(nearby)* esos,
  esas *(adj.)*, 8
those (ones) *(distant)*
  aquéllos, aquéllas
  (pron.), 8
those (ones) *(nearby)*
  ésos, ésas *(pron.)*, 8
thousand mil, 1
three tres, PI
through por, 10
Thursday jueves, PI
ticket billete *(m.)*, pasaje
  (m.), 7; entrada *(f.)*, 8; boleto
  (m.), 16
tie corbata *(f.)*, 13
till menos, 1
tire goma *(f.)*, llanta *(f.)*,
  neumático *(m.)*, 14
tired cansado(a), 3
to menos, 1; a, 3; para, 5
to the left a la izquierda, 9
to the right a la derecha, 9
to whom ¿a quién?, 3
toaster tostadora *(f.)*, 11
today hoy, PI
together juntos(as), 12
tomato tomate *(m.)*, 10
tomorrow mañana, 6
tonight esta noche, 5

too también, 4
tourist brochure folleto
  turístico *(m.)*, 7
tourist office oficina de
  turismo, 7
tow truck grúa *(f.)*,
  remolcador *(m.)*, 14
towel toalla *(f.)*, 5
town pueblo *(m.)*, 6
train tren *(m.)*, 15
  —station estación de
    trenes *(f.)*, 16
trainer entrenador(a) *(m., f.)*, 8
translate traducir, 7
trash basura *(f.)*, 11
travel viajar, 5
  —agency agencia de
    viajes *(f.)*, 7
  —agent agente de viajes
    (m., f.), 7
tree árbol *(m.)*, 18
truth verdad *(f.)*, 7
try probar (o:ue), 9
try on probarse (o:ue), 9
Tuesday martes, PI
tuition matrícula *(f.)*, 17
turn doblar, 9
  —off apagar, 11
twelve doce, PI
twenty veinte, PI
twenty-eight veintiocho, PI
twenty-five veinticinco, PI
twenty-four veinticuatro, PI
twenty-nine veintinueve, PI
twenty-one veintiuno, PI
twenty-seven veintisiete, PI
twenty-six veintiséis, PI
twenty-three veintitrés, PI
twenty-two veintidós, PI
two hundred doscientos, PII
two dos, PI
type escribir a máquina, 12;
  tipo *(m.)*, 13
typewriter máquina de
  escribir *(f.)*, 12

U

umbrella   paraguas
   (m. sing.), 10
uncle   tío *(m.)*, 8
underneath   debajo (de), 11
understand   entender (e:ie), 5
United States   Estados
   Unidos, 3
university   universidad *(f.)*,
   PII
unless   a menos que, 19
until   hasta, 15; hasta que, 19
us   nos, 7; nosotros(as), 6
use   usar, 14

V

vacation   vacaciones *(f. pl.)*, 5
vacuum cleaner   aspiradora
   (f.), 10
various   varios(as), 13
velocity   velocidad *(f.)*, 10
very   muy, 3
   —much   mucho, 2
   —well, and you?   muy
      bien, ¿y usted?, PI
veterinarian   veterinario(a)
   (m., f.), 15
visit   visitar, 3

W

wait   *(for)* esperar, 4; *(on)*
   atender (e:ie), 9
waiter   camarero *(m.)*,
   mozo(a) *(m., f.)*, mesero *(m.)*
   (Méx.), 2
waitress   camarera *(f.)*,
   mesera *(f.) (Méx.)*, 2
wake up   despertarse (e:ie), 9
walk   caminar, 11
wallet   billetera *(f.)*, 20
want   desear, 1; querer
   (e:ie), 5
ward room   sala *(f.)*, 18

wash   lavar, 9
wash one's hair   lavarse la
   cabeza, 9
washing machine   lavadora
   (f.), 10
we   nosotros(as), 1
Wednesday   miércoles, PI
week   semana *(f.)*, 5
weekend   fin de semana
   (m.), 16
weight   peso *(m.)*, 19
well   bien, PI
what?   ¿qué?, 2; ¿cuál(es)?, 3
   —is he (she, it) like?
      ¿cómo es?, 3
   —time is it?   ¿qué hora
      es?, 1
   **—is the weather like
      today?**   ¿qué tiempo
      hace hoy?, 10
when   ¿cuándo?, 4;
   cuando, 19
where?   ¿dónde?, 2
where is . . . from?   ¿de
   dónde es... ?, 2
where to   adónde, 3
which   que, 8
which (one)?   ¿cuál(es)?, 3
white   blanco, PI
whom?   quién(es)?, 3
whose?   ¿de quién?, 3
why?   ¿por qué?, 3
widowed   viudo(a) *(m., f.)*, PI
wife   esposa *(f.)*, 4
will   testamento *(m.)*, 19
window   ventana *(f.)*, 9
   —shop   mirar vidrieras, 12
windshield   parabrisas *(m.)*,
   14
   —wiper   limpiaparabrisas
      (m.), 14
wine   vino *(m.)*, 1
winter   invierno *(m.)*, PI
with   con, 3
   —whom?   ¿con quién?, 3
without   sin que, 19
   —fail   sin falta, 15

woman mujer (*f.*), PII
wood madera (*f.*), 3
work trabajar, 1
worry preocuparse, 20
worse peor, 4
write escribir, 2

X

X-ray radiografía (*f.*), 18
—**room** sala de rayos x
  (*f.*), 18

Y

year(s) año(s), PI
yellow amarillo, PI
yes sí, 1
yesterday ayer, 10
yet todavía, 9
you tú, usted, ustedes, 1; ti, 6;
  te, la, las, lo, los, 7; le, les,
  te, 8
young man chico (*m.*),
  muchacho (*m.*), 2
young woman chica (*f.*),
  muchacha (*f.*), 2
younger menor, 4
your tu (*fam. adj.*), su
  (*form. adj.*), 3
yours tuyo(s), tuya(s)
  (*fam. pron.*), 9; suyo(s),
  suya(s) (*form. pron.*), 9
yourself te, se, 9
yourselves se, 9

Z

zero cero, PI

Index